EQUITY and INCLUSION in HIGHER EDUCATION

EQUITY and INCLUSION in HIGHER EDUCATION

Strategies for Teaching

Edited by
RITA KUMAR and **BRENDA REFAEI**

UNIVERSITY OF CINCINNATI PRESS

About the University of Cincinnati Press
The University of Cincinnati Press is committed to publishing rigorous, peer-reviewed, leading scholarship accessibly to stimulate dialog among the academy, public intellectuals and lay practitioners. The Press endeavors to erase disciplinary boundaries in order to cast fresh light on common problems in our global community. Building on the university's long-standing tradition of social responsibility to the citizens of Cincinnati, the state of Ohio, and the world, the Press publishes books on topics that expose and resolve disparities at every level of society and have local, national and global impact.

The University of Cincinnati Press, Cincinnati 45221
Copyright © 2021
All rights reserved. No part of this book may be reproduced or utilized in any form or by any means, electronic or mechanical, or by any information storage and retrieval system, without written permission from the publisher. Requests for permission to reproduce material from this work should be sent to University of Cincinnati Press, Langsam Library, 2911 Woodside Drive, Cincinnati, Ohio 45221
ucincinnatipress.uc.edu

ISBN 978-1-947602-23-6 (paperback)
ISBN 978-1-947602-22-9 (e-book, PDF)
ISBN 978-1-947602-18-2 (e-book, EPUB)

Names: Kumar, Rita, editor. | Refaei, Brenda, editor.
Title: Equity and inclusion in higher education : strategies for teaching /
    edited by Rita Kumar and Brenda Refaei.
Description: Cincinnati : University of Cincinnati Press, 2021. | Includes
    bibliographical references and index.
Identifiers: LCCN 2021001180 | ISBN 9781947602236 (paperback) | ISBN
    9781947602229 (pdf) | ISBN 9781947602182 (ebook)
Subjects: LCSH: Education, Higher—Social aspects—United States. |
    Education, Higher—Curricula—United States. | Inclusive
    education—United States. | Educational equalization—United States.
Classification: LCC LC191.94 .E78 2021 | DDC 378.73—dc23
LC record available at https://lccn.loc.gov/2021001180

Designed and produced for UC Press by Julie Rushing
Typeset in Minion Pro Condensed and Acumin Variable Condensed
Printed in the United States of America
First Printing

Contents

For my parents Mulk Raj and Janak Saluja, who taught me my first lessons of equity and inclusion and my students across the globe who taught me how it truly matters.

—Rita Kumar

For my students at Taft High School, Jordan University of Science and Technology, King Saud University, and University of Cincinnati Blue Ash College, you have inspired me to be a better teacher and person.

—Brenda Refaei

Acknowledgments

A book like this is only possible because of the support of many people. First, we must thank the staff at UC Press for their unwavering support. We want to thank each of the authors in this collection for their time and patience as we worked on the book. We want to express our appreciation to the reviewers of the book whose comments and suggestions have led to a much better final product. Dr. Keisha Love was instrumental in the development of this book. It was her sponsorship of Diversity, Equity, and Inclusion (DEI) at the University of Cincinnati that served as the catalyst for this book. We want to thank Dr. Bradford Mallory for co-facilitating the first DEI workshops, which led to this book. We appreciate the support The Academy of Fellows for Teaching and Learning provided at a critical moment in the publication of this book. We would like to acknowledge our families for their support and encouragement.

Several resources mentioned throughout this book are available for free on an open access companion site. Scan the QR code to visit the site and to learn more about the materials available.

Introduction

In the current climate, equity and inclusion are under attack from those who benefit from the status quo. The Black Lives Matter movement forcefully articulates the various ways systemic racism works to marginalize and endanger racially minoritized people. Instigated by the unjust killing of Black people by law enforcement and others, the necessity of addressing systemic racism has reawakened the national consciousness. Likewise, the tragic shootings of people gathered for religious observances, such as at the Tree of Life Synagogue in Pittsburgh's Squirrel Hill neighborhood, the Quebec City and Christ Church mosques, and the Emanuel African Methodist Episcopal Church in Charleston, South Carolina, show that even houses of worship are not safe from the corruption of invective surrounding equity and inclusion. Educators have a role in overcoming this hostility toward others. They must seek out ways to include students who have often been excluded from the opportunities and advantages afforded by higher education while also working with students to develop cultural humility, which acknowledges that no one set of cultural norms should be imposed on all (Foronda et al., 2015). The role of higher education faculty in guiding students' development, so they are ready to participate as informed citizens in a pluralistic democracy, has never been more urgent than now.

As more people enroll in higher education to pursue economic opportunity, colleges and universities are seeing greater diversity among their students—not only in racial heritage, gender, and ability but in other, less apparent ways such as level of preparation, economic security, mental health, and so forth. Unfortunately, Hurtado and Guillermo-Wann (2013) found "students continue to experience negative cross-racial interactions, discrimination and bias, and harassment along multiple social identities (e.g., race, class, gender, age, sexual orientation) but rarely report it to campus authorities" (p. vii). Even more disturbing, they found that Black students noted that racism and stereotype threat negatively affected their educational experience. At the same time, more nontraditionally aged students are enrolling in higher education, which requires a greater demand for flexibility in course offerings, pedagogical approaches, and modes of instruction.

There are some who would argue that only specific disciplines have the knowledge or skills to create inclusive classrooms. We take a different position in this book. Instead, we argue that each college instructor must promote equity so that all students feel included in the classroom and that all students learn to respect the diversity present in the human experience. Equity means providing the tools and knowledge students need

1

in a manner that is accessible to each student. Equity-mindedness is the way of thinking that questions existing structures and practices to find ways to be more inclusive. Equity and inclusion should be integrated within disciplines as part of the curricula, pedagogy, and assessment. The contributors in this volume have sought to create inclusive learning environments for racially minoritized students, LGBTQ2S+ students, and students with disabilities that allow for the full participation of those who have been marginalized by higher education's practices and to promote understanding across differences. Although we acknowledge that faculty will not always reach their aim of creating inclusive class-rooms that achieve equitable outcomes, we believe that all faculty must actively work toward that goal. Developing inclusive classrooms is a continual process that involves faculty who are open to self-examination, and are willing to explore new pedagogies, to analyze different curricula, and to adopt new means of assessment.

In our own work as educators, we were fortunate to have numerous opportunities to receive guidance and support to develop inclusive teaching practices through learning communities, diversity and inclusion seminars, and workshops on inclusive pedagogy, curriculum design, and assessment. Our engagement in these activities led to receiving a competitive grant to address equity and inclusion across disciplines at our college. Faculty within disciplinary units at the college were invited to build activities or mod-ules demonstrating how equity and inclusion can be incorporated in course curriculum and pedagogy. The activities could include but were not limited to race/ethnicity, gen-der, sexual orientation, neural diversity, and socioeconomic status. Faculty teams from seven disciplines submitted proposed activities or modules that were discipline specific and focused on content as well as mode of delivery. The faculty teams then presented to their peers, generating keen interest in best practices in equity and inclusion across disciplines.

Based on the interest generated by this initiative at our college, we began exploring how others outside our college approached this work. We were curious to know what pedagogies and curricula faculty find helpful in their disciplines. The idea for the book was the culmination of years of exploration, scholarship, and experiences around equity and inclusion and its implications for learning. We were motivated to bring together resources in a book that would address the needs of instructors who want to create inclu-sive learning environments but may not have access to supportive professional devel-opment and examples of best practices. We wanted to provide guidance for reflective faculty who seek novel pedagogical approaches, curriculum, and assessment practices that would help them to create learning environments where all students have an equal opportunity to thrive.

Given the need to address the diversity present in higher education, Carbado and Gulati (2003) developed a taxonomy outlining the importance of diversity in law schools in the United States that is more broadly applicable to higher education. They argued that to promote effective education of all students, diversity is important in seven areas: inclusion, social meaning, citizenship, belonging, color blindness, speech, and institutional culture. Institutions should mirror the population of their community if they are to be inclusive. Including all members of society in higher education is necessary in a democracy. In diverse classrooms, all students benefit from the opportunity to learn from different perspectives. Unfounded social meanings, such as those associated with racism, can be challenged. When diversity is not present, those unfounded social meanings may never come up or may never be challenged. In discussing belonging, Carbado and Gulati pointed out that tokenism does not help in promoting diversity. Students need others like themselves in the classroom to feel like they belong. Strayhorn (2019) has emphasized that student success is largely affected by positive peer-to-peer relations that amplify a sense of belonging.

Perhaps the most profound and important function in their taxonomy is that of citizenship. Carbado and Gulati stated, "A third function of diversity is to facilitate the formation of a racially cooperative society" (2003, p. 1155). They elaborated: "Central to this function is the idea that universities are sites for Americanization. They naturalize us. In other words, who we become as Americans is a function of who we are as students. The nexus between school socialization and citizenship has profound implications for race. In short, school segregation produces and legitimizes societal segregation. At the most basic level, students perform in society the racial interactions they learn and rehearse in school" (p. 1155). Therefore, it is imperative that all faculty seek ways to promote inclusivity that fights against accepting prevailing social segregation that marginalizes some while privileging others. This important mandate of higher education is often given short shrift by a drive for profits over academics.

As higher education takes on the corporate model (Blum & Ullman, 2012; Mills, 2012), it loses focus on the needs of individuals. Faculty feel pressure to teach quickly so they can get back to their research or they feel pressured to teach as many students as possible without regard to the students' preparation for the courses. Berg and Seeber (2016) noted, "Yet, if there is one sector of society which should be cultivating deep thought, it is academic teachers. . . . The administrative university is concerned above all with efficiency, resulting in a time crunch and making those of us subjected to it feel powerless" (p. x). How are faculty who feel powerless supposed to empower their students? How can faculty who do not have time for cultivating deep thought find ways to create more inclusive learning environments? Faculty need to prioritize inclusive classroom design while recognizing that achieving equity is a lifelong pursuit that will not be achieved through redesigning one course. Part of the deep thinking that faculty should engage in is examining how their own values and beliefs shape their interactions with students, how they approach pedagogy in the classroom, and how they determine what should be taught in the curriculum.

However, many college educators need guidance in self-reflection, and in developing curricular designs and pedagogical approaches that support students. Regardless of discipline, educators need to engage in creating inclusive learning environments that are learner-centered. The pedagogical approaches should be theoretically situated and use active learning strategies that are culturally relevant (Ladson-Billings, 1995), culturally responsive (Gay, 2018; Hammond, 2015), and culturally sustaining (Paris, 2012). An inclusive learning environment is intentionally transparent and designed to allow all learners to succeed. Inclusive classrooms promote equity and social justice in that underserved students have opportunities to learn and all students have opportunities to learn other ways of knowing and being. In addition to inclusive pedagogies, educators need to critically examine their curricula to ensure that it does not promote inequity. Finally, inclusive pedagogies and curricula mean little if assessment practices are not equitable. Educators should explore a variety of ways to assess student learning that honors students' diverse ways of learning and knowing.

BECOMING AN INCLUSIVE PRACTITIONER

Creating an inclusive learning environment to provide opportunities for all requires the examination of our own biases. Before educators can address equity and inclusion in educational settings, they must first be willing to examine their own values, unconscious biases, and beliefs derived from the culture in which they live. Culture is "a dynamic system of social values, cognitive codes, behavioral standards, world views, and beliefs used to give order and meaning to our own lives as well as the lives of others" (Gay, 2018, p. 8). This system of values often operates below a person's level of consciousness. Effective teachers are those who are open to exploring how their values influence their behaviors, changing ineffective or harmful behaviors by constantly seeking out ways to improve their work. In deciding how to facilitate inclusive practices, faculty may discover how much their beliefs about students are influenced by deficit thinking, which places responsibility on students for poor school performance. Deficit thinking shows up when teachers believe that students are not motivated or prepared for college work and takes the responsibility off the teacher to create an inclusive learning environment. To become an inclusive practitioner, educators need to learn to reflect on how their own worldview, values, and beliefs shape the way they construct their learning environments. They also need to learn more about students' cultural systems so that those can be brought into the classroom.

When faculty begin teaching, they have often never had the opportunity to examine their own assumptions about the teaching and learning process and how those assumptions guide their behaviors and beliefs in their interactions with students. Brookfield (1995) described how assumptions are difficult to examine because they "give meaning and purpose to who we are and what we do" (p. 2). These assumptions live below instructors' consciousness yet powerfully influence all of their actions. It requires intentionality and effort to examine assumptions about effective teaching. Brookfield was focused on uncovering assumptions about teaching, but Gallaway and Zamani-Gallaher (2018, p. 5) noted that higher education also needs to reflect on how to effectively "deal with the complexity of race, identity, diversity, equity, and inclusion."

This self-examination is a necessary first step in creating an inclusive learning environment. It is important to keep in mind Tuitt's (2016) warning about the need for faculty to examine their own thinking before engaging in culturally responsive teaching: "In closing, I have come to understand that utilizing CIPs [Critical and Inclusive Practices] is not a form of praxis that all educators should embrace. In fact, educators who fail to do the self-work may cause more harm than good and, as a result, engage in the creation of unjust learning environments" (p. 218). This "self-work" is necessary for all faculty who wish to create inclusive learning environments because all faculty operate within cultural contexts that marginalizes some while privileging others.

Faculty need to uncover how these beliefs permeate their own thinking and actions—everyone has implicit biases that have been absorbed through their lived experiences in their society. Faculty should take the Implicit Association Test (IAT) (Project Implicit, n.d.). This test can help raise awareness among educators of the insidious ways that cultural and social biases influence their own beliefs and actions. Taking the test and reflecting on the results offers instructors a space to consider how they might change their behavior in their interactions with students. Educators, in particular, need to examine their assumptions to discover how these implicit biases inform their teaching.

In analyzing implicit biases, Hammond (2015) connected the physiology of the brain to the deep emotional reactions people have when they confront their implicit biases. She pointed out the function of "the amygdala and reticular activating system (RAS), is . . . to keep us safe" (p. 54). Since humans have developed implicit biases to keep them "safe," these areas of the brain are triggered when people begin to bring their awareness to them. As they become aware, they may experience the freeze, fight, or flight reactions the amygdala and RAS have developed over years of evolution. People experience deep and strong reactions when they examine their implicit biases because their brains want to protect them. Educators can minimize this strong reaction through mindfulness and other relaxation techniques (Hanson, 2013).

Educators need opportunities for mindfulness practices that enable them to build professional resiliency as they take on the difficult work of addressing inequities in higher education and society. Developing professional resiliency allows faculty to maintain their own mental health while providing needed services and instruction. Mindfulness is needed to "stay woke." Justin Michael Williams (2019) wrote, "Staying woke isn't just about awareness. It is a call to action. And it matters most when you feel like giving up" (p. 10). Once faculty become more attuned to social injustice, it is easy to feel overwhelmed and defeated. Mindfulness practices provide the needed respite to take up the work anew each day.

Many faculty entered teaching to share their knowledge of their subject matter with others. As part of their work with students, they may develop an ethic of care (Gay 2018) in which they see the importance of meeting the students where they are in order to help them learn the content. As faculty begin to better understand the experiences of their students, they may take on a social justice purpose in teaching to uplift historically marginalized students while also raising awareness of social justice issues in communities of privilege. Educators need awareness of social issues and how to facilitate social justice in the classroom.

DESIGNING INCLUSIVE CURRICULUM

Faculty must pay close attention to the structure and content of the curriculum as they prepare students for a world that needs to be freed from the shackles of Eurocentric thought and processes. Henson (2015) asserted that "successful curriculum development in the twenty-first century must prepare teachers to help *all* students to succeed" (italics in original, p. xv). Eurocentric educational systems through curriculum and pedagogy continue to dominate academia, leading to the indoctrination of students into a Western system of thought. Producing knowledge provides power to those who create it by giving the producers power over how the world is seen and creates academic hegemony marginalizing non-Eurocentric values. Educators have a duty to critically analyze and question the impact of a system that upholds "Eurocentric systems of thought, while simultaneously devaluing indigenous knowledge and multiple ways of knowing" (Wane, Shahjahan, & Wagner 2004, p. 500). Diverse members of the academic community who contribute to building the discipline need to be recognized—not as tokens but as equal participants. This means paying attention to who is represented as the knowledge experts in the field.

Knowledge cannot be divorced from the realities, beliefs, experiences, and sociocultural ethos of the people it serves if its purpose is to empower learners. Such knowledge in the form of curriculum content is necessary for empowerment and is only possible when students are offered an inclusive curriculum. However, it is equally important that such knowledge is imparted in a way that does not cause curriculum violence. Jones (2020) described curriculum violence as lessons created by curriculum writers and educators "that damage or otherwise adversely affect students intellectually and emotionally" when Eurocentric values drive the curriculum. Curriculum content that references ethnically diverse groups needs to be comprehensive, accurate, authentic, and current to not further perpetuate stereotypes and strengthen preexisting biases toward marginalized groups.

An inclusive curriculum presents students with "socially relevant and challenging new knowledge so that they, in collaboration with their teachers, can engage in a meaningful dialogue and become more informed members of their communities" (Wane, Shahjahan, & Wagner 2004, p. 507). Such a curriculum anticipates and prepares for all students' right to access and participate in a course. An inclusive curriculum is based on Croucher and Romer's (2007) definition of an approach that "does not place groups in opposition to each other. It respects diversity but does not imply a lack of commonality. It supports the concept of widening participation but does not imply an externally imposed value judgment; it values equality of opportunity but encourages all to feel that this relates to them, and that the issues are not just projected as being relevant to groups more commonly defined as disenfranchised and translated into universities' targets for equality" (Croucher and Romer, 2007, p. 3). Croucher and Romer's inclusive approach equips faculty with a foundation for building an inclusive curriculum. Morgan and Houghton (2011) described an inclusive curriculum as one that accounts for students' educational, cultural, and social backgrounds and experience in addition to any physical or sensory impairments and their mental health. They proposed that a curriculum based on principles of equity, collaboration, flexibility, and accountability benefits both educators and students (p. 5). Since the curriculum represents a crucial tool for facilitating the process of an inclusive education, its design should reflect its relevance to students and promote their participation.

Inclusive curricula ensure that the less visible part of the curriculum, "the hidden curriculum—that which is taught implicitly, rather than explicitly" (Henson, 2015, p. 13), offers opportunities for equity. Educators need to use transparent approaches to make visible the "hidden curriculum" that often alienates marginalized students. When students from different cultural, social, and economic backgrounds do not find affirmation of their identities, values, and beliefs in school and outside, it impacts their academic performance, sense of belonging, and motivation. By designing an inclusive curriculum, instructors can include different perspectives to build a multidimensional gaze that allows students to see and acknowledge the world at all its levels. Inclusive curriculum development should be adopted as an ongoing process and be closely intertwined with social inclusion.

An inclusive curriculum is one that is accessible, relevant, and engaging to all students. The course material should reflect student realities and experiences. An inclusive curriculum provides all students with opportunities to achieve the learning outcomes of their program of study. The curriculum must be open to alternative perspectives that encompass diverse realities and is meaningful to differently situated people reflective of the communities in which they work. The curriculum should not be based on a "one size fits all" model but should be designed in a way that it can be taught to mixed-ability learners. The curriculum should ensure both equity and quality. An inclusive curriculum empowers all students. "Because of the dialectic relationship between knowledge and the knower, interest and motivation, relevance and master," students must be seen as co-originators, co-designers, and co-directors of their education and not merely as consumers (Gay, 2018, p. 142). A relevant and inclusive curriculum is one that mirrors societal changes, which includes changes in the community, the school, and the students themselves (Henson, 2015). Finally, the curriculum should be both global and local in design, which means that it should be flexible, balanced, and relevant to each context and individual while addressing national, local, and learners' diversities. The broader purpose should be to strike a balance between the global, national, and local expectations, realities, and needs (Opertti, 2009). In doing so, the curriculum can effectively respond to learners' diversities and sustain long-term education for all.

Universal Design for Learning (UDL) presents a viable approach for developing an inclusive curriculum because of its core belief that "diversity exists in all shapes and throughout the entire lifespan" (Wu, 2010, p. 1). UDL transforms instruction so that adaptations for students with disabilities improves the experiences for all students in the course. For instance, offering multiple ways to present an assignment, such as providing a video with captions in addition to a document that can be read by a scanner makes the assignment more accessible to all the students in the course. The concept of accessibility makes using UDL a rational choice to guide the development of inclusive curriculum. The twenty-first-century classroom with students from a broad range of academic, social, economic, emotional, and cultural backgrounds demands a curricular approach that can meet the needs of such a heterogeneous community. A UDL curriculum allows instructors to approach learning with the mindset that the curriculum can meet diverse student needs through multiple means of engagement and action, knowledge representation, and expression. A UDL curriculum facilitates the adoption of varied course materials, technologies, pedagogical approaches, classroom activities, and assessments to meet the needs of learners.

Designing an inclusive curriculum also involves choosing curriculum content that is relevant to diverse students and can be delivered in ways that are meaningful to students. Curriculum designers should seek a wider range of sources beyond textbooks to build curriculum content. In addition to textbooks, curriculum content that is meaningful to student learning can be derived from other sources (Gay, 2018). However, course materials need to be critically evaluated to ensure that there is accurate representation of those who have contributed to the building of knowledge.

Educators can also consider co-constructing the curriculum with students. Such an approach has the potential to facilitate an innovative way of conceiving and organizing the curricular outcomes and structure as well as the syllabus with the ultimate objective of developing learners who will be autonomous, critical, and assertive citizens.

8

CREATING INCLUSIVE PEDAGOGY

Inclusive pedagogy is an intentional process of transforming the learning environment so that it respects the ways of knowing and being all students bring to the learning situation. It sustains all members of the classroom community by drawing upon the unique gifts each person brings to the learning environment by recognizing students' home cultures, dialects, and norms as equal to those of the dominant cultural norms. Inclusive pedagogy works against deficit thinking, which views learners from nondominant dialects, cultures, and literacies as deficient and in need of remediation before they can access the dominant culture's privileges. It is important to offer opportunities to critique and challenge systems of oppression, which prevent equal access to resources. Inclusive pedagogies are learner-centered. Learner-centered education occurs when the focus of educational practices is on making knowledge accessible to all students (Weimer, 2002). For this reason, inclusive pedagogies are critical to ensure that traditionally underserved students have equal access to knowledge and skills they need to attain their goals for higher education. In sum, inclusive pedagogy is a mindset, a teaching-and-learning worldview, more than a discrete set of techniques (Gannon, 2018).

Establishing and implementing inclusive pedagogy is a process of building a practice that can span a continuum beginning with equity-focused principles and ending with one that encompasses social justice principles. An inclusive pedagogical practice would develop intercultural competence as a learning goal. With the rapid internationalization of higher education, one of its objectives is helping students conceive of themselves as global citizens. In the context of this new dynamic, the development of intercultural competence as a learning goal for designing pedagogical strategies is relevant. Spitzberg and Changnon (2009) defined "intercultural competence as the appropriate and effective management of interaction between people who . . . represent different or divergent affective, cognitive, and behavioral orientations to the world." Deardorff (2006) noted that intercultural competence needs to be intentionally taught in real-world interactions that use critical reflection to develop understanding. Referencing concepts drawn from intercultural competence and pedagogy, Lee (2017) defined "intercultural pedagogy as the commitment (not just the desire) to make intentional, informed decisions that enable our courses to engage and support diversity and inclusion" (p. 15). However, the focus of intercultural competence is essentially to help bridge cultural differences between different nationalities; it does not explore social inequities within the countries or past exploitative practices between nations.

In order to address inequities that exist due to race, gender, and class, Paris (2012) offered the term Culturally Sustaining Pedagogy, which "seeks to perpetuate and foster—to sustain—linguistic, literate, and cultural pluralism as part of the democratic project of schooling. In the face of current policies and practices that have the explicit goal of creating a monocultural and monolingual society, research and practice need equally explicit resistances that embrace cultural pluralism and cultural equality" (p. 93). Such a monocultural and singular perspective needs to be challenged for public institutions to meet their mission of providing their students with tools that will prepare them for the challenges of a pluralistic society. Culturally Sustaining Pedagogy addresses the competing interests of education: replicating current society versus creating a more inclusive society.

Like Culturally Sustaining Pedagogy, Culturally Responsive Pedagogy provides a framework to assist faculty as they seek to create more inclusive classrooms. Gay (2018) described Culturally Responsive Pedagogy as "teachers acquiring more knowledge about ethnic and cultural diversity, becoming more conscious of themselves as cultural beings and cultural actors in the process of teaching, and engaging in courageous conversations about issues fundamental to social justice in society and educational equity for ethnically diverse students" (p. 80). Culturally Responsive Pedagogy intersects with the aims of Culturally Sustaining Pedagogy in their joint goal of addressing social justice through education. Moreover, both pedagogies emphasize the need for equity in meeting the needs of ethnically diverse students.

Another inclusive pedagogical approach is proposed by Tuitt, Haynes, & Stewart (2016). They suggested Critical and Inclusive Pedagogies (CIPs), which are embedded in theoretical models of teaching and use students' lived experiences to create inclusive learning environments that combine principles of equity and social justice. CIPs strive to create an identity-affirming and socially just learning environment by using a variety of interactive and dynamic teaching practices and diverse and interdisciplinary content and perspectives. In order to implement CIPs, instructors need to be courageous and transparent.

Under the broader umbrella of Culturally Sustaining Pedagogy, McCarty and Lee (2014) present the concept of Critical Culturally Sustaining/Revitalizing Pedagogy as essential to understand and guide educational practices for Native American learners. Merculieff and Roderick (2013) stressed that "It's time—past time—to build a genuinely equitable educational (not to mention social, political, and economic) system in which Native and non-Native communities function as true partners" (p. ix). Given the current linguistic, cultural, and educational realities of Native American communities, McCarty and Lee (2014) argued that Culturally Sustaining Pedagogy in these settings must also be understood as Culturally Revitalizing Pedagogy, and they advocate for community-based educational accountability that is rooted in the sovereignty of Indigenous education. Merculieff and Roderick (2013) described fourteen common Indigenous teaching practices that present a very different ontological view of reality from the one commonly held by Eurocentric systems of thought. Exploring these practices reveals a deeper understanding of interconnectedness between people and between people and nature, which influences how learning occurs. Indigenous pedagogies provide a thoughtful alternative to Eurocentric approaches to learning and challenges the notion that Eurocentric pedagogies are more effective.

In addition to culturally sustaining practices, part of inclusive pedagogy has to be a focused and intentional push to integrate universal design that recognizes diversity beyond disabilities. Grier-Reed and Williams-Wengred (2018) stated that "from the perspective of culturally sustaining pedagogy and universal design, all students are unique, and it is the systems in education that are disabling rather than the students who are disabled" (p. 2). They contend that though inclusive pedagogy has used a broad definition of inclusion, the literature has been specifically focused on disability as criteria for inclusion. The definition needs to be broadened to include other criteria such as gender, age, racial, and ethnic diversity. Waitoller and Thorius (2016) suggested that the cross-pollination of Culturally Sustaining Pedagogy with UDL can help build emancipatory pedagogies that can provide students and teachers the means to engage meaningfully with ableism and racism.

In moving along the continuum toward social justice, inclusive pedagogies should intentionally address racism. Blakeney (2005) asserted that although culturally responsive pedagogies promote inclusivity, there is a need for antiracist pedagogy to address systemic racism in education. Kishimoto (2018) argued that antiracist pedagogy, which is informed by Critical Race Theory, is needed to respond to educational contexts that have for too long been "exclusionary and functioned to assimilate students by normalizing dominant knowledge and values through the hidden curriculum" (p. 541). She rationalized that antiracist pedagogy should not be limited to teaching in its application but be adopted as an "intentional and strategic organizing effort in which we incorporate anti-racist values into our various spheres of influence" (p. 551). Kandaswamy (2020) further emphasized the importance of intentional antiracist pedagogy when she highlighted the need to push students to think beyond color blindness and multiculturalism when challenging racism and Eurocentrism.

The approaches to inclusive pedagogies described here illustrate the importance of critiquing and challenging systems of oppression, which prevent some students from achieving their educational goals. The pedagogies encourage educators to intentionally incorporate equity-minded practices in their interactions with students. These pedagogies fall along a continuum of raising students' awareness of cultural difference to empowering students to dismantle systemic forms of institutional barriers such as racism. But inclusive pedagogies and curriculum are only meaningful if they are accompanied by inclusive assessment practices.

IMPLEMENTING INCLUSIVE ASSESSMENT

Faculty often have strong feelings about the role of assessment in higher education, which is born out of a concern about being judged unfairly. Indeed, if they look to the way assessment is done in the K–12 setting, they are right to be mistrustful of powerful outside organizations making pronouncements upon what students can or cannot do in their classroom. However, thoughtful assessment processes can improve student learning by making the content relevant to students' experiences. Incorporating a culturally responsive approach to assessment allows for multiple means of demonstrating learning.

Assessment processes need to be examined in the light of how unexamined assumptions may lead to marginalization of traditionally underserved students. Whether faculty acknowledge it or not, assessment drives what is taught and what is valued in the classroom. "It [assessment] can influence not only how we see ourselves, but also our social relations with others and how we see them" (Leathwood, 2005, p. 308). For this reason, it is incumbent upon inclusive practitioners to examine their assumptions about student learning and ways that learning can be assessed. Through assessment processes, instructors convey clear messages about which students and ways of learning are valued. Traditional, one-size-fits-all approaches to assessment negate culturally responsive pedagogies and curriculum by flattening out how learning is assessed.

When we examine the most prevalent assumptions in assessment, we find that they derive from a positivist framework that views fair assessment as one that uses the same processes for all students. This attention to fairness does not acknowledge the differences among learners and the variety of ways that learning can take place. Assessment researchers Henning and Lundquist (2020), promoting inclusive assessment, suggested that educators and other assessment practitioners should use an inquiry approach to designing assessment, which is responsive to the learning environment, including the students' ways of knowing. In this approach, assessment becomes a process of telling "the stories of what students know and can do" (Montenegro & Jankowski, 2017).

Before faculty can create responsive assessments, they need to examine their own assumptions about student learning and how it can be documented. At the same time, faculty need to learn more about other ways of learning through investigating the work that has been done by researchers in areas such as Universal Design for Learning (CAST 2020) and Indigenous pedagogies (LaFever 2016; Merculieff & Roderick 2013), which can offer insights into possible ways to transform assessment practices that are fair to a greater number of students.

Transformative assessment practices begin with inclusive student learning outcomes. Faculty can use UDL and Indigenous pedagogies to rethink the language of course outcomes statements. For instance, LaFever (2016) recommended a modification of Benjamin Bloom's three-domain taxonomy based on the medicine wheel. In her revised taxonomy, she describes four domains of learning: intellectual, emotional, physical, and spiritual. She provided a scale for spiritual development that could be incorporated in course outcome statements. Similarly, Universal Design for Learning Guidelines (CAST 2020) present a different conceptualization of how a learning environment can be constructed. These are two of several different approaches that highlight there is not a one-size-fits-all model for learning or assessment of learning.

In addition to exploring options beyond discipline-specific learning-outcomes language, faculty need to involve students in the process of developing, implementing, and assessing the learning outcomes. Unfortunately, teacher and student voices are missing in the construction of course learning outcomes (McArthur, 2016; 2017; Montenegro & Jankowski, 2017). Often, course outcomes are developed by a committee and assigned to courses with little opportunity for faculty who teach the courses to provide input, while students have even less opportunity. However, inclusive practitioners use their power and positionality to push back on this inequitable situation by critically examining course learning outcomes with their students. They evaluate which ways of learning are valued in the outcomes statements and which are disregarded.

Working with students to critically evaluate course learning outcomes is one way inclusive faculty can contextualize assessment within their courses (Montenegro & Jankowski, 2020). Another way is to work with students to identify what evidence can be used to demonstrate student learning. Collaboratively, students and faculty can develop the types of assignments that would best demonstrate their learning. This collaborative approach to documenting student learning recognizes the variety of ways knowledge can be represented without privileging one above another. Portfolios are an excellent means of documenting a variety of learning demonstrations that support a more integrative approach to learning. When portfolios are done well, they provide opportunities for students to reflect upon their learning and its relevance to their own lived experiences.

Once faculty and students have identified what type of evidence should be collected to demonstrate learning, they need to identify how that evidence will be analyzed. Students and the instructor can work together to develop the criteria for success (Inoue, 2015; McArthur, 2016; 2017; Montenegro & Jankowski, 2017; Winkelmes, Boye, & Tapp, 2019). A culturally responsive rubric can be co-created with students so the criteria for success are written in language that is clear to students. After the rubric has been created, students should have the opportunity to practice applying it to sample work to clarify the language and deepen their understanding of their expected performance (Winkelmes, Boye, & Tapp, 2019). Although rubrics can help in making criteria transparent, it is important to guard against allowing them to reduce learning to basic steps students can move through without engaging in the content of the course.

Inclusive assessment practices are essential in an inclusive learning environment. "We cannot assess what students know without also attempting to understand how culture, context, and the influence of both impact learning and how we assess that learning" (Montenegro & Jankowski, 2020). When faculty have done the difficult work of examining their assumptions about teaching and learning, thoughtfully implementing inclusive pedagogy, and carefully constructing an inclusive curriculum, their assessment processes must follow the same values of honoring each student's unique lived experience in documenting their learning. Montenegro and Jankowski (2017) argued:

"What is needed is not to help learners conform to the ways of higher education, thus reinforcing inequities and expectations based on ideologies the students may not ascribe to, but to empower students for success through intentional efforts to address inequality within our structures, create clear transparent pathways, and ensure that credits and credentials are awarded by demonstration of learning, in whatever form that may take" (p. 16). Inclusive assessments promote social justice by partnering with students to identify and address barriers to demonstrating their learning.

HOW TO USE THIS BOOK

Beginning with a critical self-examination, to designing an inclusive curriculum, implementing inclusive pedagogy, and creating inclusive assessment, this book provides a comprehensive overview of why equity and inclusion are essential in the classroom. An inclusive curriculum and pedagogical strategies cannot and should not be ignored on the pretext of lack of time and content coverage challenges but need to be practiced intentionally. The authors in this book provide educators with examples of inclusive practices in different learning contexts and different disciplines so that faculty can fulfill their responsibility of developing students who are ready to function in a diverse society.

The book is divided into six parts according to broad disciplinary connections. Each part begins with an overview and a summary of the lessons learned from the chapters and ends with a series of reflective prompts to help readers consider how they can use the lessons to create their own inclusive learning environments. Readers can go to the section that most closely aligns with their discipline. All readers will find Part I on "Setting Up Inclusive Learning Environments" and Part VI on "Inclusive Assessment" applicable irrespective of their discipline.

REFERENCES

Berg, M., & Seeber, B. K. (2016). *The slow professor: Challenging the culture of speed in the academy.* University of Toronto Press.

Blakeney, A. M. (2005). Antiracist pedagogy: Definition, theory, and professional development. *Journal of Curriculum and Pedagogy, 2*(1), 119–132.

Brookfield, S. (1995). *Becoming a critically reflective teacher.* Jossey-Bass.

Blum, D., & Ullman, C. (2012). The globalization and corporatization of education: The limits and liminality of the market mantra. *International Journal of Qualitative Studies in Education, 25*(4), 367–373. https://doi.org/10.1080/09518398.2012.673031

Carbado, D., & Gulati, M. (2003). What exactly is racial diversity? *California Law Review, 91*(4), 1149–1165. https://doi.org/10.2307/3481413

CAST. (2020). *Universal design for learning guidelines.* http://udlguidelines.cast.org/

Croucher, K., and Romer, W. (2007) *Inclusivity in teaching practice and the curriculum.* Guides for Teaching and Learning in Archaeology no. 6. Higher Education Academy. https://www.heacademy.ac.uk/system/files/Number6_Teaching_and_Learning_Guide_Inclusivity.pdf

Deardorff, D. K. (2006). Identification and assessment of intercultural competence as a student outcome of internationalization. *Journal of Studies in International Education, 10,* 241–266.

Foronda, C., Baptiste, D., Reinholdt, M. M., & Ousman, K. (2015). Cultural humility: A concept analysis. *Journal of Transcultural Nursing, 27*(3), 210–217. https://doi.org/10.1177/1043659615592677

Gallaway, C., & Zamani-Gallaher, E. (2018). Community colleges, the racialized climate, and engaging diverse views through intergroup dialogue. *Office of Community College Research and Leadership, 4*(1), 1–7. https://occrl.illinois.edu/docs/librariesprovider4/news/update/racialized-climate.pdf

Gannon, K. (2018, February 27). The case for inclusive teaching. *Chronicle of Higher Education.* https://www.chronicle.com/article/The-Case-for-Inclusive/242636

Gay, G. (2018). *Culturally responsive teaching: Theory, research, and practice* (3rd ed.). Teachers College Press.

Grier-Reed, T., & Williams-Wengerd, A. (2018). Integrating universal design, culturally sustaining practices, and constructivism to advance inclusive pedagogy in undergraduate classroom. *Education Sciences, 8,* 167.

Hammond, Z. (2015). *Culturally responsive teaching and the brain: Promoting authentic engagement and rigor among culturally and linguistically diverse students.* Corwin.

Hanson, R. (2013). *Hardwiring happiness: The new brain of science of contentment, calm, and confidence.* Harmony Books.

Henning, G., & Lundquist, A. E. (2020, June 8). *Using assessment as a tool for equity and inclusion.* AAHLE Virtual Conference.

Henson, K. T. (2015). *Curriculum planning: Integrating multiculturalism, constructivism, and education reform* (5th ed.). Waveland Press.

Hurtado, S., & Guillermo-Wann, C. (2013). *Diverse learning environments: Assessing and creating conditions for student success—Final report to the Ford Foundation.* Higher Education Research Institute, University of California, Los Angeles. https://www.heri.ucla.edu/ford/DiverseLearningEnvironments.pdf

Inoue, A. B. (2015). *Antiracist writing assessment ecologies: Teaching and assessing writing for a socially just future.* WAC Clearinghouse; Parlor Press.

Iturbe-LaGrave, V. (2020). *Resources to support inclusivity in the classroom.* DU Inclusive Teaching Practices. http://inclusive-teaching.du.edu/

Jones, S. (2020). Ending curriculum violence. Yes, curriculum can be violent—whether you intend it or not. Here's what it looks like and how you can. *Teaching Tolerance, 64* (Spring).

Kandaswamy, P. (2007). Beyond colorblindness and multiculturalism: Rethinking anti-racist pedagogy in the university classroom. *Radical Teacher 80*(80), 6–11.

Kishimoto, K. (2018) Anti-racist pedagogy: From faculty's self-reflection to organizing within and beyond the classroom. *Race, Ethnicity, and Education, 21*(4), 540–554. https://doi.org/10.1080/13613324.2016.1248824

Ladson-Billings, G. (1995). But that's just good teaching! The case for culturally relevant pedagogy. *Theory into Practice, 34*(3), 159–165.

LaFever, M. (2016) Switching from Bloom to the medicine wheel: Creating learning outcomes that support Indigenous ways of knowing in post-secondary education. *Intercultural Education, 27*(5), 409–424. https://doi.org/10.1080/14675986.2016.1240496

Leathwood, C. 2005. Assessment policy and practice in higher education: Purpose, standards, and equity. *Assessment & Evaluation in Higher Education, 30*(3), 307–324.

Lee, A. (2017). *Teaching interculturally: A framework for integrating disciplinary knowledge and intercultural development.* Stylus Publishing.

McArthur, J. (2016). Assessment for social justice: The role of assessment in achieving social justice. *Assessment & Evaluation in Higher Education, 41*(7), 967–981. https://doi.org/10.1080/02602938.2015.1053429

McArthur, J. (2017, December). *Opportunities for social justice within and through assessment.* University of Illinois and Indiana University, National Institute for Learning Outcomes Assessment (NILOA). https://www.learningoutcomesassessment.org/wp-content/uploads/2019/08/EquityResponse-McArthur.pdf

McCarty, T. L., & Lee, T. S. (2014). Critical culturally sustaining/revitalizing pedagogy and Indigenous education sovereignty. *Harvard Educational Review, 84*(1), 101–124, 135–136.

Merculieff, I., & Roderick, L. (2013). *Stop talking: Indigenous ways of teaching and learning and difficult dialogues in higher education.* University of Alaska, Anchorage. https://ctl.oregonstate.edu/sites/ctl.oregonstate.edu/files/stop_talking_final.pdf

Mills, N. (2012). The corporatization of higher education. *Dissent 59*(4), 6–9. https://doi.org/10.1353/dss
.2012.0087

Montenegro, E., & Jankowski, N. A. (2017). *Equity and assessment: Moving towards culturally responsive assessment*. National Institute for Learning Outcomes Assessment (NILOA). https://www.learningoutcomesassessment.org/wpcontent/uploads/2019/02/OccasionalPaper29.pdf

Montenegro, E., & Jankowski, N. A. (2020, January). *A new decade for assessment: Embedding equity into assessment praxis* (Occasional Paper no. 42). National Institute for Learning Outcomes Assessment (NILOA). https://www.learningoutcomesassessment.org/wp-content/uploads/2020/01/A-New-Decade-for
-Assessment.pdf

Morgan, H., & Houghton, A. M. (2011). *Inclusive curriculum design in higher education: Considerations for effective practice across and within subject areas*. Higher Education Academy.

Ohio State Kirwan Institute. (n.d.). Implicit bias modules. http://kirwaninstitute.osu.edu/implicit
-bias-training/

Opertti, R. (2009,October 1-3). Inclusive education and inclusive curriculum: Moving the EFA agenda forward. [PowerPoint presentation]. Teacher Education for Inclusion Project Kick Off Meeting. Dublin, Ireland. http://www.ibe.unesco.org/sites/default/files/Teacher_Ed_Inclusive_Curriculum.pdf

Paris, D. (2012). Culturally sustaining pedagogy: A needed change in stance, terminology, and practice. *Educational Researcher, 41*(3), 93–97. https://doi.org/10.3102/0013189X12441244

Project Implicit. (n.d.). *Implicit association test*. https://implicit.harvard.edu/implicit/iatdetails.html

Spitzberg, B. H., & Changnon, G. (2009). Conceptualizing intercultural competence. In D. K. Deardorff (Ed.), *The Sage handbook of intercultural competence* (pp. 2–52). Sage Publications.

Strayhorn, T. L. (2019). *College students' sense of belonging: A key to educational success for all students* (2nd ed.). Routledge.

Tuitt, F. (2016). Pedagogy 2.0: Implications for race, equity, and higher education in a global context. In F. Tuitt, C. Haynes, & S. Stewart (Eds.), *Race, equity, and the learning environment: The global relevance of critical and inclusive pedagogies in higher education*. Stylus Publishing.

Tuitt, F., Haynes, C., & Stewart, S. (Eds.). (2016). *Race, equity, and the learning environment: The global relevance of critical and inclusive pedagogies in higher education*. Stylus Publishing.

Waitoller, F. R., & Thorius, K. A. K. (2016). Cross-pollinating culturally sustaining pedagogy and universal design for learning: Toward an inclusive pedagogy that accounts for Dis/Ability. *Harvard Educational Review, 86*(3), 366–389, 473–474.

Wane, N., Shahjahan, R. A., & Wagner, A. (2004). Walking the talk: Decolonizing the politics of equity of knowledge and charting the course for an inclusive curriculum in higher education. *Canadian Journal of Development Studies, 25*(3), 499–510. https://doi.org/10.1080/02255189.2004.9668991

Weimer, M. (2002). *Learner-centered teaching: Five key changes to practice*. Jossey-Bass.

Winkelmes, M., Boye, A., & Tapp, S. (2019). *Transparent design in higher education teaching and leadership: A guide to implementing the transparency framework institution-wide to improve learning and retention*. Stylus Publishing.

Williams, J. M. (2020). *Stay woke: A meditation guide for the rest of us*. Sounds True.

Wu, X. (2010). Universal design for learning: A collaborative framework for designing inclusive curriculum. *i.e.: inquiry in education, 1*(2). http://digitalcommons.nl.edu/ie/vol1/iss2/6

PART I
Setting Up Inclusive Learning Environments

Part I of this book is focused on setting up inclusive learning environments, which is the first logical step of any pedagogical endeavor. In this section, the chapters illustrate ways educators can intentionally create inclusive learning environments. In each chapter, the authors develop inclusive pedagogical practices and curricula to achieve equity in their classes.

Developing an inclusive classroom begins with the syllabus. The first chapter is devoted to the course syllabus, one of the first and most important steps in establishing the classroom community. The course syllabus, which historically served as a contract or agreement between the faculty and students, should evolve to become an important pedagogical tool that exemplifies the instructors' approach, their intentions, and the type of classroom they intend to create. Kirsten Helmer argues the syllabus can set the tone of a class. She examines how the way the subtext of a syllabus is interpreted can impact marginalized and underrepresented student groups. She explains how a syllabus can be written through the lens of inclusivity by following six principles of syllabus design that will promote equity.

After content, educators often state class size as a challenge to applying principles of equity and inclusion. Despite the barriers that large classes can present, Claire Lyons and Janna Taft Young make the case that even large classes need to address equity and inclusion if they are to achieve equitable outcomes for all students. They offer ways to be more inclusive under broader themes such as: How instructors can present themselves and the learning environment they create, how class structure and organization can be personalized to meet diverse needs, and finally how class content and activities can be designed to include all students. They describe how large classes can present a context for analyzing case studies, using media, engaging group work, and providing inclusive examples to illustrate core concepts. By intentionally applying culturally relevant pedagogy and curriculum, Lyons and Young show how large lecture courses can create an inclusive learning environment.

Online learning has become an increasingly necessary medium for learning. In response to the reality of online learning, educators must design inclusive learning experiences that support students in online contexts. Ruth Benander and Pam Rankey discuss how to design and facilitate equitable and inclusive online classes to meet student needs that include content and academic and technological skills. They explore how concepts of universal design, cultural humility, and multiple paths for mastery can develop inclusivity in online courses.

This section of the book brings together practical advice for syllabus design and pedagogical options that faculty can use in challenging teaching environments of large courses and online courses. Readers should consider how they might adapt the strategies presented in these chapters to their own teaching contexts to deliver content in a way that is mindful of inclusion and equity. Part I illustrates how faculty from different disciplines and institutions approach the necessary work of promoting equity in higher education.

CHAPTER 1
Six Principles of an Inclusive Syllabus Design

Kirsten Helmer

The course syllabus is typically the first point of interaction and the initial tool of communication between students and their teachers. This first impression matters (Harnish & Bridges, 2011). For instructors, the syllabus provides a critical opportunity to communicate to students not only the content and structure of the course, but also the expectations and intentions of the learning environment. While syllabi traditionally have been viewed as serving mainly administrative purposes (for example, as implicit contracts between students, instructors, and the institution), perceptions of syllabi have changed to acknowledge the role they play as important educational tools (Eberly, Newton, & Wiggins, 2001). Purposes of a syllabus include setting the tone for a course, motivating students, and showcasing instructor's pedagogical practices and intentions for the kind of learning environment they want to cultivate (Slattery & Carlson, 2005). In addition, syllabi function as socialization tools that mediate the complex social interactions within a classroom (Afros & Schryer, 2009; Sulik & Keys, 2014). In these ways, syllabi can positively shape the class climate and help to build a sense of community, respect, and mutual support (Sulik & Keys, 2014).

However, many syllabi operate as part of the hidden curriculum—those unwritten implicit rules, norms, messages, and hidden biases about students that we communicate through what Brantmeier, Broscheid, and Moore (2017) identified as the subtext of a syllabus. The hidden curriculum that flows through our syllabus can have a negative impact on students' learning experiences and academic success, particularly for students from historically marginalized and underrepresented populations. It puts students who are not familiar with the hidden curriculum at a disadvantage from the start. Examining the subtext of our syllabus to uncover its hidden curriculum is a critical step when striving to teach more inclusively and equitably. How we design our syllabi matters because they are "unobtrusive but powerful indicators of what takes place in classrooms" (Bers, Davis, & Taylor, 2000, p. 899). Intentional syllabus design allows us to be attentive to the rules, assumptions, and values that are important for students' success in our course and that inform our teaching of the course but that we often do not state explicitly.

The purpose of this chapter is to offer ideas on how to write a syllabus with an inclusive design perspective so that students do not simply treat it as "an End User License

Agreement—something for which one glances at briefly, clicks 'agree to terms,' and moves on to the product without reading any of the document" (Perry, 2014, para. 14). Womack (2017) reminded us that syllabi are informational *and* rhetorical documents; as such, we should design them with our student audience in mind. She wrote, "I had worked to make the course content diverse and accessible but had ignored the document that facilitates that content" (p. 503). As you write your syllabus, think about how you can use it to communicate your commitment to inclusive and equitable teaching and learning and to begin establishing high-quality relationships with your students.

An inclusive syllabus provides signposts for students about what they will learn, do, and need to know to succeed in the course, and it discusses options, resources, and accessibility for a more equitable learning environment. Grounded in a review of relevant literature, I synthesize existing research about syllabus design into six intersecting principles that serves as a scaffolding framework for the (re)design of course syllabi. These six principles are:

1. Focus on Student Learning

2. Course Design around Big Themes and Essential Questions

3. Application of Universal Design for Learning (UDL) Principles

4. Tone and Rhetoric—Inclusive and Motivating Language

5. Supportive Course Policies

6. Accessible Design

I will describe each principle and provide examples of how these principles translate into actual course and syllabus design options that support inclusive and equitable learning environments. Two resources, "Six Principles of Inclusive Syllabus Design" and "Syllabus Template," are available on the open access companion site for this book.

PRINCIPLE 1: FOCUS ON STUDENT LEARNING

The first principle of an inclusive syllabus design asks instructors to shift from a content-focused to a learning-focused syllabus. Traditional syllabi emphasize the course content and structure of the course. Rarely do course syllabi provide students with a nuanced understanding of the processes involved in learning and mastering the content. Palmer, Wheeler, and Aneece (2016) advocate for shifting to learning-focused syllabi, saying the syllabus should "clearly communicate that content is used primarily as a vehicle for learning" (p. 5). Their research showed that students who read a learning-focused syllabus have significantly more positive perceptions of the document itself, which importantly translates into more positive perceptions of the course and the instructor. They emphasize that learning-focused syllabi positively affect students' motivation before students even enter the classroom, thus supporting students' meaningful engagement with the course.

To check your syllabus's orientation, evaluate how it guides your students through the learning environment:

1. Do you state both high-level, long-term goals (articulated in aspirational and inspirational language) and shorter-term, measurable learning objectives?

2. Do your learning objectives address different levels of cognitive, behavioral, and affective learning?

3. Does the syllabus communicate a supportive and motivating learning environment?

4. Do you consider a variety of student interests and the learning needs of different types or groups of students?

5. Do you explain in your syllabus how the learning activities and course assignments and assessments align with the learning objectives?

6. Does your syllabus provide information about all the ways you will assess students' learning, including the use of low-stakes formative assessments throughout the course?

7. Do you pace and scaffold assessments in ways that support student success?

(Adapted from Palmer, Bach, & Streifer, 2014 and Palmer, Wheeler, & Aneece, 2016)

Consider analyzing your syllabus using one of the rubrics on inclusive and accessible syllabus design developed by Palmer, Bach, and Streifer (2014), Brantmeier, Broscheid, and Moore (2017), or the Ensuring Access through Collaboration and Technology (EnACT) project by the California State University, Sonoma.

Another way to check whether or not your syllabus functions as a tool for supporting student learning is to gather feedback from your students. Consider having your students annotate the syllabus (Kalir, 2018), or asking them to send you an email or post to an online discussion forum with questions they have about the syllabus and areas they find confusing.

PRINCIPLE 2: COURSE DESIGN AROUND BIG THEMES AND ESSENTIAL QUESTIONS

When students struggle with seeing a course as meaningful and relevant as they are reading the syllabus, they may begin the course by already seeing themselves as unsuccessful learners in that course. The second principle suggests providing a coherent narrative arc of what students will learn throughout the course. Think about framing your syllabus as containing a "promise" through language that invites students to enter the course with a sense of curiosity and high expectations about how the course will be meaningful for them (Bain, 2004; Palmer, Bach, & Streifer, 2014; Palmer, Wheeler, & Aneece, 2016). Slattery and Carlson (2005) encouraged instructors to write the syllabus as an invitation to students to take part in an "organized and meaningful journey" (p. 159). The Association of College and University Educators (n.d.) suggested building a graphic or big-ideas syllabus to support students in visualizing the organization of the course.

Wiggins and McTighe (2005) developed a backwards design process where instructors begin with the end in mind: What are the essential questions, ideas, and themes that you will explore with your students and how do they connect? They define essential questions as those that "push us to the heart of things—the essence" (p. 107) and that "serve as door-ways through which learners explore the key concepts, themes, theories, issues, and problems that reside within the content, perhaps as yet unseen" (p. 106). Cunliff (2014) emphasized how "the use of questions cues students that there will be interaction and that they are expected to engage. It also tells them that questions are OK" (para. 9). Write an engaging course description and introduce the class sessions in your course schedule with thought-provoking, intriguing questions or statements to stimulate student curiosity and signal inquiry-based learning (Eberly, Newton, & Wiggins, 2001). In doing so, you communicate to students that their voices and input matter and that you are committed to cultivating an inclusive and equitable learning community.

PRINCIPLE 3: APPLICATION OF UNIVERSAL DESIGN FOR LEARNING (UDL) PRINCIPLES

Syllabi function as organizational tools in curriculum (re)design (Eberly, Newton, & Wiggins, 2001). The third principle of inclusive syllabus design focuses on applying the principles of Universal Design for Learning (UDL) to strengthen a course's organizational structure in ways that are accessible to all students (CAST, 2018). As Womack (2017) emphasized, "Agency, for all students, comes from access" (p. 500). She advocated for framing accommodations not as "the exception we sometimes make in spite of learning, but rather the adaptations we continually make to promote learning" (p. 494). In other words, when using a UDL framework for your course and syllabus design, "accommodation is the norm, not the special case" (Womack, 2017, p. 499).

When you create your course syllabus, you have an ideal opportunity to illustrate how you design the course with variability in mind by providing students with multiple paths for learning and success. Through a UDL-informed syllabus, you communicate how you will meet the needs of diverse students by providing a variety of options and flexibility for accessing and processing course content, participating in the course, and assessing skills and knowledge (CAST, 2018). Indicate how you will present content in multiple ways beyond printed texts (i.e., through various modalities or formats, including images, graphics, videos, blogs, podcasts, or websites that feature real-world applications of content); allow choices about topics for readings, assignments, or projects; and provide options for students to demonstrate their learning that go beyond quizzes, exams, or written papers (i.e., through oral presentations, projects, performances, or products).

In addition, a UDL-informed syllabus provides explicit information that will help students plan, prioritize, and see the larger picture of how course content, learning objectives, learning activities, and assignments connect. Create a detailed course schedule, preferably in a concise table format, that provides information about what students can expect to learn, what they will need to do to be prepared for the next class session, and when assignments will be due. Let your students know what resources and supports are available to facilitate their success.

In sum, a syllabus that reflects UDL design principles allows students to see how you intend to create a flexible learning environment that will allow them to be engaged and successful.

PRINCIPLE 4: TONE AND RHETORIC—INCLUSIVE AND MOTIVATING LANGUAGE

The fourth principle of an inclusive syllabus focuses on tone and rhetoric. Wood and Madden (2014) pointed out how "syllabi function rhetorically and have consequences in terms of how students understand the classroom atmosphere, what they expect from the teacher's relationship to students, and how they predict the semester will go for them" (para. 10). The syllabus as a rhetorical text communicates issues about power and authority between instructor and students. The language we choose and the way we frame course content, student engagement, and our course policies communicate explicitly and implicitly our values, expectations, and how we view our students as learners. Many syllabi present problematic assumptions because instructors write them with the "problem" student in mind (Womack, 2017). They often use a confrontational, authoritarian, or condescending tone (Sulik & Keys, 2014), communicate mistrust by using negative punishment language (Wasley, 2008) or defensive and even combative policies (Baecker, 1998; Perry 2014), and have a generally cold tenor (Womack, 2017). Such language distances students instead of inviting them as learners into our classes. This can be especially problematic for historically marginalized students who often struggle with finding a sense of belonging in academic settings.

Research has shown that syllabi characterized by friendliness, enthusiasm, and anticipation of student success evoke "perceptions of the instructor being warmer, more approachable, and more motivated to teach the course" (Harnish & Bridges, 2011, p. 319). Palmer, Bach, and Streifer (2014) advocated for a positive, respectful, and inviting tone throughout the document that addresses the students as competent and engaged learners. Such language fosters positive motivation by emphasizing a collaborative spirit and an orientation toward learning and possibility rather than performance and punishment. Womack (2017) suggested establishing a tone of negotiation and flexibility in the classroom by writing in terms of invitations rather than commands and in ways that highlight common ideals and community building.

One simple but powerful shift is to use personal pronouns (e.g., I, you, we, us) instead of the traditional "the students," "the course," or "they" (Palmer, Wheeler, & Aneece, 2016). However, we need to be mindful of how we use the pronouns so that we do not unintentionally exclude rather than include. As Baecker (1998) cautioned, the personal pronoun *we* is ambiguous because it is often used to blur responsibilities and coerce cooperation instead of showing genuine intent to cultivate community.

Palmer, Wheeler, and Aneece (2016) further suggested replacing the predictable, mundane section headings in the syllabus (e.g., Course Overview, Due Dates, Grading) with ones that are learning-oriented, such as "What will help you to be successful in this course?," "What will you learn along this way?," and "What will you be doing?" Harnish and Bridges (2011) found that providing a rationale for assignments, sharing personal experiences, using humor, and showing enthusiasm for the course positively influence students' perceptions of the instructor and the course.

PRINCIPLE 5: SUPPORTIVE COURSE POLICIES

Many institutions require standard policy statements on matters like attendance, academic honesty, and disability accommodations. It is important to recognize how the language and the use of policies, procedures, and rationales within the syllabus reflects cultural norms and expectations. Interestingly, many course policies, particularly those about attendance, punctuality, deadlines, and more recently, classroom civility, take a punitive approach and stress accountability and students' self-presentation as keys to success. However, few course policies focus on the importance of students' active engagement with learning processes and advise students to raise questions, be involved, and embrace active learning (Sulik & Keys, 2014). The fifth principle of inclusive syllabus design therefore focuses on writing supportive course policies. Such policies help students understand the rationale behind expectations and values, and they provide comprehensive information about resources and supports that will help students be successful learners.

DIVERSITY AND INCLUSION STATEMENTS

Consider including a statement in your syllabus in which you explicitly acknowledge your values and beliefs, and your commitment to cultivate an inclusive and equitable learning environment where differences are respected and valued (Sheridan Center, n.d.). As you write this statement think about how you define diversity and how diversity, equity, and inclusion inform your teaching philosophy. Let your students know how you intend to shape a positive class climate that will provide students with a sense of belonging within a mutually supportive community. You can find a variety of examples online and adapt these to fit your own personality, teaching style and philosophy, and disciplinary context.

DISABILITY ACCOMMODATION AND INCLUSIVE LEARNING STATEMENT

Many institutions have official disability statements that inform students with disabilities about their legal right to reasonable accommodations. While this information is critical, disability statements typically do not consider issues of access for students who do not meet the minimum legal guidelines for accommodations. Think about how to craft a statement that demonstrates to your students your intention to provide wide access beyond legal obligations. Consider expanding the disability statement required by your institution into a "Disability Accommodation and Inclusive Learning Statement." As Womack (2017) wrote, "When all course policies have been theoretically subordinated to accommodation, it makes sense to begin the list with an inclusive learning statement" (p. 513). Such an inclusive learning statement should include hyperlinks to important student services on your campus, such as a disability services office, a campus writing center, a learning resource center, a center for counseling, and a program for non-native speakers of English. By placing such an inclusive learning statement at the top of your syllabus, rather than at the end, as is typical, you can further enhance the supportive tone of your syllabus.

OFFICE HOURS STATEMENT

Simply listing office hours in the syllabus does not encourage students to visit an instructor. Many students, especially those from historically underrepresented populations, hesitate to contact their instructors or they do not understand the purpose of office hours. This can create social barriers to their learning. Craft a statement that motivates students to meet with you. Consider using a term like "'Student-Instructor Hours'" and explaining to your students what they gain from connecting with you. Offer brief greeting chats at the beginning of the semester so that you and your students can get to know each other. Tell your students that more traditional longer meetings are for helping them with specific course content questions, assignments, other course-related problems, or to talk about other school and life matters, including future plans. Consider offering group meetings to support students as they work on projects, presentations, or other assignments. Flexible and/or virtual meeting hours are a wonderful opportunity to demonstrate availability, caring, and support. Many students have other obligations so that they cannot make it to office hours that are offered only on specific days and times. Use an online scheduling system or an online document for sign-up.

ACADEMIC HONESTY STATEMENT

Similar to the disability accommodation statement, most institutions require an academic honesty statement in the syllabus. In writing this statement through the lens of inclusiveness, assume your students' best intentions and ask yourself what they need to know to be able to comply with academic honesty. Adopt a warm tone that explains what plagiarism is and is not, let students know they can consult with you to clarify any points of confusion, and provide hyperlinks to the institutional policy, campus resources on the topic, and external resources, such as the Purdue Owl Online Writing Lab.

ATTENDANCE AND DEADLINES

Consider flexibility in attendance as well as assignment deadlines. Fixed deadlines and strict mandatory attendance policies often function as barriers to student success. As Womack (2017) pointed out, "Extended time is a common disability accommodation because learners perform at different speeds, and college students juggle multiple commitments" (p. 517). She suggested empowering students through flexible course plans that extend the time frame for deadlines by including an instructor-set range and student-determined deadlines. Build extended time for all students into timed exams and offer assessments that do not rely on one opportunity only to be completed based on a predetermined schedule.

PRONOUN POLICY

Increasingly, students have the opportunity to identify chosen names and pronouns in learning management systems. Including a name and pronoun policy in the syllabus can contribute to an increased sense of belonging for transgender and gender-nonconforming students. Include hyperlinks to additional resources on the use of pronouns in this policy.

PRINCIPLE 6: ACCESSIBLE DESIGN

The final principle for an inclusive syllabus design addresses the visual and text design of the syllabus. Traditional syllabi are often dense, text-heavy, and very hard to read, especially for students with dyslexia, AD(H)D, learning disabilities, or non-native speakers of English. In addition, many syllabi do not comply with accessibility requirements because screen readers cannot read them, or they are hard to navigate. The following basic steps will help you create a syllabus that is accessible and easy to read and navigate.

BASIC STEPS

- Assign styles (Title, Heading 1, Heading 2) to establish a hierarchical structure within the document. By doing so, you can easily create a table of contents on the first page of the syllabus with document-internal hyperlinks that will allow readers to easily navigate the syllabus on their electronic devices.

- Create document-internal hyperlinks to connect to information located later in the document and hyperlinks to external resources and your course learning management system (LMS). Make sure to use meaningful labels that indicate where a link goes. For example, provide the name of the website or the name of the author and the title of the reading to which you are linking instead of "click here." External hyperlinks allow you to cut text related to information that students can find elsewhere.

- Arrange the text in discernible chunks by breaking up the text into smaller paragraphs, or by using text columns, text boxes, tables, and bulleted or numbered lists.
- Align text to the left.
- Use a 12–14 point sans serif font.
- Use at least 1.25 line spacing.
- Create accessible tables by designating defining header rows and first columns and repeating headers across page.

USE OF VISUAL REPRESENTATION OF CONTENT

Consider using graphic design principles that highlight and focus attention, enhance clarity, strengthen the organization, and add visual interest to your syllabus. Williams (2015) suggested using contrast (such as size, color, and spacing), repetition (consistency in style elements, fonts, color, spacing), alignment (how the elements of the text visually connect), and proximity (placing related things together) to guide your design.

To add interest and to enhance the content in your syllabus, trade some text for accessible images and visual representations of content. Using images and visual representations of information quickly conveys information and increases understanding, particularly when students quickly skim a document (Womack, 2017). A collage of images, a single provocative image, photographs of key authors, the textbook logo, or a word cloud visualizing key terms can indicate themes of the course. Make sure to cite the image source and use alt text to briefly describe it. Block together icons to illustrate essential course information, such as your email, office hours, the class location, class meeting times, and course texts. Use graphic representation for important information; for example, create a colored pie chart to illustrate the weight of different assignments for the grade (Womack, 2017).

ELECTRONIC HYPERTEXT

Document-internal links and hyperlinks to external web-based resources offer instructors more organizational possibilities and foster the scaffolding of learning (Afros & Schryer, 2009). For students, such interactive tools provide easy access to academic and social support services on campus (i.e., disability services, counseling services, support groups, writing center, tutoring help, a program for non-native English speakers) and off campus (tutorial videos, study aids) as well as to administrative information (i.e., institutional policies on academic integrity and disability accommodations, academic calendar, schedule of classes, dean's office).

CONCLUSION

Within a context in higher education that recognizes how important it is to center diversity, inclusion, and equity in course design and pedagogical practices, we need to rethink how we communicate such values to our students right from the start. Literature on syllabus designs highlight the importance of the syllabus for shaping the conditions for teaching and learning. More attention needs to focus on the syllabus as a significant tool to promote inclusive and accessible learning environments for the increasingly diverse students in our classes. Consequently, instructors should take care in developing their syllabi. The six principles of an inclusive syllabus design presented in this chapter provide a guiding framework for more inclusiveness in learning by design.

Writing an inclusive and accessible syllabus is of practical and ethical importance. By making explicit the hidden curriculum and communicating that we are committed to helping our students succeed in our classes, instructors can contribute to more equity in learning. Designing syllabi through the lens of inclusiveness may contribute to student success for a broader range of students and the promotion of a more inclusive and equitable campus climate.

REFERENCES

Afros, E., & Schryer, C. F. (2009). The genre of syllabus in higher education. *Journal of English for Academic Purposes, 8*(3), 224–233. https://doi.org/10.1016/j.jeap.2009.01.004

Association of College and University Educators (n.d.). *Preparing an effective syllabus.* https://acue.org/courses/modules/preparing-an-effective-syllabus/

Bain, K. (2004). *What the best college teachers do.* Harvard University Press.

Baecker, D. L. (1998). Uncovering the rhetoric of the syllabus: The case of the missing I. *College Teaching, 46*(2), 58.

Bers, T. H., Davis, B. D., & Taylor, B. (2000). The use of syllabi in assessments: Unobtrusive indicators and tools for faculty development. *Assessment Update 12*(3), 4–7.

Brantmeier, E., Broscheid, A., & Moore, C. S. (2017, September 11). *Inclusion by design: Tools helps faculty examine their teaching practices.* Faculty Focus. https://www.facultyfocus.com/articles/course-design-ideas/inclusion-by-design-tool-helps-faculty-examine-teaching-practices/

CAST. (2018). *Universal Design for Learning Guidelines version 2.2.* http://udlguidelines.cast.org

Cunliff, E. (2014). Tonic for the boring syllabus. *Teaching Professor, 28*(2), 5. https://www.usi.edu/media/4668536/12-Cunliff-Tonic-for-the-Boring-Syllabus.docx

Eberly, M. B., Newton, S. E., & Wiggins, R. A. (2001). The syllabus as a tool for student-centered learning. *Journal of General Education, 50*(1), 56–74. https://doi.org/10.1353/jge.2001.0003

Ensuring Access through Collaboration and Technology (EnACT)–California State University, Sonoma (n.d.). *UDL-Universe: A comprehensive faculty development guide: UDL syllabus rubric.* http://enact.sonoma.edu/c.php?g=789377&p=5650618

Harnish, R. J., & Bridges, K. R. (2011). Effect of syllabus tone: Students' perceptions of instructor and course. *Social Psychology of Education,14* (3), 319–330.

Kalir, R. (2018, December 19). Annotate your syllabus 2.0. [Blog post]. http://remikalir.com/blog/annotate-your-syllabus-2-0

Palmer, M. S., Bach, D. J., & Streifer, A. C. (2014). Measuring the promise: A learning-focused syllabus rubric. *To Improve the Academy, 33*(1), 14–36.

Palmer, M. S., Wheeler, L. B., & Aneece, I. (2016). Does the document matter? The evolving role of syllabi in higher education. *Change, 48*(4), 36–47. https://doi.org/10.1080/00091383.2016.1198186

Perry, D. M. (2014, March 17). Faculty members are not cashiers. *Chronicle of Higher Education.* https://www.chronicle.com/article/Faculty-Members-Are-Not/145363

Purdue Writing Lab. (n.d.). OWL // Purdue Writing Lab. https://owl.purdue.edu/

Sheridan Center at Brown University. (n.d.). Diversity & inclusion syllabus statements. https://www.brown.edu/sheridan/teaching-learning-resources/inclusive-teaching/statements

Slattery, J. M., & Carlson, J. F. (2005). Preparing an effective syllabus: Current best practices. *College Teaching, 53*(4), 159.

Sulik, G., & Keys, J. (2014). "Many students really do not yet know how to behave!": The syllabus as a tool for socialization. *Teaching Sociology, 42*(2), 151–160.

Wasley, P. (2008, March 14). The syllabus becomes a repository of legalese. *Chronicle of Higher Education.* https://www.chronicle.com/article/the-syllabus-becomes-a-repository-of-legalese/

Wiggins, G. P., & McTighe, J. (2005). *Understanding by design* (2nd ed.). Association for Supervision and Curriculum Development.

Williams, R. (2015). *The non-designer's design book: Design and typographic principles for the visual novice.* Peachpit Press.

Womack, A. (2017). Teaching is accommodation: Universally designing composition classrooms and syllabi. *College Composition & Communication, 68*(3), 494–525.

Wood, T., & Madden, S. (2014). Suggested practices for syllabus accessibility statements. *Kairos 18*(1). https://praxis.technorhetoric.net/tiki-index.php?page=Suggested_Practices_for_Syllabus_Accessibility_Statements

CHAPTER 2
Student-Centered Teaching for Equity and Inclusion in Very Large Multidisciplinary Classes

Claire W. Lyons and Janna Taft Young

Large classes are a common and enduring part of the higher education landscape (Salz, 2014; Whisenhunt et al., 2019), particularly for introductory courses. Nevertheless, there is a common perception that large classes are less effective and engaging. For example, in their ranking of Best Colleges, *U.S. News* gives no credit for classes larger than fifty students (*U.S. News*, 2019). One consequence of these negative perceptions is that researchers addressing educational innovation seem to neglect the very large class.

Notably, any educator looking for advice on how to make their class more inclusive and equitable will quickly discover that the recommended approaches are difficult to implement in the very large class (Hartwell et al., 2017). For example, intergroup dialogue is a well-established approach to addressing equity and inclusion. It typically involves sustained communication between students in the class, while raising consciousness and bridging differences (Zúñiga, Naagda, & Sevig, 2002). Creating dialogue in a meaningful way in the very large class can be difficult. In fact, the optimal number for intergroup dialogue is considered to be eight to fifteen students.

Moreover, some aspects of the very large class seem to work against the establishment of dialogue. Students frequently say that they feel anonymous in these large group settings, feeling distant from their instructor and other students. This perceived distance makes it difficult for the instructor to sustain student engagement (Whisenhunt et al., 2019). Furthermore, lecturing tends to be the methodology of choice in the large class (Panjawani & Cipollina, 2017). Instructors can easily fall into a stand-and-deliver style of teaching, which may seem antithetical to the goals of promoting equity and inclusion.

Given these challenges, it can be tempting for those of us who teach very large classes to leave issues of equity and inclusion to our colleagues who can work with smaller groups. We resist this temptation for a number of reasons. Themes of equity and inclusion are evident in our classes whether we are aware of it or not. They are in the subject matter (e.g., sociocultural influences on behavior) and structure of our classes (e.g., diverse populations of students). They are also part of the group dynamics in our classroom and part of our students' lives outside of the classroom. It would be naive of us to think that privilege and oppression are not part of our classes. So, we have a duty to address these issues in the most efficient and effective way that we can. In our case, preparing students to be citizens of a diverse society is one of the established goals for undergraduate psychology education (American Psychological Association, 2011). Indeed, education for diversity and inclusion has become a primary focus across a variety of disciplines (Association of American Colleges & Universities, 2019). If we do not address inclusivity directly, we run the risk that students' misconceptions about equity and inclusion will go unchallenged.

In our opinion, large general education classes are an ideal setting to begin to address equity and inclusion. Addressing inclusivity in these settings allows us the opportunity to influence a large number of students across a variety of majors and diverse cultural backgrounds. Our specific approach to equity and inclusion in the large class involves three primary elements: presentation of self and learning environment, class structure and organization, and class content and activities.

DESCRIPTION OF PRACTICE
OUR TEACHING CONTEXT

The authors each teach large-section survey courses in the Department of Psychology at James Madison University (JMU). JMU is a comprehensive public university with over twenty-two thousand students, about 90 percent of whom are undergraduates (see http://www.jmu.edu/about/index.shtml). We typically teach two- to three-hundred-student sections. Our courses are part of JMU's general education curriculum within the sociocultural domain. A majority of our students are in their first year, especially in the fall semester. Given the number of students served each term, these classes are held in a large auditorium with tiered seating. We use undergraduate teaching assistants to help with learning activities, office hours, and grading. In the following sections, we discuss ways of addressing equity and inclusion in large classes that are applicable across a range of disciplines.

PRESENTATION OF SELF AND LEARNING ENVIRONMENT

If we want to make our classes inclusive learning spaces where diversity is valued, we need to build nurturing, supportive relationships with our students. We need to engage them emotionally and cognitively. Furthermore, we need to let students know what to expect because engaging with issues of equity and diversity is going to be challenging for them (Adams, 2016). In this section we discuss how we begin to build positive relationships with our students and how we set clear expectations for our learning environment through our syllabi.

As instructors, we set the tone for our class. In our presentation of ourselves, we make sure to convey that the class is a welcoming space for all students. We are energetic and enthusiastic, and we try to very clearly let the students know that we want them to succeed and for us to learn together. We set ground rules for positive engagement in the class to ensure that students are as safe as possible. Whenever possible, we also use our own stories as a basis for the discussion of equity and inclusion. Sharing a part of our experiences can make a large class feel much more personal. For instance, we might share our feelings about being a first-generation college student or how depression can be isolating. Our students report that they are more engaged, and the class size feels more intimate, when we use our own real-life examples. When the students see us as approachable and genuinely interested in our students' success, even the large class can seem more equitable and inclusive.

The tone and attitude you take with your students in your teaching, and even in your handouts, is important to consider. Since we will not get the chance to speak with each of our students individually, we must convey a welcoming environment in every public aspect of our course. To that end, we include syllabus statements that directly address diversity and inclusion, such as: "James Madison University is a community dedicated to diversity and inclusivity. As faculty, we believe that learning environments should support a diversity of thoughts, perspectives, experiences, and identities. We invite you to share anything with us that might help create a more inclusive and welcoming learning environment" (see https://www.jmu.edu/facultysenate/_files/div_syllabi_motion.pdf).

We enact this syllabus statement by getting to know our students as much as possible. To support students, we need to get some idea of their experiences and perspectives. Students are more likely to give us feedback on how to create a more inclusive classroom environment if we know them and if they trust us. Before class starts, a welcoming email can be sent to students. In our introductory email, we encourage students to come visit during office hours so we can get to know as many students as possible.

Students could complete an entry questionnaire in which they are invited to share information that will help the instructor get to know them. Questions that can be asked include: students' nationalities, whether they have ever taken a large class before, what they expect learning in the large class will be like, their learning needs, how they identify their race or ethnicity, whether they are first-generation students, and their motivation for taking the class. The questionnaire can be anonymous, or students can be invited to share their name if they wish. Students should always be given the option not to answer a question, without penalty. The questionnaire should be seen as an invitation, not a requirement.

Having this information sensitizes the instructor to issues that the class, or specific students, may be facing. For example, students have shared their anxiety that they will not be able to keep up with the pace of the class. To address this anxiety, we monitor the pace of instruction and repeat important explanations and examples, pausing to make sure that students can take adequate notes. Instructors can reassure students that they will be supported in their learning and emphasize the support that is available, such as regular office hours. Aggregate data from the questionnaire can be used to create empathy in the class. With this kind of data, instructors can share information such as half of the students have never taken a class like this before, which helps more advanced students understand the pace of the class.

Another way to recognize diversity among your students and promote inclusivity is to implement a survey such as the Inclusive Introduction Questionnaire developed by Bethany P. Bryson, JMU's safe zone coordinator (Bryson, n.d.). This questionnaire allows students to let the instructor know how they would like to be addressed (e.g., preferred name and pronoun), since official class rosters do not always accurately reflect students' identities. They are also asked to share anything that will help the instructor to get to know them. It is not feasible for instructors with over three hundred students to get to know each one of them individually. However, the instructor can review data before meeting with a student. They can also reach out to specific students through email based on comments (e.g., a student with concerns). In our experience, students have responded enthusiastically to these communications. For example, students have told us they are grateful for the personal contact and they are subsequently more comfortable looking for help.

CLASS STRUCTURE AND ORGANIZATION

In large classes, it is important to intentionally design the structure and organization in order to create inclusive learning environments. We do this by providing access to resources, assessing students in different ways, learning students' names, practicing content with clickers, online timed testing, and the use of teaching assistants.

Universal Design for Learning (UDL) involves designing learning environments that are accessible to as many students as possible (Ostiguy, Peters, & Shiasko, 2016). This accessibility is achieved by flexible presentation and assessment of learning, and multiple modes of engagement. Drawing on the principles of UDL, we present material in accessible ways and assess students in a variety of ways (Center for Teaching Innovation, n.d.; Dean, Lee-Post, and Hapke, 2017). For instance, we provide the primary content of lecture concepts and discussion questions on the learning management system. We also use a combination of performance (e.g., quizzes and tests) and effort (e.g., class participation) measures for assessing students. In this way, students earn points in a variety of ways to augment their chances of success.

As a means of promoting engagement, it is advisable to learn as many students' names as possible. One way to do this is to incorporate discussion activities, perhaps in place of in-class testing. We make an effort to learn the students' preferred names by making name tags on the discussion days and adjusting the names as students share their preferences with us. This effort does not go unnoticed. Students have reported

33

that this makes a large lecture class personal by encouraging students to socially collaborate, discuss concepts, and develop critical thinking while applying class concepts to real life.

A seating plan with all the students' names and where they commonly sit can help the instructor to get to know students. We label the seats in the auditorium and make a sign-in sheet with the seat row and number; students sign their name in the corresponding seat. The seating plan allows the instructor and/or teaching assistants to find students more quickly in the classroom, if necessary. It also alerts us to student absences. If it appears that a student is repeatedly missing, an email can be sent to check on the student.

As an application of UDL, one could use captioned videos for individuals with hearing disabilities and read out loud all clicker questions and answers in case there are students with visual deficits and/or individuals with processing difficulties. Reading questions out loud might be especially helpful to students who end up seated far away from a projection screen in a large classroom. PowerPoint slides with general information can be posted in advance of the class. This affords students the opportunity to process the information both in and out of class, allowing them to focus on the details and examples discussed in class. Providing outlined slides does not deter student attendance, especially when there are additional participation activities (for points) such as group work and/or concept practice with clickers.

Whether one is teaching a seated section, online, or hybrid course, chapter quizzes and exams can be administered online so as to minimize test anxiety. This makes the assessments more accessible, in line with principles of UDL. We keep our timed quizzes/tests open for at least a day and a half and allow two attempts on each quiz (keeping the highest score) with the correct answers indicated. This allows students who may need to use on-campus facilities (e.g., computer and Wi-Fi) the time to access these resources. It also gives all students (not just those requiring accommodations) permission to take the quiz/test at a time and place of their choosing, plausibly in a less distracting and more relaxed environment. Several students have left comments on evaluations that the online quizzes and tests alleviated stress and helped build confidence. The cognitive benefits of being comfortable in your own environment and completing (even timed) tasks in your own space and time should not be taken for granted.

The aforementioned strategies could be implemented by instructors themselves. In addition, access to undergraduate teaching assistants opens up more ways of making our classes accessible. In our case, teaching assistants interact with students during class (e.g., help with use of clickers, distribute handouts, facilitate activities) and often hold office hours. These assistants, however, will need to be carefully selected and trained; they may be students who have taken the class before, but they should not be current members of the class. Teaching assistants with prior experience in the class often make for excellent peer tutors. They can be assigned to monitor low-performing students throughout the semester via email and encourage them to utilize office hours. Although many students may not visit the instructor's office, they are more likely to utilize resources with this personal, peer contact.

CLASS CONTENT AND ACTIVITIES

So far, we have discussed how we endeavor to make our class inclusive through presentation of self and learning environment and class structure and organization. The third way we attempt to create inclusivity in the large classroom is in the content for our course and in-class activities. The activities that we choose to develop or connect with the course content may help with equity and inclusion.

Approaches to designing student-centered classes for equity and inclusion involve dialogue, reflection, and critical thinking. These elements can be included in the very large class through the judicious design of activities, allowing time and space for students to collaborate and to reflect. These discussion activities might not only raise awareness of other perspectives but also give the students an opportunity to get to know each other, thus allowing for a personal experience in what otherwise may be a large and segregated classroom.

While it has been well-documented that a strong sense of belonging at a university promotes educational success, social involvement, and psychological adjustment, it is equally clear that predominantly White institutions (PWIs) like ours struggle to create a context in which diverse students feel they belong (Strayhorn, 2020). One way in which we can make it clear to students that they belong is to represent diverse experiences and identities in our class content. Instructors in large classes do need to be cautious, however, about what they ask of their students. Instructors with hundreds of students are not in a position to facilitate in-depth processing of issues of equity and diversity. They need to be careful to ensure that their class activities do not further marginalize already marginalized students. We suggest focusing on activities that raise awareness of diversity and allowing for structured dialogue and reflection. For instance, the reflection can be focused on the literature and evaluating the evidence rather than personal experience.

We can implement some elements of intergroup dialogue by selecting course material and examples that address equity and inclusion (Gallor, 2017). The instructor can take on the bulk of the responsibility of presenting diverse perspectives and experiences by using published material. With our desire to represent different sociocultural factors in explaining behavior, we can find a variety of good exemplars in psychological research. We can highlight, for instance, how some racial groups are at lower risk of developing Alzheimer's disease or how climate might impact the incidence of mental illness (Pinel, 2014). While the discussion of equity and diversity will still challenge marginalized students more than privileged students, instructors can lessen the cognitive and emotional load on marginalized students by taking responsibility for voicing diverse perspectives and providing guiding questions for a safe discussion.

Even in a very large class, group discussion can be an opportunity for encouraging engagement and inclusion through dialogue, reflection, and critical thinking. Media, such as movies or video clips, can be a way to connect with the students and elicit discussion with a sharing of ideas. For our discussion activities, students are told they will be alphabetically assigned (by last name) to groups of about eight members and that they will have a team leader (e.g., instructor or teaching assistant). We ask each student to be responsible for knowing their group number, team leader, and where to sit in the room; seating is arranged by colors and numbers. Each team leader manages between five and eleven student groups (at about fifty students). For each discussion, the instructor visits with and leads a different color group, in order to get to meet each group at least once. Students are asked to discuss, come to a consensus as needed, and write out their short answers to the (three to five) questions as a group. There is typically a clicker question to assess student conceptualization and understanding of the critical concepts.

As part of critical thinking, students are encouraged to evaluate the purpose, importance, and implications of the information presented before each discussion. This may include a short video clip, a blog, or brief summaries of research findings. Students are specifically instructed that these activities are to help them build team working skills and to strengthen and develop their critical thinking. As such, we ask them to *Analyze* (i.e., what was learned) and *Reflect* (i.e., why is it important) and think about how the information relates to current (or future) classroom topics. Additional instructions are to creatively discuss ideas and concepts by connecting to topics in the discipline. We also highlight how they should *Relate* (i.e., make connections from the material to psychology and life) and *Generate* (i.e., create and answer new questions about the material).

As an example of dialogue, reflection, and critical thinking, students can be tasked with making connections between movie concepts and class material. The movie *Crash* (Haggis, 2005) is particularly eye-opening for many of our rural-based students because of its depiction of race, prejudice, and discrimination. Through the lens of the movie, students can better understand how classroom concepts might be applicable in life. Question prompts, for instance, can be provided in advance of the viewing and discussion to guide the students. The instructor can challenge the students to evaluate the media and discover ways in which class concepts can be connected to themes, scenes, or ideas in the film. Exercising these critical thinking skills can help the students to be more knowledgeable and observant of ideas, even those different from their own. Students have said that these discussions helped them to process information at a deeper level and encouraged learning over memorization since the focus was on making connections and asking questions rather than trying to arrive at a single correct answer.

Group discussion may also be an opportunity to raise awareness of sociocultural factors. One specific example of a sociocultural theme centers on how perspectives on mental illness may vary by culture, time, and age. Students are given advance notice of the content of the discussions to ensure that they are prepared. The professor first reviews a blog from *Psychology Today* about reactions to trauma and cultural perspectives on offering aid to other countries (Muller, 2013). In addition to highlighting the traditional development of PTSD in response to war or rape, there is an opportunity here to educate the students that trauma might also be induced by a natural disaster (e.g., a tsunami obliterating communities) or an attack (e.g., a school shooting). The students then discuss varied perspectives on how trauma is handled in different countries. They are strongly encouraged to reference and apply specific concepts and ideas in the field to support their stance.

As another example of reflection and critical thinking, instructors can encourage students to consider the role of sociocultural and ecological factors in their discipline. The instructor can apply this approach by presenting students with a description of someone's behavior. They are then asked to come up with as many reasons as possible for the behavior from a variety of domains (e.g., biosocial vs. cognitive). Students are asked to explicitly consider the influences of culture. To facilitate the implementation of this kind of activity in the large class, instructors can begin by asking students to select from a set of closed options. Once students become more competent at the task, they can be asked to generate their own answers. These tasks illustrate diversity because they ask students to consider other people's perspectives and apply a sociocultural lens to their discipline. The activity is a first step toward inclusive participation as the instructor validates different cultural interpretations and norms. Such awareness and validation provide a platform for students to interact more inclusively with each other. Instructors in the large class may not always be able to monitor student participation, but they can publicly validate different perspectives and set the tone for inclusive interaction.

Another way to address equity and inclusion, and encourage reflection, is to teach diversity. Questions of diversity, such as the nature of race and ethnicity, can be explicitly taught. Examples and case studies from one's discipline can be chosen to reflect this diversity. An example of a class activity is exposing students to the challenges faced by immigrant families and the strengths of those families. As an additional reflection of diversity, the instructor can use names from around the world in examples and test questions.

Instructors also can put diversity to the forefront in their exploration of core concepts. Teaching from a diverse standpoint encourages students to reflect on their assumptions about "normality" and to think critically about their understanding of the human experience. Ordinarily we teach about average or majority experience and then talk about exceptions. Instead of this sequence, why not start with an inclusive example

37

and use it to illustrate core concepts? Multiple lecture segments can be redesigned in this way, to normalize the diversity of development. For example, one can teach about the features of long-term relationships from the perspective of same-sex couples.

The following is an example of how the topic of identity has been taught using this approach. The class begins with the students reflecting on their own experiences. They write as many answers as possible to the question "Who am I?" Students are then presented with an inclusive case study. They watch a YouTube clip of the Black Latina hip-hop musician Amara La Negra and read an interview in which Amara challenges colorism and racism in the music industry (Meraji & Richmond, 2018; *Vice News*, 2018). The next step is to ask students to engage in critical thinking. Students identified the experiences that shaped Amara's identity on a worksheet. A quick scan of a subset of the worksheets enables the instructor to get feedback from the class. Using student responses, the instructor can explain that identity is formed through exploration and commitment. This example can also illustrate how identity is fluid. With this focus, the instructor has spotlighted diversity while also covering core disciplinary concepts. The instructor could ask students to consider how what they have learned about identity theory helps them to understand their own identities. Care needs to be taken in asking students to share reflections about their own identities with other students, since there is a potential for marginalized students to be exposed in this process. If the instructor is asking students in the large class to share reflections on their own identities, we recommend that those reflections are shared directly with the teaching team in the first instance. The instructor could then summarize some key themes from the class and present them in aggregate. In this way, vulnerable students can be protected, while still given a voice.

These examples of class activities present an ideal opportunity to explore equity and inclusion in an engaging manner. The instructor can present some of the key issues in the case and, depending on the sensitivity of the topic, begin by asking students to reflect on their own experience with that issue. Even in the large class, students can share their reflections with others near them. Instructors can guide discussion of the case and students can respond to the example using structured worksheets or clicker questions. The clicker questions provide immediate feedback on students' understanding and can be used as a springboard for further discussion. We have found a word cloud to be a most effective and engaging way of presenting student feedback.

CONCLUSION

Our experience in making very large classes student-centered shows that these classes can promote and teach about equity and inclusion. Currently, the evidence supporting the approaches described in this chapter comes from our own reflections, our course evaluations, and the informal reactions of our students. The support for our approach is promising. Reaching out to students and presenting a welcoming and open class environment creates a positive teaching and learning experience for us and for our students. Students frequently comment that they feel far more connected to the instructors and to the other students in the class than they anticipated. They comment on the approachability of the instructors and their belief that the instructors want them to succeed. Opportunities to earn points in many different ways, with performance and effort assessments, are appreciated by students. Furthermore, students of diverse backgrounds have praised the focus on equity and inclusion in our classes. Traditionally underrepresented groups, such as first-generation college students, indicate that they do not feel excluded or tangential, despite the size of the class.

The exploration of student-centered teaching is invigorating for us as instructors. In the future, we aim to gather data about the effectiveness of the approaches to inclusion that we have developed. We could envision the use of an experimental manipulation comparing two different sections of the same course: one with inclusivity at the forefront and the other without, or one with team-based group reflection and one with individual work. Although we cannot guarantee that large classroom activities do not isolate marginalized students, keeping the tone of the learning environment, the organization of the class, and diverse and inclusive class activities in the forefront might prevent this.

Faculty who want to implement our approach could begin with a redrafting of their syllabi. They could also examine how they present themselves to their students and decide if they should use entry questionnaires to learn more about their students. In addition to an organized presentation, the goal is to be inclusive and accessible. We suggest that the next step would be to reevaluate course content to include more diverse examples and literature. Once faculty have feedback on these approaches, they could then take on the challenge of designing class activities that require critical thinking and reflection before moving on to activities that involve structured dialogue. Our experience to date tells us that teaching with equity and inclusion in mind is not only possible in the very large class, but also enriches the class experience for students and instructors.

REFERENCES

Adams, M. (2016). Pedagogical foundations of social justice education. In M. Adams, L. A. Bell, D. J. Goodman, & K. Y. Joshi (Eds.), *Teaching for diversity and social justice* (3rd ed., pp. 27–54). Routledge.

American Psychological Association. (2011). *APA principles for quality undergraduate education in psychology.* American Psychological Association.

Association of American Colleges & Universities. (2019). *High impact practices.* https://www.aacu.org/resources/high-impact-practices

Bryson, B. P. (n.d.). *Inclusive introduction questionnaire.* https://www.jmu.edu/safezone/IIQ.shtml

Castle, Cerise. (2018, January 26). *"Love & Hip Hop" star Amara La Negra is calling out racism—and colorism.* Vice News. https://www.vice.com/en/article/kznvmv/this-love-and-hip-hop-star-is-calling-out-racism-and-colorism

Center for Teaching Innovation. Cornell University. (n.d.). *Universal design for learning.* https://teaching.cornell.edu/teaching-resources/building-inclusive-classrooms/universal-design-learning

Dean, T., Lee-Post, A., & Hapke, H. (2017). Universal design for learning in teaching large lecture classes. *Journal of Marketing Education, 39*(1), 5–16. https://doi.org/10.1177/0273475316662104

Gallor, S. (2017). A social justice approach to undergraduate psychology education: Building cultural diversity, inclusion, and sensitivity into teaching, research, and service. *Psi Chi Journal of Psychological Research, 22*(4), 254–257. https://doi.org/10.24839/2325-7342.JN22.4.254

Haggis, P. (Director). (2005). *Crash.* [Film]. Lions Gate Films.

Hartwell, E. E., Cole, K., Donovan, S. K., Greene, R. L., Burrell Storms, S. L., & Williams, T. (2017). *Breaking down silos: Teaching for equity, diversity, and inclusion across disciplines.* http://digitalcommons.fairfield.edu/education-facultypubs/129

Meraji, S. M., & Richmond, J. (2018). *'Se que soy': Amara la negra embraces her afro-latinidad.* National Public Radio, Inc. (NPR).

Morse, Robert, Eric Brooks, and Matt Mason. (2018, September 9). *How U.S. News Calculated the 2019 Best College Rankings.* U.S. News. https://www.usnews.com/education/best-colleges/articles/how-us-news-calculated-the-rankings

Muller, R. T. (2013, October 4). Culture and PTSD: Lessons from the 2004 tsunami [Blog post]. https://www.psychologytoday.com/us/blog/talking-about-trauma/201310/culture-ptsd-lessons-the-2004-tsunami

Ostiguy, B. J., Peters, M. L., & Shiasko, D. (2016). Abelism. In M. Adams, L. A. Bell, D. J. Goodman, & K. Y. Joshi (Eds.) *Teaching for diversity and social justice* (3rd ed., pp. 299–337). Routledge.

Panjawani, A., & Cipollina, R. (2017). The elephant in the room: Fostering participation in large classes. In R. Obeid, A. Schwartz, C. Shane-Simpson, & P. J. Brooks (Eds.), *How we teach now: The GSTA guide to student-centered teaching. Society for Teaching of Psychology.* https://teachpsych.org/ebooks/howweteachnow

Pinel, J. P. J. (2014). *Biopsychology* (9th ed.). Pearson Education.

Salz, M. (2014). Economies of scale and large classes. *Thought and Action, 30,* 149–159.

Strayhorn, T. (2020). *College students' sense of belonging: A key to educational success for all students* (2nd ed.). Routledge.

Whisenhunt, B. L., Cathey, C., Visio, M. E., Hudson, D. L., Shoptaugh, C. F., & Rost, A. D. (2019). Strategies to address challenges with large classes: Can we exceed student expectations for large class experiences? *Scholarship of Teaching and Learning in Psychology, 5*(2), 121–127. https://doi.org/10.1037/stl0000135

Zúñiga, X., Naagda, B. A., & Sevig, T. D. (2002). Intergroup dialogues: An educational model for cultivating engagement across differences. *Equity & Excellence in Education, 35*(1), 7–17. https://doi.org/10.1080/713845248

CHAPTER 3
Designing and Facilitating Equitable and Inclusive Online Courses

Ruth Benander and Pam Rankey

Online learning has become an expected part of curricula (Allen & Seaman, 2017; Lederman, 2018; Snyder, Brey, & Dillow, 2019) and can be a required mode of learning in some cases. With the expansion of computers, software programs, and web applications, the definition of online learning has become more diverse (Singh & Thurman, 2019). Most simply, online learning is an experience mediated by electronic communication where the student and instructor may not be not face to face. Of course, with the common use of learning management systems and video conferencing, even classes that meet face to face will still have online learning components. Students in higher education who are learning this way are increasingly diverse, including first-generation students, international students, and students from a variety of ethnic backgrounds and identities and different levels of socioeconomic status (SES). This rich diversity means our course design must be as inclusive as possible. Diversity has been extensively discussed in reference to in-person courses, and since online learning becomes an expected part of students' experiences, it is equally important to design inclusive online learning experiences. Our approach asks the instructor to consider three principles that allow them to support a wide diversity of students: make expectations explicit, create multiple paths for mastery, and make the recognition and value of diversity explicit.

Online learning requires a series of agreements between the instructor and the student about technology, time management, self-regulation, and how to negotiate online social relationships. Students who choose to learn online, and increasingly need to learn online whether they choose to or not, come from a wide variety of experiences with all of these elements. Face to face, we can negotiate these elements in the moment; online, the instructor must plan for them. Not only must an instructor be aware of all the possibilities, often without being able to immediately check to see how students are experiencing the course, but they must also provide online opportunities for students to negotiate their experiences with each other and with the course content in supportive and respectful ways, using the diversity of their shared beliefs and understandings of what it is to learn and interact with others online.

It is important to acknowledge that the definitions of online learning became much more fluid during the challenges of the 2020 pandemic when much learning went online. This move exacerbated what some defined as the "digital divide" since not everybody has the means to access online learning (Strauss, 2020). For the purposes of this chapter, we concentrate on how to intentionally design asynchronous online learning experiences. Even if the class has synchronous or face-to-face meetings, instructors who include an online component may also benefit by implementing these suggestions to support students while they are online.

Designing and facilitating equitable and inclusive online courses requires attention to supporting a variety of student needs including content skills, academic skills, and technological skills. Universal Design (Mace, 2008) and Culturally Responsive and Culturally Sustaining Pedagogies (Gay, 2010; Paris, 2012) help inform approaches to designing equitable and inclusive online environments. Instructors need to be aware of their own hidden biases and preconceptions as they develop online activities that will support students with a variety of backgrounds. They can use principles of access and inclusion to design an array of online activities that allow students multiple paths for participation and demonstration of their learning in a context that respects and supports their life experiences. The Peralta Community College District (2019) has created an "Online Equity Rubric" to be used in conjunction with the California community colleges' more general course design rubric, which presents the elements of equity and inclusion that can inform the design of an online course to take into account key elements of equity and inclusion. The rubric creators have outlined important elements to consider:

- Offering alternatives for technology access
- Explicitly acknowledging a commitment to diversity and inclusion
- Including images and representation that reflect diversity
- Acknowledging human interaction bias
- Connecting content to student experience
- Fostering student-to-student interaction
- Using Universal Design for Learning (UDL) elements
- Explaining how to access online student support resources

As most learning is becoming mediated by technology, these general principles for creating an equitable and inclusive online course apply to any course, regardless of medium. A syllabus can begin to address these elements with explicit statements of the value of equity and inclusion, recognition of implicit bias, and directions for online technology support and student services (see Chapter 1). This discussion focuses on the asynchronous part of the online learning experience, the more specific realization of the learning experience when students are alone in front of their computer with only the syllabus and learning management system to guide them.

Providing equitable learning experiences for diverse populations has been suggested as a benefit of online learning since students are initially identified only by their names. However, there are other elements that also need to be considered, including instructor access to roster photos, ethnic association through names, access to appropriate technology, and knowledge of academic cultural norms. Kronk (2017) reported online courses are often more diverse than in-person courses, so bias is important to consider. We should note that Hansen and Reich (2015) found students of lower socioeconomic status experienced lower access and success in online learning. In addition, Baker et al. (2018) reported on gender and ethnicity bias in online discussion boards, possibly influenced by student name markers. Hidden bias may also be folded into online courses through using culturally specific videos, only portraying dominant ethnicities in visual materials, and only using the dominant accent or language in videos.

Often the first step in course (re)design for equity and inclusion involves an attitude of "cultural humility," first codified by Tervalon and Murray-García (1998). The instructor must acknowledge personal biases, be open to learning how others approach a problem, and appreciate multiple paths to a common end. A predisposition to cultural humility can help an instructor create online learning experiences designed to take into account student choice and personal experiences in both topic and approach to demonstrating learning outcomes.

PRINCIPLES

Universal Design for Learning (UDL) originated in the accessibility movement, which extended into online instructional design. Culturally Responsive Pedagogy (Gay, 2010) and Culturally Sustaining Pedagogy (Paris, 2012; Paris & Alim, 2014) promote learning activities that support and respect all students in an increasingly diverse student population. In the online learning environment, we design for readability and navigation, but also for the multiple ways students understand materials, demonstrate learning and mastery, and express their evolving academic identities.

UDL was championed by Mace (2008). The principles Mace and his colleagues outlined include equitable use, flexibility, simplicity, perceptible information, tolerance for error, low effort, and approachability (Connell et al., 2006). In 2008, the Center for Universal Design for Learning published its own principles, which built on Mace's vision, including multiple means of representation, multiple means of action and expression, and multiple means of engagement. Student choice and multiple paths to success are the cornerstones of Culturally Responsive Pedagogy, which involves establishing inclusion, offering choice, valuing previous knowledge, and offering multiple ways to represent knowledge (Wlodkowski & Ginsberg, 1995). Paris and Alim (2014) argued that culturally sustaining design also creates opportunities in a course to "foster linguistic and cultural flexibility" in practice and perspective (p. 87). In this chapter, we review different activities that can be designed to support students from diverse linguistic and cultural backgrounds and help them work in an online environment that is accessible not only electronically but also socially and culturally.

As courses and activities are designed for a wide range of learners, allowing for personal interactions in the course and structuring activities where instructor expectations are transparent is essential. The following sections present specific, asynchronous, online approaches to making academic skills, technology, and content presentation more equitable and inclusive through transparency of expectations, multiple paths to success, and facilitation of multiple perspectives through sharing experiences. When we think about supporting all students in online courses, we can think about different strategies in the following areas: academic skills, technological skills, and content skills. The following activities are not an exhaustive list; rather, they are examples of how to apply the principles of valuing all students, respecting everybody's circumstances, and providing support for success.

ACADEMIC SKILLS: GIVING ALL STUDENTS STRATEGIES FOR SUCCESS
TIME MANAGEMENT
Being able to stay on task and negotiate deadlines has long been noted as a key element of success in online classes (e.g., Baker, Evans et al., 2018; Broadbent & Poon, 2015; Roper, 2007). Helping students learn to use a calendar, negotiate family and work priorities, and create a consistent schedule can support students in developing self-regulation skills. Baker et al. (2018) noted that while interventions support students in scheduling their coursework, it is more effective if the time management support lasts throughout the course rather than just in the early weeks. Time management strategies to support all students include:

- Submitting a weekly study scheduling plan that includes study time as well as assignment working time
- Sending a viewing survey after the deadline to view a video
- Requiring a reading summary at the time that a reading is due to be completed

In addition, it is helpful for the instructor to provide an explicit breakdown of how long an assignment is expected to take. Students may not view deadlines in the same way that instructors do, so being clear about expectations can increase the likelihood that the expectations will be met.

ONLINE COMMUNICATION
Just as time management expectations need to be transparent, discussion board instructions and communication etiquette must be clearly outlined so that all students are sharing the same understanding. In a diverse group of students, expectations for effective

communication can vary, and these expectations may sometimes be in stark contrast with the more restricted communication of an online discussion board (Yeboah & Smith, 2016). Communicating effectively in online discussions is dependent on grammar, punctuation, syntax, and vocabulary choices. Instructors can help students deal with these language choices and communicate clearly by addressing this diversity directly in the first discussion board of a class. Students can discuss how they perceive effective online communication and collaborate on creating a supportive set of guidelines for the class discussion boards. In this collaboration, students work together to negotiate their expectations and find a common ground that includes everyone while acknowledging the differences.

LANGUAGE

The language of instruction in much of American higher education is "standard English," a form of English that is regularized in form and usage, often associated with print and media. Nevertheless, other languages and other Englishes (Nelson, Proshina, & Davis, 2020), such as Nigerian English or Indian English, or other varieties of English spoken in North America, can be valuable parts of the learning experience. To create equitable instruction and to value the diversity of the student experience, instructors in online classes can broaden their view of how language is used (e.g., Young et al., 2014). Part of this broadened view is being transparent and explicit about language-use opportunities in the course, written, spoken, read, and heard. The first step is being aware of expectations; the next is fostering opportunities for a variety of language usage.

WRITING

Assignments and discussions often rely on writing in online, asynchronous classes. As an alternative, it is possible to consider the many video options that are available in learning management systems and web-based applications. Offering assignments that require writing along with assignments that are spoken video presentations creates a variety of opportunities for expression. In addition, the expectations for language usage can be explicit about the breadth of choices students can make to express themselves. Instructors can specify writing expressly formal English for one assignment's audience, and for another assignment's audience, offering an opportunity to take advantage of multiple forms and expressions of English and other languages. Instructors also need to be transparent about how they will assess language use. If instructors assess language use as part of a grade, regardless of discipline, they need to be clear about the criteria for assessment.

SPEAKING

Speaking can be a source of stress for students. In requiring spoken presentations, instructors can be supportive of all students by encouraging personal expression and welcoming all forms of English in the assignment instructions so that students know it is safe to speak in their own voices. If a student is fluent in another language and struggles in English, one might consider accepting a presentation in another language that is captioned in English. Encouraging all students to find their voices in the language of the discipline can also be supportive of their professional growth. Thus, asking students to use course-specific vocabulary in short spoken videos can help them feel confident as full participants in the academy. Encouraging students to view their ability to use all their language resources can help them see this as a professional success skill (e.g., Obama White House, 2015).

READING

Students new to college and university life may not be well practiced in academic reading. Supporting students in academic reading includes making expectations clear for how to read the course texts and use them in their coursework. For example, instead of the instructions for an online reading assignment being "Read pages 6–21," consider explaining what is required in reading and using this text, such as, "Read pages 6–21, give an opinion on the text, ask a question of the text, make a connection to your own experience, and select a significant passage from the text and explain why it is important." In addition, if research is required for an assignment, in the instructions for the research assignment, students who are literate in more than one language can be encouraged to use all their languages in researching a course topic. Instructors might consult with their librarians for help in recommending international databases for newspapers, magazines, and other publications, whether in English or in other languages. Framing multilingualism as a skill, and not a hindrance in academic life, and offering opportunities for using and mixing varieties of English can support students in seeing their abilities as strengths.

LISTENING

Students are supported in feeling like they belong in college when they see people like themselves in course materials, and they are also supported when they hear Englishes like their own. In addition, all students benefit from learning to hear multiple Englishes. Instructors might find videos communicating the course content in different Englishes, supporting comprehension with transcripts or captioning. Finally, encouraging students to create videos in their own voices that present course material, work problems, or create projects can allow students to hear each other being experts in the course material in their own voices, with their own Englishes.

TECHNOLOGY SKILLS: GIVING ALL STUDENTS THE TOOLS THEY NEED

Providing students information about technology tools that will be used in the course, and assistance with learning how to use those tools and obtain help for problems, is critical to students' success in the online environment. Likewise, online students need easy access to support services, which could include academic support, accessibility resources, psychological support, financial aid or registration, and veterans' services.

Technology expectations should also be directly addressed. Faculty should directly state requirements for items such as headphones and microphones, computers with webcams, and internet access. When working in the online environment, students (and instructors) need to be prepared for student internet outages, computer malfunctions, or even families sharing a computer, resulting in competing priorities. Policies should be both clear and inclusive to show recognition and reasonable accommodation for these situations. Ideally faculty should develop policies or solutions that can accommodate varying priorities between students regardless of individual situations. For example, an inclusive policy is dropping the lowest grade on one or two low-stakes assignments, which eliminates the need for the instructor to evaluate reasons for missed assignments and provides students flexibility and autonomy.

CONTENT SKILLS: GIVING ALL STUDENTS A VOICE IN THE COURSE

It is common to adapt a variety of in-classroom techniques in developing activities to engage online students. Many of these activities may be revised to accommodate the online environment and support student engagement. This section identifies considerations to make online activities more equitable and inclusive as students are encouraged to engage with the content and share as equal voices in the online classroom.

GALLERY WALK

In this activity, students share something they created and engage in dialogue about it. In the traditional classroom, it might be a poster, a document, a concept map, or other artifacts. In the online environment, this is easily accommodated through a discussion board, blog, or an eportfolio for students to share and comment on each other's work. Students could reflect on and ask questions in the comments area about other students' work. Questions and respectful responses value differences and help the students understand concepts better by being able to hear multiple perspectives. Bringing this activity into the online environment invites the fragmented community of online participation to view the individual contributions to the course as expressions of each person's individuality in addition to knowing each other through their names or their texts.

In a scholarly teaching assessment study, Benander (2015) noted that alternative paths for presenting personal identity seemed to increase engagement in an online course. In a gallery walk activity in an online English course, students shared posters that described the discourse communities they participated in. Students responded to each other's posters that were posted in the online blog. One online student commented, "The assignment that most impacted me this semester was the discourse community essay, and the map we made for our peers to see. I absolutely loved this assignment, because it allowed us to get to know our peers on such a deeper, more personal level rather than just a simple blog post with a couple fun facts included about ourselves." When viewing each other's work as a community effort, students felt included and comfortable sharing group work. In an online English course, students commented on how the amount of student-to-student interaction through gallery walks and Four Corners discussions in the blog area was surprising and supportive in creating inclusion and community.

While equity has not been an explicit focus of studies of online group work, the principle of giving all students an equal and supported chance to participate fully in a course is demonstrated in these examples of online group work. When students can support each other in creating new knowledge together, their multiple perspectives can be valued and showcased.

FOUR CORNERS AND JIGSAW ACTIVITIES IN DISCUSSION BOARDS

In these activities, students are assigned one of four small group discussion topics, either individually or in group discussion areas. In Four Corners, they participate in one small group discussion, read each other's threads, and create a summary of the group's conclusions. Each student submits his or her own summary as an assignment. This activity cultivates multiple points of view and allows the instructor to view everyone's understanding of the small group discussion. The conversation can then be broadened through a Jigsaw Discussion. In the Four Corners small group discussions, students become experts on a topic through independent research and collaboration in their group. They can be working in a discussion board thread, a shared online document, or in a shared webpage that all members can edit. Then, in the Jigsaw activity, new small groups are created, each with their own new collaborative online space. In each of these small groups includes one member from each of the Four Corners groups. In each of these new Jigsaw groups, experts from the previous activity contribute their perspectives on a new problem posed by the instructor that requires input from multiple perspectives.

This type of online discussion promotes equity by allowing all students the opportunity to become an expert and then share their knowledge with others. This preparation allows all students to become well informed and participate instead of privileging participation to those who have had access to previous experiences others may not have had. To make this inclusive, it is important team roles be clearly defined. This activity makes a diverse group feel more unified because everyone becomes an expert, and everyone has a support system. When designing any type of discussion, interactional guidelines for civil discourse should be included.

VIDEO LECTURE

Video lectures must be made equitable through captioning and transcripts to allow students who may be learning the language of the classroom or students who simply need more time to review to slow down content delivery. To emphasize inclusiveness, the images and accents in videos should represent a diversity of people beyond the dominant ethnic group and language/accent. Additional considerations regarding videos and diversity include who makes the videos. The engagement is even better if students create their own videos. When students make their own videos, they can approach the material from their own perspective. When students watch each other's videos, they learn from multiple perspectives, which honors each student's voice and experience as knowledge creators in the discipline.

STUDENT-CREATED SURVEYS

A common problem for students with little experience outside their own communities is thinking that their personal perspective is representative of all perspectives. To help students learn to take multiple perspectives into account, instructors can ask students to survey their class on a course topic or a personal research topic. In a survey, sometimes students who might not speak up may be able to offer their perspectives to other students. Students or instructors can create surveys concerning course topics using online survey applications, such as Google Forms. Students can post their surveys in discussions or on their eportfolios, class members can anonymously take the survey, and each student can analyze survey data to present their interpretation of the survey data. This inclusive activity focuses on the online class as a coherent community and prompts students to value the variety of ways to understand responses to the surveys. In creating a survey, and inviting class members to offer their perspectives, participants value the diversity of the group as important input for each individual's consideration of the course content. This approach may be useful in history, English, behavioral sciences, or economics courses, for example, where different stakeholders often perceive a problem from different viewpoints.

BRINGING ACADEMIC, TECHNOLOGY, AND CONTENT SKILLS TOGETHER

In an online course, academic, technical, and content skills are actually experienced together. We recommend two keystone practices that integrate these three skills in the course experience. A readiness assessment assignment at the start of a course helps students practice the essential academic and technology skills of the course as well as preparing them for the content of the course. Using a class eportfolio allows both the students and the instructor to have a holistic view of the course experience.

READINESS ASSESSMENT

The readiness assessment as the first set of activities in a course helps students learn the expectations of the course, learn about managing online due dates, have a place to express their concerns about the course, and have an opportunity to connect with the instructor and other students right from the start of the course. To create a readiness assessment, instructors introduce students to the skills they are expected to use through short, simple assignments that relate to basic course content or expected previous knowledge. These short assignments should be accompanied by links to resources and instructions for the required course technologies for students who need more information. These assignments can also be an opportunity for pretesting, especially in sequenced courses. Instructors can model an introduction using preferred pronouns, first and second languages, or other information that might make students from diverse backgrounds feel

Table 3.1. Sample sequence of readiness assessment activities

ACADEMIC SKILL	TECHNOLOGY SKILL	CONTENT SKILL
How to send professional email	Institutional email system	Send an email to the instructor outlining personal goals for the course or concerns about the course.
Applying previous knowledge to the course and using an online quiz	Accessing the learning management system testing application	Take a short test of expected background knowledge for the course.
How to read a textbook	Online textbook access and the assignment submission function	Preview the chapters of the text: ask a question about the content, make a connection from the content to your personal experience. Discuss the chapters of the text that you feel confident about and the chapters of the text that you are most concerned about being able to understand.
How to present yourself in an online academic setting	Learning management system discussion application such as discussion boards or blogs	Post a personal introduction to the class starting with, "If you knew me, you would know . . ." Post your personal goals for the course and what you need to do to achieve them.
Time management	Using a planning calendar (submitted through the assignment submission function)	List the roles you have in your life and the responsibilities you have for each role (including college student). Create a calendar where you make time for these roles in your day (including time to study). Reflect on what you may need to ask others to do so you can fit your role of college student into your life.

they can share more about themselves. A key element is to make the activities relevant to the course content. For an example of a series of readiness assessment activities, see Table 3.1.

This type of readiness assessment activity demonstrates the UDL principle of making spaces naturally comfortable and usable for any person, regardless of previous academic and online experience. Students who come to the course without previous college experience benefit from low-stakes practice in the online environment in which they will be learning. By offering a readiness assessment set of exercises, the instructor creates a more equitable environment by not privileging students with more online experience over those who are new to this type of learning. In addition, a more inclusive environment is cultivated by beginning the course with social introductions that value the group and each person in the group. In our anecdotal experience, providing practice in the academic skills and online learning tools specific to the course results in more successful completion of assignments from the start, establishment of an online community where each person is valued, and the opportunity to support students who may need more help right at the start of the course.

ePORTFOLIOS

The American Association of Colleges and Universities (2019) includes eportfolios as a high-impact practice both for assessment and for fostering deeper learning. An eportfolio is an online collection of a student's work that can include process work, final projects in multiple media, and reflective writing. Because an eportfolio is highly personalized and represents a student's individual journey through a course, students express themselves as participants in the discipline. Additionally, eportfolios facilitate the ability of students to see the progress of their own learning and reflect on that progress. As Terrel Rhodes (qtd. in Carey, 2016) noted, "Eportfolios are much more than a technology; they are a way of thinking about one's learning." For first-generation students and students from underrepresented minorities, taking control of their own learning, and thinking critically about their learning, are skills that support them throughout their academic careers.

In research on the effectiveness of engaging students using online eportfolios, Benander et al. (2018) found using eportfolios to document an academic plan and discipline-specific skills helped students in a first-year biology and chemistry course feel more engaged in their discipline. The students who completed the first-year eportfolio also reported more self-regulated learning habits than students who attended the first-year course but who did not experience the eportfolio activity. For students who may feel marginalized, building a professional eportfolio that emphasizes how they are full participants in their chosen field may support them in feeling on an equal footing with their peers (Christy & Fasina, 2017; Oehlman et al., 2016).

In the online environment, students can feel isolated in their learning, and they may approach their work as a series of discrete assignments submitted into the anonymity of the learning management system. However, if they keep an eportfolio of their work, they can review it over the course of the semester for a long view of their learning. This review can give their online work a coherence that may have been lacking without such a review (Benander & Refaei, 2016). Many students comment on how structured reflective assignments helped them realize how much they had learned and how they felt increased confidence as a result. Some students may not feel confident that they can be in control of their learning or even that they can be successful learners. The opportunity to review their individual work and see their success helps them see themselves as confident, competent members of an academic community that values their contribution. This type of reflection invites students to share their perspectives of the learning as a means of including their own lived experience of the course and shows that the instructor values the individual student's perception of their own learning journey.

CONCLUSION

Designing online learning experiences that support diversity and inclusion requires two key principles: making expectations explicit and creating multiple paths for mastery. Instructors must keep in mind Tervalon and Murray-García's (1998) principles of cultural humility and Gabriel's (2008) advice that "the climate we want to sustain must be introduced from the beginning" (p. 25). Practicing cultural humility, instructors can create learning experiences that allow students to share the way they understand the course content and create a climate of community support, which helps students want to share their understanding. Online assignments that ask students to learn in multiple modalities from essays to reflections to infographics to videos allow students to explore different ways of learning and sharing what they know. In this way, individuals are valued, and no student needs to guess what is needed to succeed in the class. An essential step in increasing equity and inclusion is full transparency of expectations and the option to leverage one's personal strengths to achieve success. Requiring students to guess how to succeed and narrowly defining what success looks like is a sure path to inequality of opportunity and easy exclusion of those who don't know the implicit rules of the game. Equity and inclusion in learning means supporting students' agency and sense of belonging in the classroom community, which can be done through clear expectations, making technology tools easily available, and creating opportunities to build a community that supports all students.

REFERENCES

Allen, I. E., & Seaman, J. (2017). *Digital learning compass: Distance education enrollment report 2017*. https://onlinelearningsurvey.com/reports/digtiallearningcompassenrollment2017.pdf

American Association of Colleges and Universities. (2019). *High-impact practices*. https://www.aacu.org/leap/hips

Baker, R., Dee, T., Evans, B., & John, J. (2018). *Bias in online classes: Evidence from a field experiment*. CEPA Working Paper No. 18–03. https://cepa.stanford.edu/sites/default/files/wp18-03-201803.pdf

Baker, R., Evans, B., Li, Q., & Cung, B. (2018). Does inducing students to schedule lecture watching in online classes improve their academic performance? An experimental analysis of a time management intervention. *Research in Higher Education, 60*, 521–552.

Benander, R. (2015, April 10). *ePortfolios: Assessment without standardization*. Paper presented at the meeting of the 3Ts Conference, Clermont College, Batavia, OH.

Benander, R., Greer, M., & Dematteo, M. (2018, November 9). *Using eportfolios in STEM first-year experience courses to increase engagement, success, and persistence*. Paper presented at the American Association of Colleges and Universities, Atlanta, GA.

Benander, R., & Refaei, B. (2016). Reflections: Developing metacognitive habits of mind. In K. Coleman and A. Flood (Eds.), *Enabling reflective thinking: Reflection and reflective practice in learning and teaching* (pp. 22–33). Common Ground Publishing.

Broadbent, J., & Poon, W. L. (2015). Self-regulated learning strategies and academic achievement in online higher education learning environments: A systematic review. *The Internet and Higher Education, 27*, 1–13.

Carey, S. (2016). From the editor. *Peer Review 18*(3). https://www.aacu.org/peerreview/2016/summer/editor

Christy, A., & Fasina, O. (2017, June 25). *Student eportfolios for undergraduate professional development: A comparison of two programs*. Paper presented at the meeting of the 2017 ASEE Annual Conference & Exposition, Columbus, OH. https://www.asee.org/public/conferences/78/papers/20035/view

Connell, B., Jones, M., Mace, R., Mueller, J., Mullick, A., Ostroff, E., Sanford, J., Steinfeld, E., Story, M., & Vanderheiden, G. (2006). *The principles of universal design*. North Carolina State University College of Design. https://projects.ncsu.edu/design/cud/pubs_p/docs/poster.pdf

Gabriel, K. (2008). *Teaching unprepared students*. Stylus Publishing.

Gay, G. (2010). *Culturally responsive teaching: Theory, research, and practice*. Teachers College Press.

Hansen, J., & Reich, J. (2015). Democratizing education? Examining access and usage patterns in massive open online courses. *Science, 350*(6265), 1245–1248. https://doi.org/10.1126/science.aab3782

Kronk, H. (2017). The most diverse U.S. universities are online. *eLearning Inside*. https://news.elearninginside.com/diverse-u-s-universities-online/

Lederman, D. (2018, November 7). Online education ascends. *Inside Higher Ed*. https://www.insidehighered.com/digital-learning/article/2018/11/07/new-data-online-enrollments-grow-and-share-overall-enrollment

Mace, R. (2008). *About UD*. Center for Universal Design: Environments and Products for All People. https://projects.ncsu.edu/design/cud/about_ud/about_ud.htm

Nelson, C., Proshina, Z., & Davis, D. (2020). *The handbook of world Englishes*. Wiley-Blackwell.

Obama White House. (2015, April 9). *President Obama speaks at a town hall with young leaders of the Americas in Jamaica*. YouTube [Video]. https://youtu.be/636mgw1THpc

Oehlman, N., Haegar, H., Clarkston, B., & Banks, J. (2016). Maximizing the function of student eportfolios. *Peer Review, 18*(3). https://www.aacu.org/peerreview/2016/summer/Oehlman

Paris, D. (2012). Culturally sustaining pedagogy: A needed change in stance, terminology, and practice. *Educational Researcher, 41*(93), 93–97. http://edr.sagepub.com/content/41/3/93

Paris, D., & Alim, H. (2014). What are we seeking to sustain through culturally sustaining pedagogy? A loving critique forward. *Harvard Educational Review, 84*(1), 85–100.

Peralta Community College District (2019). *Online equity rubric*. https://web.peralta.edu/de/files/2019/01/Peralta-Equity-Rubric-V6-January-2019.pdf

Roper, A. R. (2007). How students develop online learning skills. *Educause Quarterly, 30*, 62–65.

Singh, V., & Thurman, A. (2019). How many ways can we define online learning? A systematic literature review of definitions of online learning (1988–2018). *American Journal of Distance Education, 33*(4), 289–306. https://doi.org/10.1080/08923647.2019.1663082

Snyder, T., Brey, C., & Dillow, S. (2019). *Digest of education statistics 2017.* International Center for Education Statistics, NCES 2018–07. https://nces.ed.gov/pubs2018/2018070.pdf

Strauss, V. (2020, April 29). Coronavirus pandemic shines light on deep digital divide in U.S. amid efforts to narrow it. *Washington Post.* https://www.washingtonpost.com/

Tervalon, M., & Murray-García, J. (1998). Cultural humility versus cultural competence: A critical distinction in defining physician training outcomes in multicultural education. *Journal of Health Care for the Poor and Underserved, 9*(2), 117–125.

Universal Design for Learning. (2008). *Universal Design for Learning guidelines version 1.0.* http://udlseries. udlcenter.org/presentations/learner_variability.html?plist=explore

Wlodkowski, R., & M. Ginsberg. (1995). *Diversity and motivation: Culturally responsive teaching.* Jossey-Bass.

Yeboah, A., & Smith, P. (2016). Relationships between minority students online learning experiences and academic performance. *Online Learning, 20*(4), 1–26.

Young, V. A., Barrett, R., Young-Rivera, Y., & Lovejoy, K. (2014). *Other people's English: Code-meshing, code-switching, and African American literacy.* Teachers College Press.

REFLECTION ON
Setting Up an Inclusive Learning Environment

Creating an inclusive learning environment requires an intentional focus on practitioner beliefs and behaviors, pedagogy, curriculum, and assessment processes. The syllabus is often one of the first ways students are introduced to the expectations and norms for the class. As the authors in Part I suggest, it is important to use it to set the tone for equity and inclusion for the course. The setting for the course also has an impact on creating an inclusive learning environment. Large classes and online classes have unique challenges and opportunities in setting up inclusive spaces where all students can learn. The authors recommend making expectations explicit, so students have a clear understanding of the expectations for their performance. Courses taught online or in large lectures should provide multiple paths to success through a variety of activities and assignments. Even in these challenging environments, the classes should be student-centered and involve active learning approaches that engage students in learning the material. If educators can create inclusive online courses and large lecture courses, then the process should be achievable in a more traditional classroom.

These questions are designed to help readers consider how they might adopt some of the strategies and approaches described in the preceding chapters.

PRACTITIONER BELIEFS AND BEHAVIORS

1. How does your syllabus reflect your values for diversity? Does your teaching persona match your values?

2. How is diversity present in your classes? How do you learn about your students' interests, backgrounds, and thoughts about the course? How could you use an entry questionnaire in your teaching context? How do you address inclusivity directly?

3. How do you seek out responses to your syllabus from students and peers or community stakeholders?

4. As students read your syllabus, what will they expect from the classroom climate, your relationship with them, and how the semester will go? Is your syllabus easy to read and navigate in an accessible format?

5. How does your syllabus empower your students as learners, especially those from historically marginalized student populations?

PEDAGOGY

1. How can you design course activities that promote students helping each other, sharing their different perspectives, and feeling a sense of belonging to the group?

2. How can you design course activities online that include student voices in presenting and discussing materials? How can you encourage students to use all their language skills in assignments, whether it be multilingual research, visual, or spoken presentations?

3. How could you use eportfolios to help students connect their personal lives and educational experiences to create an inclusive learning community?

CURRICULUM

1. What are the academic and technology skills required for your course? How can you provide an introduction to these academic expectations in a readiness assessment series of activities that allow students to use the tools required by the course to get to know each other, to create a time management plan, and reflect on the course content?

2. How can your course materials such as lectures, textbook, and activities reflect the diversity of your students?

3. How do you communicate through your syllabus that you designed the course with learner variability in mind by providing students with multiple paths for learning and success?

ASSESSMENT

1. How do you apply your values for diversity when creating your assessments?

2. How do you communicate through your assessments that you designed the course with learner variability in mind by providing students with multiple paths for demonstrating their learning and success?

PART II
Creating Inclusive Classrooms in the Social Sciences

Time-starved faculty may find it helpful to work with others to create inclusive classrooms. In Part II, faculty across disciplines and courses worked to develop pedagogy, curriculum, and assessment processes that promote inclusion of all students in their courses. Sharing approaches across disciplines opens up the possibility to share the variety of ways a culturally sustaining pedagogy and inclusive curriculum can be designed to ensure that all students succeed. The contributors describe the philosophies that guided the development of classroom activities that can be integrated in courses across the curriculum.

Angela Miller-Hargis, Tamika Odum, Taylor Wadian, and Helene Arbouet Harte, who represent faculty across the five disciplines of psychology, sociology, education, criminal justice, and social work, describe a process that is centered around "perspective taking." They argue that by using this process they encourage and teach their students to identify inequality, evaluate their own behavior and skills, and then to reflect and engage respectfully with those who are different. Through an interdisciplinary lens this chapter offers strategies of perspective taking and building skills of inclusivity.

Professors of sociology, communication, English, and American studies Cynthia Ganote, Tasha Souza, and Floyd Cheung examine how microaggressions in educational settings can impact feelings of self-worth, leading to isolation and low academic performance. They explore the power of teaching microresistance strategies in the classroom context to counter microaggression and empower students. Using interventional skills such as Open the Front Door (OFTD) and ACTION (Ask Questions, Come from Curiosity Not Judgement, Tell Observation, Impact Exploration, Own Thoughts/Feelings re: Impact, Next Steps), which extends OFTD by adding inquiry questions, they help students to practice microresistance and become better equipped to handle inequity both in the classroom and beyond.

CHAPTER 4
Perspectives of Inclusion in the Social Sciences

Angela M. Miller-Hargis, Tamika C. Odum, Taylor W. Wadian, and Helene Arbouet Harte

The authors of this chapter are members of the Behavioral Sciences Department on a regional campus that is part of a large public university. This urban university offers approximately three hundred undergraduate programs of study, spread across eleven colleges and three campuses (one main campus and two regional campuses). As an open access college, our campus offers fifty majors and associate degree programs. In addition, students have the option to transition from our college to the main campus if they wish to pursue a baccalaureate degree. The student profiles of the college in which we teach indicate that, during the 2017–2018 academic year, 60 percent of the student population identified as White, 21 percent identified as African American or Black, 3.3 percent reported as Asian, 5 percent considered themselves Hispanic or Latinx, 4.4 percent indicated they were biracial, and 3.3 percent went unreported. Within this college, there is also a range of ages: 4.2 percent of the student body is under the age of eighteen, 63 percent are between the ages of eighteen and twenty-one, 25 percent report they are between the ages of twenty-two and thirty-four, with 7.2 percent of the total student population being over the age of thirty-five.

SUPPORTING AN INCLUSIVE PEDAGOGY IN THE BEHAVIORAL SCIENCES
The Behavioral Sciences Department itself comprise a highly diversified faculty, disciplines, and courses offered. There are thirteen full-time tenured or tenure-track faculty across five disciplines: psychology, sociology, education, criminal justice, and social work. As a department, we offer a vast array of introductory courses, mostly at the 100- and 200-level, with typical class sizes ranging from fifteen to thirty students, depending on the course itself, the time offering, and the overall student enrollment.

Because of the student demographics at our college and within our department, the authors and the department plan for an inclusive pedagogy across disciplines that promotes an understanding of individuals who differ from us. Students must understand and appreciate diversity in order to operate collaboratively on our campus and within our classrooms, and it is important to note that many of our students indicate a desire to work in occupations that will require them to have cultural competence (i.e., the knowledge, skills, and dispositions to interact effectively with those they may perceive as "others"). These occupations include educators at every level, social workers, child advocates, literacy coaches, special education teachers, assistant teachers, teacher aides, paraprofessionals, and others.

Research has indicated that classroom environments are greatly enhanced when students are educated about human difference, biases, and the historical context of these within our communities (Rankin & Reason, 2005). Our goal as behavioral science instructors is to offer a range of classes that allow students to safely explore this knowledge and develop the requisite skills required to meet several objectives. First, we want students to identify and analyze systems of inequality based on race, gender, social class, and ability. Most of the activities discussed here are built on introductory readings and lectures that allow for personal reflection after deep and respectful class discussions. Second, we expect that students will be able to assess and evaluate their own practices, tools, and personal narratives in order to uncover and challenge deeply held attitudes, beliefs, and implicit biases. Each of the activities reviewed in this chapter involve either writing assignments or classroom dialogues that are designed to respectfully engage all student perspectives and voices as a starting point for transformative conversations. Third, we expect students to express their thoughts and positions respectfully and thoughtfully in difficult discourse about and with those who differ from themselves, not only in their courses but also in their chosen professions.

One of the ways in which we attempt to create a transformative dialogue in our individual classes is through perspective taking, which requires instructors to generate opportunities for students to engage in personal reflection while considering perspectives different from their own. Using an intersectional lens and a multidisciplinary approach, we hope to encourage our students to appreciate the need to embrace diversity and inclusion in their classes, on campus, and in their daily personal and professional lives. The process of becoming a reflective practitioner who considers issues from a range of perspectives requires students to consciously engage, take responsibility to inquire, and entertain alternative ways of being (Lewison, Leland, & Harste, 2008). This approach is integrated across our many disciplines in order to encourage students to understand human behavior from a psychological, sociological, and educational standpoint. In disrupting the commonplace and "accepted" way of seeing the world, our students learn to interrogate their own understanding from multiple viewpoints. Furthermore, through the use of an intersectional lens, our students can challenge their own understanding of equity and inclusion, test revisionist histories as they relate to marginalized groups, and eventually adopt a deep appreciation of human difference in order to act with cultural sensitivity and competence.

The four activities presented here were created to demonstrate the myriad ways that diversity and inclusion concepts can be integrated into disciplinary-specific course content. The goal is to develop hands-on and interactive lessons that facilitate an experience our students can use as a basis for understanding themselves more fully and approaching their learning from a reflective stance and widened perspective. The activities were designed to help students examine historical information related to inequality while establishing a basis for them to create new ideas about how fairness and equity might look and exist in our world. Additionally, our goal includes a desire to introduce our students to the value of perspective taking and critical reflection when challenging oneself and others and when looking at the systemic nature of inequality.

The next four sections of this chapter represent each of the activities and explicate the coursework in which these activities are embedded. Activity 1 is embedded in an education course, and it introduces students to the concept of sexism, then branches out to investigate the other "-isms" represented in traditional teaching. Activity 2 introduces students to the concept of disability by having students unpack and challenge their understanding of the word "disability" from an educational point of view. Activity 3 is developed in a psychology course and centers around helping students understand the dangers of adopting a "single story" and cautions against stereotyping. Activity 4 uses imagery in a sociology course to better understand the concepts of race and racism.

ACTIVITY 1: FOCUS ON SEXISM IN EARLY CHILDHOOD EDUCATION THROUGH CHILDREN'S LITERATURE

The Foundations of Early Childhood course is one of the first classes that early childhood preservice teacher candidates take. The course introduces preservice teacher candidates to the historical, philosophical, and social foundations of contemporary early childhood programs as well as familiarizes them with current theories of child development and pedagogy. The course incorporates three state teaching standards. Specifically, the objectives include helping preservice teacher candidates understand student learning and development, express respect for the diversity of the students they teach, and assume responsibility for their professional growth and development.

When working with students in the diversity section of the course, we begin by doing a feminist reading of *The Giving Tree* (Silverstein, 1962). This text was chosen because it is commonly used in early childhood classes, has a great deal of familiarity among preservice educators, and is considered a classic among literacy educators. Because of its publication date and author, it provides a context for a historical analysis of feminism, as well. The text is read aloud via online text, and the students are required to write down issues of sexism that they recognize in the children's picture book. The plot of the book follows a female apple tree and a boy who communicate and interact throughout their lives. In the beginning, the boy is simply happy to eat her apples, swing from her branches, and rest in her shade. As the boy enters adolescence, he wants what every emerging adult wants: money. At this point, the tree proposes the boy take her apples and sell them, which he does. Later, after reaching adulthood, he wants a home and a family, so the tree suggests he cut her branches to build a house, which he also does. Upon reaching middle age, the boy wants a boat and the tree offers to let him cut her trunk to build one. This he does also, and at the end of each interaction, the book states that "the tree was happy." The story ends when the boy, now an old man, returns a final time, at which point the tree indicates she has nothing left to give. But the boy now requires only a "quiet place to sit and rest," which the tree *can* provide, and the book ends with the sentence, "And the tree was happy."

In the discussion that follows, students talk about how women are often characterized as givers, while men are portrayed as takers; how women are expected to be nurturers and caregivers; how women alter themselves to suit men like the tree does, who literally cut off parts of herself to please the boy.

The class explores the ways in which sexism is so pervasive and implicitly embedded in our culture that we often do not "see" it. The lesson generally ends with two YouTube videos that explore sexism (Danubata24, 2007) and representations of masculinity in Disney films (Newton, 2007). Students examine the covertness of these messages and the cumulative effect these messages might have over the course of a child's lifetime. Classroom discussions also explore the ways in which they, as future educators, may become complicit in perpetuating bias through their choice and use of instructional materials. The background, experiences, and occupation of *The Giving Tree*'s author, Shel Silverstein, is also explored, as well as the historical context of the text and issues related to sexism in contemporary society.

As a follow-up, students are presented with Disney clips that represent the latent but pervasive sexism in traditional fairy tales and princess stories. The students watch the assigned clips as part of a homework assignment and are required to analyze the ways in which sexism is exemplified in various fairy tales and stories (e.g., *The Little Mermaid, Aladdin, Beauty and the Beast, Cinderella*, and *Tangled*) with regard to women. They are also required to examine messages being sent to males within these fairy tales and stories, such as the need for men to have a certain body type, the importance of physical prowess, the ways in which violence and dominance are used to maintain masculinity, and the need to "get the girl" for status maintenance. In class, students discuss their findings and investigate the cumulative effects of "princess culture" for both males and females.

As a follow-up to this experience, the students are divided randomly into small groups of three to five and are given a children's picture book. They are required to read their assigned text and consider the issue of bias in light of both the text itself and the illustrations. They are provided with a list of guiding questions to help them consider a wide range of inclusive concepts. Specifically, they evaluate the text based on its portrayal of gender, issues of power and dominance, the amount and type of diversity with regard to race and ethnicity, the accuracy and appropriateness of the depiction of gender and cultures, and issues of body image, sexual orientation, language, religion, and socioeconomics. Each group creates a poster about their assigned text and reports out to the rest of the class during a subsequent class meeting.

ACTIVITY 2: PERCEPTIONS OF DISABILITY

The introductory special education course entitled Individuals with Exceptionalities aims to prepare education professionals to work with diverse learners. In addition to reviewing developmental characteristics, this survey course covers ethical principles and dispositions. Attitudes about individuals with disabilities could impact behavior toward individuals with disabilities. Teacher perceptions matter, and influence practices. Preservice teachers may be less anxious about the inclusion of students with disabilities in their classrooms after an introductory special education course (Shippen et al., 2005). In order to examine, reflect on, and challenge perspectives, the course intentionally begins with activities that explore students' current thinking, rather than immediately providing definitions of specific disabilities.

This lesson on disability is planned keeping Universal Design for Learning (UDL) in mind. Universal Design for Learning reaches the widest range of learners, planning for those in the margins rather than teaching to those in the middle. Presenting material in varied ways, allowing for a range of responses, and engaging students in multiple ways builds support for students (CAST, 2018). Using UDL accounts for the presence of students with disabilities in class and prevents their further marginalization in several ways. Most importantly it includes considerations for varied responses and needs at the onset rather than as an afterthought or "what if" by providing guidelines and scaffolds for students both with and without disabilities. As most disabilities are invisible and students may or may not choose to disclose their disabilities, UDL provides options for diverse needs and avoids putting undue obstacles into activities.

In addition, intentionality and guidance for group interaction serves to prevent possible challenges or issues. Ground rules or agreements for interaction might include treating others with respect and staying engaged. Examples of what those behaviors look like would be discussed. Clearly defined group roles help enhance the group. Group member roles might include facilitator, recorder, reporter, timekeeper, and materials manager (Barkley, Major, & Cross, 2014).

Rather than being put on the spot as experts or ignored, students with disabilities become collaborators in the experience with their peers. Ultimately this activity aims to empower individuals with disabilities and disrupt possible misconceptions and assumptions of those without disabilities.

The students begin by writing a quick list of words that come to mind regarding the word "disability." They then get into groups of four to six and collaboratively develop a definition of disability based on their lists. Each group writes its definition on large sheets of paper, and students then walk around the room to analyze the different definitions created. During this "gallery walk," each student uses colored adhesive dots to vote on the two definitions deemed most accurate. Following the gallery walk, the professor initiates a class discussion that highlights common themes as well as identifying the "winning" definitions as evidenced by the students' votes. In an effort to introduce students to the importance of listening to the voices of individuals with disabilities, students watch the TED talk by Aimee Mullins, titled "The Opportunity of Adversity." In this talk, Mullins (2009) highlighted the dictionary definition of disability, shared her own experiences, and came up with her own revised definition that is more strengths-based. After viewing the TED talk, students individually create bumper stickers summarizing the theme of the talk. After comparing their bumper stickers with a partner, students engage in a class discussion about what changes they might make to the definitions of disability that they created at the beginning of class.

Following the in-class activities, which allow students to collaborate, some individual exploration provides an opportunity to delve further into the subject. As homework, students complete the online IRIS module "What do you see? Perceptions of Disability" (IRIS Center, 2016). The module reinforces the themes introduced in the previous class session. It includes myths and facts about disability. In addition, there are interactive activities, images, videos, and poems to examine how perceptions of disability may have positive or negative impacts on individuals with disabilities. After completion of the module, students write a one-minute paper summarizing what they learned to prepare for the next class. The next class session begins with sharing the one-minute summaries. Following discussion, the instructor provides a mini-lecture about the social construction of disability, person-first language, and identity-first language. This lecture builds on content introduced in the online module. Students examine a list of terms and work in groups to identify if they are "acceptable" in terms of person-first language. If they are not acceptable, students determine an appropriate replacement. The class then reviews the work and discusses why the terms may or may not be acceptable, as well as exceptions for identity-first language. The class discusses how language might connect to assumptions, perceptions, ableism, interactions, and expectations.

ACTIVITY 3: CHALLENGING SINGLE STORIES

Introduction to Psychology is a general education course that provides students with a broad overview of psychology as a scientific discipline and field of study. As a survey course, Introduction to Psychology covers a wide range of subfields within the discipline including one where students are exposed to psychological research on prejudice. Unfortunately, discussing prejudice can be challenging. Many students feel uncomfortable sharing their experiences with and views on prejudice (Bolgatz, 2005). The activity described below was created to help students engage in a meaningful discussion of this challenging topic with the express purpose of fostering intergroup perspective-taking among students.

It is important to note that prior to introducing the activity, professors must recognize the challenges associated with discussing prejudice and discrimination and set some basic ground rules for discussion moving forward. The class discussion begins by providing students with a trigger warning about the activity by informing them that, through the activity, they will be challenged to engage in discussions that may result in uncomfortable dialogues about their own and others' experiences with prejudice and discrimination. Students are told that although these discussions are difficult, they are important. A good deal of research (see Paluck & Green, 2009, for review) finds that open and reciprocal discussions about people's unique experiences with prejudice and discrimination can positively impact intergroup relations and foster understanding and acceptance. Students engage in a discussion about some basic ground rules for the activity. First, students acknowledge that institutional/systematic forms of oppression (e.g., racism and sexism) exist in society and that they should not blame themselves or others for the existence of these institutional/systematic forms of oppression. Second, students are made aware that although stereotypes are a natural byproduct of human cognition (i.e., we all fall prey to them), they are inherently illogical/false and should be discussed as such. Third, students agree not to demean or devalue themselves or others for sharing their own or others' personal experiences with prejudice, discrimination, or institutionalize forms of oppression. Fourth, the class is informed that no individual should ever be thought of or forced to serve as a representative for an entire group of people. It is emphasized that although we may share experiences, we all are unique individuals. Students are asked to refrain from labeling others based on their social identities or perceived group memberships.

The lesson begins with a brief discussion highlighting the distinctions among stereotypes, prejudice, and discrimination. Students then watch Chimamanda Ngozi Adichie's TED talk, "The Danger of a Single Story" where Adichie (2009) highlighted how people, even those with the best intentions, can fall prey to stereotypes or "make one story about a group of people the only story" (i.e., the single story). The dangers of "single stories," Adichie concluded, is that they deprive people from understanding one another, and realizing that we are all more similar than we are different. After watching the TED talk, students are asked to think about a time when (a) they relied on a single story to form an impression of another person, and (b) someone else has used a single story to form an impression of them. Students are then randomly assigned into small groups (of three or four) to share their stories with their peers. During this time, students are told that their groups will be creating a "blog" that challenges one of the single stories shared within their group as part of an out-of-class activity. Instructions for this assignment state that students must (1) introduce a single story, (2) explain how people have come to believe this single story, (3) describe how the single story can and has impacted people's impressions of and actions toward others, and (4) provide accurate information that challenges the single story.

At the beginning of the next class period, students are asked to form new groups with at least one representative of each blog is represented. After sharing their blogs with one another in these groups, the professor leads the students in a large group discussion highlighting how stereotypes are pervasive in society and foster prejudice, discrimination, and moral exclusion (i.e., perception of certain individuals or groups as outside the boundary within which one applies moral values and rules of fairness). The professor presents and asks students to provide examples of sources of stereotypes and prejudice and how the "single stories" that the students explored in their blogs may breed prejudice and discrimination or even moral exclusion. The professor then introduces the students to the psychological research on out-group homogeneity (i.e., the perception that all members of a particular out-group are the same) and asks them to highlight how their blogs demonstrated and then challenged this idea. Students are then asked to share their perspectives on how we, as individuals or a society, could (a) counteract our tendency to demonstrate out-group homogeneity, and (b) foster moral *inclusion*. After this discussion, the professor introduces how social psychologists have attempted to reduce people's endorsement of stereotyped beliefs, negative prejudiced attitudes, and discriminatory actions toward others, highlighting the role of perspective taking and intergroup contact in mitigating prejudice and fostering moral inclusion. As a concluding out-of-class activity, students are asked to write a short journal entry reflecting on what they learned from the activity and how it will impact them in the future.

ACTIVITY 4: EXAMINING RACE AND RACISM THROUGH IMAGERY

Introduction to Sociology is a general education course that introduces students to the discipline of sociology by examining major research findings and theories related to the social causes and consequences of human behavior. Students are introduced to research methods, social structure, institutions, culture, socialization, inequality, and social change. This course, although only an introductory level course, is developed around seven major learning outcomes. Sociology is the systematic study of society and sociologists are particularly interested in examining social patterns in interactions, relationships, institutions, and social problems. Sociology is useful for explaining important matters in our personal lives, our communities, and our world.

The pedagogical approach used to teach Introduction to Sociology positions students to participate in the active construction of knowledge; "perspective taking" becomes a foundational pedagogical tool. When challenged with acknowledging that racism, classism, sexism, heterosexism, and other institutional forms of oppression exist in our world, students often have a hard time grappling with these ideas if not facilitated in a safe learning environment. Perspective taking helps to create a learning environment in which students learn to consciously engage, take responsibility, ask questions, reflect, and examine diverse viewpoints (Lewison, Leland, & Harste, 2008). Examining race and racism through imagery seeks to encourage critical reflection of the diverse experiences of others and the experiences of students themselves from multiple perspectives.

This activity begins by assigning a reading related to race and racism. The textbook chapter on race and ethnicity is assigned; the assigned textbook reading could be substituted with a journal article, book chapter, or essay outlining definitions, concepts, and theories related to race and ethnicity. Once class begins, students are asked to find a partner and discuss the following question: How do you define yourself racially? Explain your answer. As an instructor, it's important to recognize that students will come to this activity identifying with different stages in their personal identity development and this can be challenging for some. Students of color specifically are often more self-aware and can think more critically about their race and may find it challenging to respond to classmates who are much less critical and self-aware. Building a safe space for this activity is crucial. Using an antiracist course design with clear guidelines for students should be built into the foundation of the course. More tactical tips faculty can use to navigate a safe environment for students to explore their identity include: becoming more self-aware as an instructor; being present when small groups explore the prompt; spending time with each group to help guide more difficult conversations; holding space for students of color so that the responsibility is not on them to help White students become more critically aware; and acknowledging these challenges prior to beginning the activity. Pairs are then asked to share their answers with the larger class.

The purpose of the larger group discussion is to help students begin to think more deeply about how race operates in their personal lives. After the opening discussion, students are asked to form groups of four to five and begin a gallery walk using imagery that illustrates different aspects of race and ethnicity in our society. The gallery walk is a useful discussion technique as it requires students to leave their seats and actively participate (Gonchar, 2014). Each image is accompanied by a thought-provoking question, which groups must answer by writing their response on the sheet of paper provided next to the image. Groups are given three to five minutes to respond to the text associated with each image before moving to the next image. Once students have circled through and responded to all prompts, they return to their seats with the image and responses to the prompts from which they began. They will discuss as a small group what other students wrote, and this will serve as a foundation to open the discussion on race and racism. Groups then share responses that stood out or helped them think more critically about the material with the entire class.

This activity uses images of the following: (1) a timeline outlining the changing definitions of race (*Learning Outcome:* Explain the social construction of race and ethnicity); (2) images of four African American women who made significant strides in the advancement of African American people (*Learning Outcome(s):* a. Identify influential women of color throughout time and b. Identify and explain incidences of structural racism); (3) images of racially ambiguous individuals (*Learning Outcome:* Explain the social construction of race and ethnicity); (4) a Wordle of key terms with *discrimination* and *prejudice* standing out (*Learning Outcome:* Distinguish discrimination from prejudice); (5) a picture of a Native American family before and after forced assimilation (*Learning Outcome:* Identify examples of assimilation and racism); and (6) *racism* written in graffiti art (*Learning Outcomes:* a. Identify examples of racism and b. Identify and explain incidences of structural racism). Instructors can use images that best fit the needs of the course but should pay particular attention to the rationale used when selecting images, as they should connect back to the learning outcomes.

After participating in this activity students are asked to complete an online exit ticket where they are asked to respond to the following questions:

1. Name one important thing you learned in class.

2. What did you think was accomplished by the activity we did today?

3. Write/ask one question about today's content—something that has left you puzzled.

Examples of interesting student responses that helped facilitate more thought-provoking discussion include the following:

- "With all the information we now have about race and that it is a social construct, why have we continued to use it even though there is no concrete or standard way to define it?"

- "Every group seemed to identify one of the four women pictured without issue, while nobody in any of the groups could identify the other three . . . I am curious as to whether this could be attributed to a systemic educational issue or if it stems more from individual tendencies, as a largely White class, to focus on White historical figures."

- "Why when asked to write down a personal, everyday example of discrimination in your life did only one group write down something that actually happens directly to them?"

- "I wonder if there will ever be a time when I will not try to find categories and classifications for individuals, based on their appearances?"

These thoughts demonstrate the students' ability to examine historical information related to inequality and the value of perspective taking when challenging oneself and others while looking at the systemic nature of inequality. Students were also able to create new ideas about how fairness and equity might look and exist in our world. Critical reflection on the diverse experiences of others and themselves is a consistent theme throughout most completed exit ticket responses.

After the unit is complete students are also given a selected-response quiz related to the content. When assessing how well students performed on the unit quiz prior to including this activity only 60 percent of the class scored a B or higher on the quiz.

After incorporating the activity 76 percent scored a B or higher on the unit quiz. While many factors may contribute to the improvement in performance, the addition of this activity is indeed one factor that positively enhanced the learning environment. This activity is extremely versatile and could be used with almost any reading on race and ethnicity. Examining race and racism through imagery is best designed to be facilitated in one twenty-minute course or over two days in a fifty-five-minute course. Images and thought-provoking questions could be changed to more relevant images and questions that relate to more specific course content and learning objectives instructors plan to cover in class.

DISCUSSION

While the authors recognize that both our college (a regional, open access campus that is part of a large university) and our department (inclusive of highly diversified faculty, disciplines, and courses) is unique, the applicability of these pedagogical techniques is generalizable to include most other institutions. Emphasizing the significance of cultural competence in coursework, while not always indicated by individual course learning outcomes, is also not a concept foreign to most postsecondary educators (Deardorff, 2004). Whether the need for such competence is derived from the rapid changes precipitated by students from around the world entering US classrooms with a variety of backgrounds or from the capacities and attitudes required to facilitate classroom exchange that "emphasizes a penetration at the interpersonal level, thus requiring an . . . emphasis on the building of relationships to facilitate collaboration and the resolution of common problems" (Cushner, 2015, p. 203), most postsecondary educators understand the increasing need for helping their students develop inclusive perspectives. Creating a plan for an inclusive pedagogy across disciplines requires that postsecondary educators commit to an understanding of individuals who differ from us and seek ways to explore and appreciate diversity in ways that make sense within the context of the content they teach. As Bender-Slack (2019) indicated, "Changing curriculum should be done in conjunction with altering pedagogy. Critical pedagogy is a teaching approach based in critical theory that can be radical and transformative by exploring the power relations within and outside of school, starting with analyzing a person's lived reality" (p. 160). We offer here one integrated way of working toward this goal, but there are many ways in which other institutions can move toward cultural competence in ways that make sense for them and their students.

Pinar (2004) has indicated that classrooms can become unpleasant spaces for educators, especially in light of the diverse populations with which they must engage. As a result, even educators in higher education may withdraw into the "safety of their subjectivities. But in so doing, they have abdicated their professional authority and ethical responsibility for the curriculum they teach" (Pinar, 2004, pp. 3–4). Contrary to Pinar's assessment, the authors of the current chapter have opted not to relinquish our professional power and our ethical duty to teach in an inclusive classroom. Instead, we explored the ways in which we could develop activities, facilitate conversations, and challenge ourselves and our students to engage in difficult discourses. The classroom is the most appropriate place for students to challenge and unpack their own belief systems; it is critical that we organize, modify, and facilitate a robust classroom conversation that allows our students a safe space to explore their thinking, their values, and the systems in place that form both. We suggest that educators consider following Mansilla and Jackson's (2011) global competencies as they plan for pedagogy in their classrooms:

1. Investigate the world beyond their immediate environment, framing significant problems and conducting well-crafted and age-appropriate research.

2. Recognize perspectives, others' and their own, articulating and explaining such perspectives thoughtfully and respectfully.

3. Communicate ideas effectively with diverse audiences, bridging geographic, linguistic, ideological, and cultural barriers.

4. Take action to improve conditions, viewing themselves as players in the world and participating reflectively.

According to hooks (1994), the classroom is the most radical space of possibility because in it one can think, rethink, and create new visions. Teachers can utilize classroom discourses in order to acknowledge that the structure of education, as a microcosm of the wider society, is often shaped by racism, sexism, and classism. The result is that students from diverse backgrounds may or may not find themselves reflected in the curricular structure and classroom discourse, widening the gap of misunderstanding and mistrust of "others," even in an educational setting. Greene (1998), too, indicated that few students enter coursework with an inclination to problematize, question cultural assumptions and ideologies, or examine their feelings.

The activities put forth here are just some examples of what instructors can do to close that gap and encourage the inquiry, the conscious engagement, the reflection, and the entertainment of alternative ways of being that Lewison, Leland, and Harste (2008) suggested are necessary for the development of cultural competence and cultural responsiveness that can lead to purposeful perspective taking and moral inclusion. We encourage instructors who undertake such activities to think critically about the population they serve and explore the ways in which course content, design, and learning outcomes can be a starting point to supporting these important, but difficult discourses in the classroom.

REFERENCES

Adichie, C. N. (2009). *The danger of a single story* [Video]. https://www.ted.com/talks/chimamanda_adichie _the_danger_of_a_single_story/transcript

Barkley, E. F., Major, C. H., & Cross, K. P. (2014). *Collaborative learning techniques: A handbook for college faculty* (2nd ed.). Jossey-Bass.

Bender-Slack, D. A. (2019). *Going global: Internationalization in the classroom*. Rowman and Littlefield.

Bolgatz, J. (2005). *Talking race in the classroom*. Teachers College Press.

CAST. (2018). *Universal Design for Learning Guidelines version 2.2*. http://udlguidelines.cast.org

Cushner, K. (2015) Development and assessment of intercultural competence. In J. Thompson, J. Levy, & M. Hayden (Eds.), *The SAGE Handbook of Research in International Education* (pp. 200–216). SAGE Publications.

Danubata24 [screen name]. (2007, December 3). *Racism in Disney* [Video]. https://youtu.be/LibK0SCpIkk

Deardorff, D. (2004). The identification and assessment of intercultural competence as a student outcome of internationalization at institutions of higher education in the United States. https://repository.lib.ncsu .edu/bitstream/handle/1840.16/5733/etd.pdf?sequence=1&is

Gonchar, M. (2014, October 7). 50 ways to teach with current events. *New York Times*. https://learning.blogs. nytimes.com/2014/10/07/50-ways-to-teach-current-events/

Greene, M. (1998). Teaching for social justice. In W. Ayers, J. Hunt, & T. Quinn (Eds.), *Teaching for social justice: A democracy and education reader* (pp. xxvii–xlvi). Teachers College Press.

hooks, b. (1994). *Teaching to transgress: Education as a practice of freedom*. Routledge.

IRIS Center. (2016). *What do you see? Perceptions of disability*. https://iris.peabody.vanderbilt.edu/module /da/

Lewison, M., Leland, C., & Harste, J. (2008). *Creating critical classrooms: Reading and writing with an edge*. Taylor and Francis.

Mansilla, V. and A. Jackson (2011). *Educating for global competence: Preparing our youth the engage the world*. Asia Society, New York.

Mullins, A. (2009, October). *Aimee Mullins: The opportunity of adversity* [Video]. https://www.ted.com/talks /aimee_mullins_the_opportunity_of_adversity?language=en

Newton, S. (2007, April 12). Sexism, strength and dominance: Masculinity in Disney films [Video]. https:// youtu.be/8CWMCt35oFY

Paluck, E. L., & Green, D. P. (2009). Prejudice reduction: What works? A review and assessment of research and practice. *Annual Review of Psychology, 60*, 339–367. https://doi.org/https://doi.org/10.1146/annurev.psych .60.110707.163607

Pinar, W. (2004). *What is curriculum theory?* Lawrence Erlbaum.

Rankin, S. R., & Reason, R. D. (2005). Differing perceptions: How students of color and white students perceive campus climate for underrepresented groups. *Journal of College Student Development, 46*, 43–61.

Shippen, M. E., Crites, S. A., Houchins, D. E., Ramsey, M. L., & Simon, M. (2005). Preservice teachers' perceptions of including students with disabilities. *Teacher Education and Special Education: The Journal of the Teacher Education Division of the Council for Exceptional Children, 28*(2), 92–99.

Silverstein, S. (1962). *The giving tree*. Evil Eye Music.

CHAPTER 5

Pedagogies of Microresistance
for Equity and Social Justice

Cynthia Ganote, Tasha Souza, and Floyd Cheung

"To educate as the practice of freedom is a way of teaching that anyone can learn. That learning process comes easiest to those of us who teach who also believe that there is an aspect of our vocation that is sacred; who believe that our work is not merely to share information but to share in the intellectual and spiritual growth of our students. To teach in a manner that respects and cares for the souls of our students is essential if we are to provide the necessary conditions where learning can most deeply and intimately begin."—bell hooks (1994, p. 13)

As educators, we aim to provide students with the knowledge, skills, and confidence necessary to engage in the classroom and public sphere with the ultimate goals of equity and social justice. We, as professors of sociology, communication, English, and American studies—and indeed teachers of any courses with social justice aims—can interrupt patterns and systems of inequity by enabling students to identify, name, and challenge them. Microaggressions, or brief, commonplace, and derogatory verbal, nonverbal, or environmental slights and insults (Sue et al., 2007), are rooted in larger systems of oppression and often occur in everyday interactions. When studying college students who faced racial microaggressions, Nadal and colleagues (2014) found that "while all microaggressions are harmful, microaggressions that occur in educational settings (i.e., by professors or other students) or work settings (i.e., by employers or coworkers) may particularly hurt individuals' self-worth" (p. 468). In addition, Sue (2010) found that microaggressions negatively impact students' academic achievement and feelings of inclusion. Microaggressions, then, must be addressed head-on if we want to create vibrant and equitable learning environments in our educational institutions.

Our proposed antidote for microaggressions is microresistance—small-scale individual or collaborative efforts that empower targeted people and allies to cope with, respond to, and challenge microaggressions with a goal of disrupting systems of oppression as they unfold in everyday life, thereby creating more inclusive institutions. By "targeted people," we mean those who are directly affected by that system of oppression (e.g., racism, classism, etc.). By "allies," we mean those who move "beyond awareness of privilege to take risks, call out inequities, . . . dismantle systems of exclusion and oppression," and avoid centering themselves and expecting recognition (Hernández, 2020, p. 150). Allyship should not be seen as an identity (Bebout, 2016); it requires continuous action. Teaching students how to practice microresistance can increase their resilience in the face of microaggressions and empower students to counter them. Our belief in teaching students how to face microaggressions is echoed in the findings of Nadal and colleagues (2014), who asserted that students should be taught how to address microaggressions in college, as a formative experience (Navarro-Garcia, 2016).

While pedagogies of microresistance can be applied in many different contexts, including faculty development and residence life, this chapter will focus on teaching microresistance strategies to students in a classroom context. In particular, we will describe how we teach microresistance, unpacking its various forms and asking students to apply specific communication tools that can be used to respond to microaggressions. In addition, we will analyze the results of a case study in which a majority of undergraduate students reported feeling more empowered to address the microaggressions they experienced or witnessed after learning about and applying microresistance strategies. Teaching students about microresistance helps them feel more prepared to communicate intentionally and act consciously in the face of microaggressions, both inside and outside the classroom.

CONTEXT: TEACHING AT THE UNIVERSITY OF LOUISVILLE

While all three of us teach microresistance at our institutions—Tasha Souza at a large, public university and Floyd Cheung at a small, private college—this chapter will focus on data collected by Cynthia Ganote on the impact of teaching microresistance to her students at the University of Louisville. The University of Louisville is a public, metropolitan university with an enrollment of 22,459 students, located in Louisville, Kentucky. Within the Department of Sociology, Cynthia Ganote teaches classes like Sociology 202: Social Problems, with approximately fifty-five students per section, and Sociology 210: Race in the US, with approximately fifty-five students per section. Both of these classes are 200-level offerings that meet "Cardinal Core" general education requirements in the dual areas of social and behavioral sciences and diversity 1, which focuses on US diversity. For that reason, students in both of these classes come from colleges and majors across the entire university. In other words, sociology majors do not make up the majority of the students in these classes; they are integrated with many other majors and minors. Students often take their core courses in their first or second year of university, but there are also junior and senior students in the classes who need to pick up these course requirements later in their programs of study.

SOCIAL JUSTICE EDUCATION AND THE DEVELOPMENT OF CRITICAL CONSCIOUSNESS

In order to advance equity as social justice educators, we strive to provide students with the skills and confidence necessary to engage in the classroom and public sphere with the aim of responsible social action (Adams et al., 2016). Goodman (2011) emphasized that social justice addresses issues of power, privilege, and psychological well-being. Attaining social justice requires changing larger unjust institutional structures as well as problematic everyday practices in order to challenge dominant ideology (Navarro-Garcia, 2016). Gewirtz (1998) described social justice as actions that support a process built on care, respect, recognition, and empathy while disrupting arrangements that promote marginalization and exclusionary processes. "In the case of social justice education, the stakes are high because we are dealing with historic and current differentials in power, privilege, and access that are manifesting concretely (even as their existence is denied)" (Sensoy & DiAngelo, 2009, p. 348). Integrating social justice into our classrooms means guiding students in critical self-reflection of their socialization into systems of oppression, analyzing the mechanisms of oppression, and empowering them with the ability to challenge these hierarchies (Cochran-Smith, 2004).

One way to engage students in this kind of critical self-reflection and analysis of the mechanisms of oppression, while offering tools to challenge these hierarchies, is to focus on the development of *conscientização*, or critical consciousness, as it is often translated in English (Freire, 2000). Critical consciousness is an awareness of systems of oppression as they unfold in everyday life, combined with action taken to transform these oppressive structures (Freire, 2000). The development of critical consciousness is an integral component of Paolo Freire's critical pedagogy, and it serves as a way for students and teachers together to unveil the mechanisms of oppression in everyday life through a method called co-intentional education. Once the mechanisms of oppression have been revealed, Freire suggests that students become agents of change who can transform reality by taking action against oppressive practices (Ganote & Longo, 2015).

The development of critical consciousness can be broken into three stages, performed iteratively: awareness, analysis, and action—what we and our students decided to call the "triple A's of critical consciousness." In our particular case, using pedagogies of microresistance, we can help students become aware of microaggressions as they occur in everyday life in the awareness stage. In the analysis stage, we teach them that microaggressions are everyday, commonplace manifestations of larger systems of oppression (e.g., systemic racism, patriarchy, heterosexism, classism, ableism, ageism, and American imperialism, to name a few), and we ask students to analyze how and when they occur in different social contexts. And finally, after raising awareness of and unveiling the root causes of these microaggressions in broader systems of oppression, we can teach students productive ways to take action to address them.

TEACHING MICRORESISTANCE IN THE CLASSROOM

In order to teach students to use microresistance, we first raise awareness of microaggressions by defining the term as "brief and commonplace daily verbal, behavioral, or environmental indignities, whether intentional or unintentional, that communicate hostile, derogatory, or negative ... slights and insults" (Sue et al., 2007, p. 271). We unpack each part of the definition, asking students for examples of verbal, behavioral (nonverbal), and environmental (occurring in symbols or in access to buildings, etc.) indignities. Next, we identify different types of microaggressions, asking students for real-world examples without expecting them to self-disclose, which sharpens their awareness of microaggressions that occur in everyday life. Of course, many students are the victims of microaggressions themselves, so it's important to give content warnings and permission for all to care for mental health by, for instance, taking a break if necessary. In the analysis phase, we situate microaggressions within broader systems of oppression, using a sociological framework that asserts that they are the everyday, interactional forms of, for example, systemic racism, patriarchy, heterosexism, classism, ableism, ageism, and American imperialism that we encounter in today's society.

Simply raising student awareness of microaggressions and analyzing their roots in broader systems of oppression, however, is insufficient. At best, students gain the ability to recognize them. At worst, they fall into hopelessness. Thankfully, there are many ways to empower students to respond to microaggressions. Teaching students microresistance is one promising practice. Over time, they learn that they can respond when a microaggression occurs, shore up their own defenses, and build a network of support. With practice, they can grow in confidence and sophistication with regard to practicing microresistance.

RESPONDING TO MICROAGGRESSIONS IN THE MOMENT

As instructors, it is our responsibility to respond to microaggressions and give a sense of agency to our students to do the same, whether confronted with a microaggression in the classroom or any other context. Teaching students about microresistance helps them feel more prepared to communicate intentionally and act consciously. Although there are various communication tools (e.g., Rosenberg, 2003) that can organize one's thoughts and words when faced with a microaggression, we will describe one in detail that we find especially useful and easy to remember for organizing thoughts and responses. We introduce it to students visually at first, on a slide, and we read through each stage. This tool is called OTFD, which stands for Open the Front Door to communication (Learning Forum, 2016). The phrase "open the front door" is a mnemonic device for the four steps of this tool:

- Observe: *State in clear, unambiguous language what you saw happening.* Seek common ground here by stating an observation without evaluation or judgment so that all involved could agree on the speech act, behavior, or incident.

- Think: *Express what you think and/or what you imagine others might be thinking based on the observation.* This is your interpretation step based on the evidence you have.

- Feel: *Express your feelings about the situation.* It's important to take responsibility for one's own feelings using "I" statements ("I feel upset when . . .") instead of placing blame ("You made me feel upset when . . ."). It is also important to actually name an emotion so if the words "I feel" are followed with "like," this is unlikely to happen. For example, "I feel like leaving" is not naming an emotion.

- Desire: *State the concrete action you would like to happen next, your desired next step.* For example, this request could be for more conversation about the microaggression or a request for the behavior to change.

The strength of this tool is that it encourages transparent communication yet allows for flexibility. The following is an example of what the use of this tool might look like employed by a professor or a student in a classroom in response to a tokenism microaggression: "I noticed that an individual was asked to speak for an entire group (Observe). I think we need to resist the temptation because it's a lot to place on someone to ask them to speak for a whole community (Think). I feel uncomfortable with this request (Feel) and would like us all to simply ask others to speak for themselves (Desire)."

After explaining and modeling OTFD with a microaggression example, we then separate the students into pairs and offer two different scenarios for them to apply the steps of OTFD and receive feedback on their application. The microaggression scenarios range from a tokenism example to an example involving a pattern of interruptions. For instance, the latter scenario, projected on a screen and read aloud, looks like this: "You are in the middle of a group discussion at your table, and you observe Jane (a White woman) interrupting Tanya (a woman of color) two times. You've noticed that Jane has done this same thing before, in other class periods." Again, content warnings and permission for self-care should precede this activity.

After initial OTFD practice, we offer an additional communication framework called ACTION (Souza, 2018), which expands upon OTFD with the addition of inquiry questions directed at the microaggressor, along with impact exploration.[1] So rather than beginning with the Observation, students can respond with questions to get clarification and unpack intent (e.g., "Can you tell me a bit more about what you mean by the word 'feminazi'?"). The next step is to summarize what they observed and ask questions to encourage the microaggressor to explore the impact on others of what was stated/done (e.g., "How do you think other people who are Jewish or who identify as feminists may

---

1. **ACTION** stands for **A**sk Questions, **C**ome from Curiosity Not Judgment, **T**ell Observation, **I**mpact Exploration, **O**wn Thoughts/Feelings re: Impact, **N**ext Steps.

feel when hearing that word?"). The following steps in ACTION are similar to the TFD part of OTFD: students share their thoughts and feelings about the microaggressive act and ask for a desired next step. We then guide students in applying ACTION to hypothetical microaggression scenarios (ones in which person A plays the observer of the microaggression, and person B plays the perpetrator), which are set both in and outside of classroom contexts. We always note that we are practicing these communication tools in an environment where a microaggression has *not* just occurred, so that we may be more prepared in a moment when one actually occurs in the future.

After these application opportunities, we debrief with students about their experience. What was easy, difficult? What did you learn from using the communication tools? How might you use these in the future? The debrief assists students in thinking about their own communication skills in terms of strengths and areas for improvement as well as reflecting on how they can respond to microaggressions with microresistance, which increases their sense of agency. We make sure to inform students that they don't have to use the tools perfectly; a clunky response is often better than no response at all, as silence can suggest complicity. We are simply trying things out with each other in a low-stakes environment in an attempt to find microresistance approaches that work for each of us in future situations.

SHORING UP DEFENSES AND BUILDING A NETWORK OF SUPPORT

Shoring up defenses and building a network of support increase one's ability to endure, resist, and respond. These promising practices develop personal resilience and social capital, both of which can serve one well when faced with microaggressions. One key step in the pedagogy of microresistance is to remind students that self-care is a resistant and even revolutionary practice, especially for those who constantly face microaggressions. For inspiration, we share with students Audre Lorde's assertion that "Caring for myself is not self-indulgence, it is self-preservation, and that is an act of political warfare" (1988, p. 131). After hearing Lorde's words, students have talked about how liberating it feels to learn about the importance of caring for themselves, especially since dominant US culture does not often promote self-care.

Faculty can promote self-care by highlighting wellness programs that many campuses sponsor. For instance, Goucher College promotes wellness with the memorable acronym SWEET, which stands for Sleep, Water, Exercise, Eat, and Time (Bowen, 2018). Not surprisingly, getting enough sleep, keeping hydrated, exercising, eating healthfully, and managing time efficiently are foundational to leading a good life. All of these behaviors shore up one's defenses before a microaggression occurs.

Social networks are also crucial, as found in Irey's (2013) research on how women faculty of color practiced microresistance at Bellevue College. While individuals can practice microresistance on their own, having a network of colleagues who look out for one another provides additional strength. Irey credited these networks, which were often affinity groups created by faculty and staff colleagues, with fostering an "alternative leadership paradigm," based on shared personal values like the "strong desire to empower and advocate for others" (p. 165). Irey called this paradigm "the ultimate form of microresistance" (p. 166).

Felten and Lambert (2019) argued that students, too, can join and build similar "webs of relationships." Ready-made student groups or spaces on most campuses include gender equity centers, cultural or intercultural centers, sports teams, affinity organizations, and performance groups. Students can be encouraged to find such groups and spaces or develop them with student, staff, or faculty collaborators. We, as teachers, can support them in the development of networks in class by employing simple techniques like making sure students learn one another's names and asking them to use them when building off classmates' comments during a discussion, along with more complex ideas like designing and implementing thoughtful group projects that require collaboration and accountability. Books like *Collaborative Learning Techniques* by Barkley, Major, and Cross (2014) have offered advice on how to do this successfully. The goal is to create opportunities for students to develop relationships that can lead to empowerment and advocacy for others. As Wheatley (1999) observed, quoting Grace Lee Boggs, "We never know how our small activities will affect others through the invisible fabric of our connectedness. In this exquisitely connected world, it's never a question of 'critical mass.' It's always about critical connections" (p. 45).

Rowe (2008) called these small acts "microaffirmations," which she defined variously as "tiny acts of opening doors to opportunity, gestures of inclusion and caring, and graceful acts of listening," as well as "providing comfort and support when others are in distress" (p. 46). Hence resistance need not look aggressive or hard. It can be subtle and soft. Microaffirmation is a powerful form of microresistance.

EXAMPLES AND EVIDENCE OF SUCCESS

In our microresistance unit, we first raised students' awareness of microaggressions and taught them different microresistance techniques while giving them an opportunity to practice in a low-stakes environment. Next, we asked students to provide written feedback on the experience of learning and practicing OTFD with a partner, and whether they might use microresistance in their own lives. Students were asked to write these short reflections for a minimal number of points, and they received points based on their depth of reflection, not on whether they said they found OTFD useful or were likely to use microresistance in the future.

The data we analyzed for this chapter are from Ganote's Sociology 202: Social Problems class (n = 44) and Sociology 210: Race in the US class (n = 34), both in Fall 2018 at the University of Louisville (total n = 78). After collecting student responses, we used a grounded theory qualitative analytical approach in order to identify themes that emerged from the data (Glaser & Strauss, 1967). In the grounded theory method, instead of applying existing concepts to the data, coding is done through labeling words and phrases that emerge. After labeling words and phrases, we identified broader themes.[2] In analyzing the student response data, we realized that the data grouped around the third A, the action stage, of the "triple A's of critical consciousness" model (awareness, analysis, action). Because microresistance is a form of action that can be taken in the face of microaggressions, the majority of student responses centered on OTFD in particular, and microresistance in general, as an antidote to microaggressions. For that reason, we will amplify nuances in the action stage of critical consciousness that emerged from our student response data.

The themes that emerged were echoed by a majority of undergraduate students and include that microresistance was easy and useful, took little effort but offered a big impact, and gave them strategies to become an effective ally. In addition, they agreed that OTFD was an effective teaching and accountability tool that can be deployed beyond the classroom, ultimately aiding social justice aims. Taken as a whole, these emergent themes reinforce the idea that microresistance is a useful tool for supporting equity and social justice from the students' perspectives.

EASE AND UTILITY

A majority of students reported that the OTFD tool was easy to learn and put into action, and that they believed that OTFD would be effective in addressing microaggressions. Students reported that a lack of plan or structure can lead to inaction, but as one student noted, OTFD can be "modified based on the situation and person and can be used when dealing with any microaggression." Another student, in a representative comment around this theme, wrote: "The OTFD exercise with a partner showed how easy it is to put this tool into action. It didn't take very long at all for me or my partner to come up with an OTFD response to a microaggression example. This makes me feel like I will use this tool in the future because it is very simple and also very effective in standing out against a microaggression."

SMALL STEP, BIG IMPACT

Mulitple students wrote about microresistance as taking small actions that can lead to a much greater impact. For example, one student claimed that "if everybody would show resistance, then things would not get blown away. . . . Microresistance will prevent a bigger problem by squashing the smaller one and if everybody comes together there would be

---

2. In the classic grounded theory method, respondents would be interviewed until theoretical saturation is reached. In this case, we modified the approach, simply using the responses of students on the day that we presented the unit on ways to meet microaggressions with microresistance.

more peace." Another student offered the following comment, asserting that microresistance, as a small response in proportion to the microaggression itself, can be very effective: "I think that microresistance can definitely be helpful because it works in the same way that microaggressions do. If a small insult (microaggression) can be powerful then a small effort against that insult (microresistance) can be just as powerful. If people speak out against microaggressions it shows that we will not stand for this behavior and we are willing to show you just that. Microresistance is how we put a stop to microaggressions."

ALLYSHIP

Many students highlighted the role of microresistance in helping people become effective allies. For example, one student wrote that OTFD gives them "an idea of how to stand up for another human! It is a concept I am very grateful to have learned." One Black student noted that microresistance could encourage White bystanders to follow the lead of those targeted and step up as allies. She stated, "If more people of all races would speak up about them [microaggressions], then we could progress as a nation." Another student found that before learning OTFD, "I would have not known the proper steps on how to resolve this sort of problem, and would have either had no idea what to say, or not known how to help another individual that was being victimized from these microaggressions. . . . Being able to be placed in a scenario that I might actually face in life, and knowing how to respond allowed me to feel more beneficial if someone needed my assistance, and made me feel like I'd be less of a bystander."

Those who are typically targets of microaggressions described how reassuring it is to have allies using microresistance. For example, one student wrote that "when people feel like they have someone or others who can back them up, it gives them strength. When you feel like you're the only one who faces something, and others witness it, but no one backs you up, it's like putting you down all over again because that's telling you that they feel like it's acceptable. Even if the microaggression was not toward you or your group, I do believe it is important to be the strength someone needs. It can help prevent future microaggressions from that aggressor or other aggressors."

A TEACHING AND ACCOUNTABILITY TOOL

Similar to the previous student, several others mentioned that microresistance is important because it lets people know that their actions are problematic. One student said, "Microresistance is so important because it calls individuals out and lets them know that their actions are not okay. It is helpful in the way of ending racism." Another student said, "I think it could be helpful just to start the conversation because if you never stop them, the person will think that's okay. It will help address the situation and start to fix that perception." Another student expressed how dangerous they thought it would be to brush off microaggressions as ignorance: "I think that the most helpful thing that you could do to help increase the amount of microresistance against these discriminatory comments is to not just brush off these comments as ignorance. If you just let these kinds of comments be made then the person who stated them is just going to keep making them and similar ones because they aren't being told not to. Ignorance will only continue to grow if you continue to let it do so."

DEPLOYING MICRORESISTANCE BEYOND THE CLASSROOM
A majority of students reported that they planned to use OTFD in the future in various contexts. For example, a student claimed, "I will most likely be utilizing it with some of my family during the holidays, which should help me gain enough proficiency and confidence in the method to apply it in other social situations." Another student, in a representative comment around these themes, wrote: "I feel like I was able to practice an appropriate response to racist comments in a nonhostile environment, with a level head. It was something I would be 100 percent comfortable repeating to a parent, coworker, relative, friend, or acquaintance. It felt like I could actually have a conversation and connect with someone enough to educate!"

SOCIAL JUSTICE
A majority of students asserted that they believed that microresistance would be an effective tool for creating social change. One student expressed the power of one person to make a change, stating that "microresistance creates hope that microaggressions will fade away. Many people believe that one person cannot make a difference or change within society, however, with the belief of hope then we will see change in the long term." Another student put it in the following way: "Microresistance is, in my view, a vital strategy going forward. I believe that most microaggressions are committed out of ignorance rather than malice, and microresistance methods are excellent tools to combat that ignorance without inciting malice. This is an important step moving forward in society and bridging the divides that segregate us." Another student emphasized that "creating awareness, listening, and acting against microaggressions with the help of microresistance will hopefully one day change our society for the better and destroy microaggressions."

CONCLUSION
While there were a few students who claimed they would not use microresistance or would use it only in certain contexts, an overwhelming majority of students asserted that microresistance was easy and useful, took little effort but offered a big impact, and gave them strategies to become an effective ally. In addition, they agreed that OTFD was an effective teaching and accountability tool that can be deployed beyond the classroom, ultimately supporting social justice aims.

Microaggressions can occur anywhere, including colleges and universities. In our classrooms, we can leverage our role as professors to examine microaggressions through an academic lens. Furthermore, we can teach our students about microresistance to help them feel more prepared to communicate intentionally and act consciously in the face of microaggressions, both inside and outside the academy. With practice in the relatively safe space of the classroom, students may develop interventional skills like OTFD, which they can deploy in any context. If they take our advice to shore up defenses and build networks of support, they will have greater personal and social resources to draw upon when faced with microaggressions. Of course, some injustices occur at the macro level and call for macro-scale response. Through small acts of resistance, however, we and our students can live to fight another day toward equity and social justice and take positive steps toward changing the microclimates that we touch.

ACKNOWLEDGMENTS

The authors wish to thank Lindsay Bernhagen and Pamela Roy, who first invited us to present on microresistance at the annual meeting of the Professional and Organizational Development Network (POD) in 2015. In addition, we are grateful to the students at Saint Mary's College of California who codeveloped the language of the "triple A's of critical consciousness" with Cynthia Ganote.

REFERENCES

Adams, M., Bell, L. A., Goodman, D. J., & Joshi, K. Y. (2016). *Teaching for diversity and social justice: A sourcebook.* Routledge.

Barkley, E., Major, C., & Cross, K. (2014). *Collaborative learning techniques* (2nd ed.). Jossey-Bass.

Bebout, L. (2016). *Whiteness on the border: Mapping the U.S. racial imagination in Brown and White.* New York University Press.

Bowen, J. (2018, November, 16). *Nudges, the learning economy, and a new 3Rs: Redesigning for student relationships, resilience, and reflection.* Keynote speech at Professional Organizational Developers Network conference, Portland, OR.

Cheung, F., Ganote, C. M., & Souza, T. J. (2016). Microaggressions and microresistance: Supporting and empowering students. In *Faculty focus special report: Diversity and inclusion in the college classroom.* Magna Publications. http://provost.tufts.edu/celt/files/Diversity-and-Inclusion-Report.pdf

Cochran-Smith, M. (2004). *Walking the road: Race, diversity, and social justice in teacher education.* Teachers College Press.

Felten, P., & Lambert, L. (2019, January 25). *Relationships matter.* Presentation at AAC&U Conference, Atlanta, GA.

Freire, P. (2000). *Pedagogy of the oppressed* (30th Anniversary Edition). Continuum.

Ganote, C., & Longo, P. (2015). Education for social transformation: Infusing feminist ethics and critical pedagogy into community-based research. *Critical Sociology, 41*(7–8), 1065–1085.

Gewirtz, S. (1998). Conceptualizing social justice in education: Mapping the territory. *Journal of Education Policy, 13*(4), 469–484.

Glaser, B. G., & Strauss, A. L. (1967). *The discovery of grounded theory: Strategies for qualitative research.* Aldine.

Goodman, D. J. (2011). *Promoting diversity and social justice: Educating people from privileged groups* (2nd ed.). Routledge.

Hernández, L. H. (2020). Silence, (in)action, and the downfalls of White allyship. *Women & Language, 43*(1), 147–152.

hooks, b. (1994). *Teaching to transgress: Education as the practice of freedom.* Routledge.

Irey, S. (2013). How Asian American women perceive and move toward leadership roles in community colleges: A study of insider counter narratives [Unpublished doctoral dissertation]. University of Washington, Seattle, WA.

Learning Forum. (2016, December 15). *OTFD: A powerful communication technique.* https://prezi.com /tszt1slnknpa/otfd-a-powerful-communication-technique/

Lorde, A. (1988). *A burst of light: Essays.* Firebrand.

Nadal, K. L, Wing, Y., Griffin, K. E., Davidoff, K., & Sriken, J. (2014). The adverse impact of racial microaggressions on college students' self-esteem. *Journal of College Student Development, 55*(5), 461–474.

Navarro-Garcia, G. (2016). Integrating social justice values in educational leadership: A study of African American and Black university presidents [Unpublished doctoral dissertation]. UCLA, Los Angeles, CA. https://escholarship.org/uc/item/7fz0z9ps

Rosenberg, M. B. (2003). *Nonviolent communication: A language of life* (2nd ed.). Puddledancer Press.

Rowe, M. (2008). Micro-affirmations and micro-inequities. *Journal of the International Ombudsman Association, I*(1), 45–48.

Sensoy, O., & DiAngelo, R. (2009). Developing social justice literacy: An open letter to our faculty colleagues. *Phi Delta Kappan, 90*(5), 345–352.

Souza, T. J. (2018). Responding to microaggressions in the classroom: Taking A.C.T.I.O.N. *Faculty Focus Premium.* https://www.facultyfocus.com/articles/effective-classroom-management/responding-to -microaggressions-in-the-classroom/

Sue, D. W. (2010). *Racial microaggressions in everyday life: Race, gender, and sexual orientation.* Wiley.

Sue, D. W., Capodilupo, C. M., Torino, G. C., Bucceri, J. M. Holder, A., Nadal, K., & Esquilin, M. (2007). Racial microaggressions in everyday life: Implications for clinical practice. *American Psychologist, 62*(4), 271–286.

Wheatley, M. (1999). *Leadership and the new science.* Berrett-Koehler.

REFLECTION ON
Inclusive Social Sciences

Equity and inclusion are clearly integrated in the curricula, pedagogy, and assessment practices of the authors in this section. They illustrate how educators can create a safe environment to discuss and explore human difference while respecting those differences. They expect students to identify and analyze difference, so they can assess and evaluate their own exclusionary practices. They use UDL principles to actively engage students to take responsibility to inquire, be reflective, and entertain alternative ways of being. They work to make the familiar strange, so students are able to see inequity in their everyday lives. They start where students are by drawing upon their experiences as the starting point. Students' development is assessed through a variety of activities and reflective assignments that require students to assimilate the learning.

PRACTITIONER BEHAVIORS

1. How can you use your disciplinary guidelines to create an inclusive and equitable learning environment?

2. What practices or policies do you put in place in your course to interrupt patterns and systems of inequity?

3. In reflecting on the ways in which you respond to microaggressions in various contexts, what personal work do you have yet to do?

PEDAGOGY

1. What concerns do you have regarding the facilitation of difficult discourses about systemic inequality regarding your students of color or marginalized populations within the classroom?

2. What hands-on and interactive lessons have you attempted in your coursework that you feel successfully facilitated a perspective-taking experience for your students?

CURRICULUM

1. What challenges would your institution, college, or department face if an institutional decision was made to include diversity and inclusion concepts into disciplinary-specific content?

2. How can you integrate principles of social justice into your curriculum?

3. What are some ways to create a curriculum that supports the development of critical consciousness?

ASSESSMENT

1. Given the nature of your subject matter and courses, how might the teaching of microresistance align with your learning outcomes? How might teaching microresistance strengthen other aspects of your course(s)?

2. How can you assess inquiry, conscious engagement, reflection, and entertainment of alternative ways of being necessary for the development of cultural competence and cultural responsiveness?

PART III
Inclusive Humanities

Part III on humanities includes examples drawn from the foreign-language classroom where Susan Hildebrandt provides the sample strategies she uses to promote inclusivity for students with learning disabilities. She describes universal design for instruction principles such as perceptible information, tolerance for error, creating a community of learners, and an inclusive instructional climate, which when leveraged in the foreign-language classroom, can help better meet the needs of diverse learners and help them develop proficiency in a foreign language.

The English classroom, specifically first-year composition courses, has the distinction of seeing every undergraduate on campus since it is a required course at most higher education institutions and students must pass the course in order to graduate. The stakes are high because it is required for graduation and serves as a gatekeeper course. A negative experience in such a course can frequently be perceived as a barrier to success by college students. English literature courses, predominantly Eurocentric, patriarchal, and biased in favor of certain socioeconomic classes, need to change to be more representative of the diverse population that enrolls in these courses. Brenda Refaei and Rita Kumar suggest using both inclusive strategies and an equitable curriculum to address diversity in the English composition classroom and the literature classroom.

CHAPTER 6

Increasing Inclusion and Lowering Student Anxiety in the Postsecondary Foreign-Language Classroom

Susan A. Hildebrandt

This chapter outlines specific strategies grounded in Universal Design for Instruction (UDI) (Scott & Edwards, 2012; 2019; Scott, Hildebrandt, & Edwards, 2013), that include diverse student voices in the second- or foreign-language classroom. With a focus on student anxiety and attitudes toward student and instructor target language (e.g., French, German, Spanish) use, it highlights the spontaneous use of the spoken target language as the medium of communication in the classroom and explores inclusive pedagogy to help students with and without disabilities be more successful users of a second language. Too often language classes can provoke anxiety and, thereby, diminish the in-class participation and language acquisition of students who may fear correction, causing them to focus on small linguistic errors, or feel disconnected from the language, instructor, or fellow classmates. Inclusive language teaching strategies can provide ways for all students to increase their involvement in class and their investment in the language learning process. This chapter includes the voices of students who have various diagnosed disabilities to demonstrate how UDI can help them, as individuals, to learn a second language, while allowing them to have a similar learning experience as that of their peers in the classroom. The chapter closes with an exploration of how the existing literature and information gained from interviews with students with disabilities informed pedagogical modifications to a fifth-semester Spanish conversation class.

RATIONALE FOR INCLUSIVE PEDAGOGY

Research grounded in Universal Design for Instruction (UDI) (Scott & Edwards, 2012; 2019; Scott, Hildebrandt, & Edwards, 2013) has helped foreign-language instructors and universities' language programs better meet the needs of all learners in the classroom and move toward fulfilling the vision of all students developing proficiency in a language other than English. UDI is a social model of disability that anticipates and plans for student diversity instead of modifying instruction or conditions for individual students after the fact, as a medical model of disability does. It focuses on perceived barriers to learning for all students, instead of only the challenges that learners with disabilities bring to the language-learning experience. The medical model, on the other hand, focuses on "special help" to be offered to the exceptional individual and may perpetuate a deficit model of students with disabilities, as opposed to the social model that highlights the interaction between an individual's differences and his or her environment.

While many in this volume use Universal Design for Learning (UDL), this chapter uses Universal Design for Instruction (UDI) as its framework. These two models originate from Universal Design and focus on improving teaching and learning for all students. UDI was developed for postsecondary settings and UDL was originally implemented in K–12 classrooms (McGuire, Scott, & Shaw, 2006). UDL focuses on multiple means of engagement, representation, action, and expression with a focus on the curriculum, while UDI has nine different principles that instructors can use to improve instruction for the most students possible. UDI was chosen as the framework for this chapter because of its use as a "tool for reflective practice that can lead to more inclusive instruction in an increasingly diverse population of college students" (McGuire, Scott, & Shaw, 2006, p. 169).

UDI applies Universal Design to instruction, drawing upon Universal Design's architectural and design-based concepts of usability for the maximum amount of people possible. UDI principles, according to Scott, McGuire, and Foley (2003), "are intended to be a framework to inform faculty planning and practice rather than a rigid procedure or prescription for instruction" (p. 43). These principles are: (1) equitable use, (2) flexibility in use, (3) simple and intuitive, (4) perceptible information, (5) tolerance for error, (6) low physical effort, (7) size and space for approach and use, (8) a community of learners, and (9) instructional climate. These principles, generally speaking, can increase students' perceptions of safety and lower perceived threats, as they build community with the instructor and other students, lowering barriers for all learners.

Proactive modifications to the classroom environment can alleviate some anxiety-related language-learning challenges and help students be more successful, while fostering a more natural acquisition of the second language. By anticipating diversity, instructors can diminish or remove barriers to learning and using a second language for all students, not just those with disabilities (Scott, Hildebrandt, & Edwards, 2013). Scott, Hildebrandt, and Edwards (2013) explained that "rather than single out specific individuals for their uncommon needs, adherents to the social model anticipate those needs and design the environment with them in mind" (p. 172). That focus on the environment, whether physical space, curriculum, or pedagogy, benefits all students. That proactive stance can concern the physical space of the classroom, instructional materials, course syllabi, and instructor dispositions, which all can *set the stage* for successful language teaching and learning (Scott & Edwards, 2019).

Many high school students may take foreign-language classes in order to qualify for university admission. Later, during university studies, they may also need to complete up to four additional semesters of a language as part of general education requirements. Unfortunately, university beginning-level classes may be taught by instructors who may not have had very robust pedagogical preparation. Even with some pedagogical grounding, instructors may not always have much preparation or experience teaching students with special needs, many of whom had numerous supports at the secondary level. Students with disabilities have been all too frequently overlooked in the second-language classroom, despite the vision of the *World-Readiness Standards for Learning Languages* that "ALL students will develop and maintain proficiency in English and at least one other language" (National Standards Collaborative Board, 2015, p. 7, emphasis in the original).

Introductory language courses require students to read, write, listen, and speak in the target language; that is, they must interact in the language that is being taught. It is generally advised that students take these introductory classes as soon as possible in their university studies, although course availability, student anxiety around the second language, or other variables may delay their completion until shortly before graduation. In particular, the need for spontaneous use of the second language during class can raise student anxiety and adversely influence student affect. Student anxiety in the language classroom has been a rich topic of investigation historically (Horwitz, 2000), including among students with disabilities (Scott, Hildebrandt, & Edwards, 2013). As more and more students with disabilities enter American universities, it becomes increasingly important that second-language instructors implement pedagogical practices that include as many learners as possible so that language course requirements don't become an impediment to finishing a university degree (Scott, Hildebrandt, & Edwards, 2013).

Contemporary language teaching is based on communication, rather than memorizing decontextualized verb conjugations and endless lists of vocabulary words. The emphasis is no longer on what students know *about* language; rather, it is on what students can *do* with language (Clementi & Terrill, 2017). Therefore, the second-language classroom has become focused on communication between students and the instructor and among students in the target language. The three modes of communication are interpretative (in which learners understand or interpret information that is heard, read, or viewed), interpersonal (in which learners negotiate meaning and interact in conversations, whether written or spoken), and presentational (in which learners engage in a one-way presentation of information to others) (National Standards Collaborative Board, 2015). The flagship organization of K–16 second-language teachers, American Council on the Teaching of Foreign Languages (ACTFL), recommends that 90 percent or more of the discourse in the language classroom be in the target language—that is, the language being studied (ACTFL, 2010). The council suggests the following ways of maximizing target language use:

1. provide comprehensible input that is directed toward communicative goals;

2. make meaning clear through body language, gestures, and visual support;

3. conduct comprehension checks to ensure understanding;

4. negotiate meaning with students and encourage negotiation among students;

5. elicit talk that increases in fluency, accuracy, and complexity over time;

6. encourage self-expression and spontaneous use of language;

7. teach students strategies for requesting clarification and assistance when faced with comprehension difficulties; and

8. offer feedback to assist and improve students' ability to interact orally in the target language. (ACTFL, 2010, para. 1)

For decades communicative approaches to teaching world languages have recognized the importance of comprehensible input (Krashen, 1982), both in the form of authentic written and audio resources created by native speakers for native speakers and in the form of written and spoken language created by the instructor. Comprehensible input, according to Krashen (1982), should be gauged to just above the language learners' current level of proficiency, or at "$i + 1$," in order to provide learners with language that is generally understood but just challenging enough to remain engaging. At present, however, not all language classrooms put into practice linguistic input that arrives at "$i + 1$." Instead, instructors may provide input that is too advanced, use English to teach the target language, focus exclusively on grammatical accuracy instead of meaning, or move quickly through the curriculum without ensuring student understanding.

Related to the use of the target language in the classroom, student affect can play a critical part in the success or struggle of individuals attempting to learn languages. With motivation and self-confidence, anxiety makes up the phenomenon of student affect. According to Krashen (1982), "low anxiety appears to be conducive to second language acquisition, whether measured as personal or classroom anxiety" (p. 31). Those with higher motivation and self-confidence and lower anxiety, Krashen (1982) argued, will seek out opportunities for increased target language input and more occasions for target language creation.

Foreign language anxiety has been a topic of intense interest in the language teaching profession for decades (e.g., Horwitz, 2000; Horwitz, Horwitz, & Cope, 1986; Rassaei, 2015). Student anxiety and the unexpected, inconsistent use of comprehensible input in the target language may act as barriers to language learners from a variety of backgrounds, including those with disabilities. That mixture of variables can also increase withdrawals from language classes, thereby delaying time to graduation and increasing educational expenses (Scott & Edwards, 2012). Inclusive language teaching practices, however, can positively impact the language learning experiences of learners with and without disabilities.

There are a number of ways that the target language can be maximized during class, while encouraging all students to participate. In particular, Edwards (2011) suggested that instructors "establish a rhythm" to the class, with "easy-to-anticipate steps within instruction time" (p. 3). She went on to highlight a number of practices that increase equity and inclusion as students attempt to create the target language, including dispelling inaccurate assumptions through "reassurance that speaking in the target language gets easier as time is devoted to the practice" (p. 2) and communicating realistic expectations through open conversations about course outcomes. She established a parallel with an exercise class in which students must prepare in advance in order to fully take advantage of the class time, like completing homework based on the material to be addressed in the upcoming class, working on a warm-up activity in the target language at the beginning of class, addressing new material afterward, and finishing the class with "review, reinforcement, and teasers for the next class meeting" (p. 3). With a routinized classroom schedule, students are able to anticipate what is to come during class and can, therefore, be more able to participate with diminished anxiety.

Edwards (2011) pointed to other ways to encourage target language use, such as the regular use of visuals in the class. These visuals can include engaging pictures that represent vocabulary being studied or the written language being spoken, whether on the whiteboard in the moment or digitally through subtitles on videos. She went on to highlight the importance of using cognates, or words in the target language that resemble and mean the same thing in English, while teaching the second language. Finally, circumlocution or rephrasing aids students in understanding target language produced by the teacher and can be taught as a communication strategy for students to use if a target language word does not occur to them in the moment it is needed. All of these strategies can be implemented in any language classroom to increase the inclusion of all students and the equity of the classroom.

Scott and Edwards (2019) suggested that instructors "use the target language from the very first day" (p. 98), while pointing out that support should also be offered in the form of strategies to help students use the target language and evolving lists of frequently used classroom expressions. Additionally, they suggested that a ten-minute conversation about the importance of using the target language during class "will establish high expectations while demonstrating an awareness of student anxiety and concern" (p. 98).

Utilizing the UDI framework (Scott, McGuire, & Foley, 2003), the remainder of this chapter highlights student voices as they discuss learning languages in a classroom setting and then moves into the pedagogical implications and suggested modifications for the language classroom to be a more inclusive space for students with and without disabilities. It focuses on students' reactions to pedagogical practices based on four of the nine UDI principles: *perceptible information* (Principle 4), encouraging a *tolerance of errors* (Principle 5), promoting a *community of learners* (Principle 8), and designing a welcoming *instructional climate* (Principle 9). Ways for practitioners to put into practice strategies for including as many student voices as possible, while lowering overall student anxiety, are included. The chapter closes with an examination of how UDI can address the issues of power and inequity in the second-language classroom.

UNIVERSITY SETTINGS

Student reactions to inclusive language teaching practices were gathered on two campuses: Illinois State University in Normal and Longwood University in Farmville, Virginia. Illinois State University, the first public university in the state and a former teachers' college, has 18,330 undergraduate and 2,454 graduate students (Illinois State University, 2019). Students wishing to earn a bachelor of arts degree in all colleges must complete at least three semesters of language study, while those seeking a bachelor of science degree in the College of Arts and Sciences must complete at least two semesters. Those seeking a bachelor of science degree in other colleges are not required to complete any additional language study beyond what was completed in high school and required for admission to the university.

Six Illinois State students with disabilities who are supported by the on-campus Office of Disability Concerns, recently renamed Student Access and Accommodation Services, participated in semi-structured interviews. The participants have the following documented disabilities: ADHD (2), ADD (1), mild to profound hearing loss (2), reading processing difficulties (1), cognitive learning disability (1), and bipolar disorder (1). They had one to six years of experience taking classes in French, German, Italian, and Spanish prior to entering postsecondary education and one to four semesters of experience at the university level. One participant also had four semesters of experience taking American Sign Language.

Longwood is a former teachers' college for the commonwealth and has 4,574 undergraduate and 522 graduate students (Longwood University, n.d.). At the time of the study, all students were required to pass an intermediate level or higher course in a second language to earn an undergraduate degree. Seven students with disabilities from Longwood participated in interviews using the same protocol and were registered with the Office of Disability Resources on campus. Diagnosed disabilities among participants included learning disability (4), ADD (2), cerebral palsy (1), autism spectrum (Asperger's syndrome) (1), visual impairment (1), and psychological disability (1). Each participant completed foreign-language requirements in high school and had taken between one and six semesters of language coursework at Longwood. The data from the seven interviews carried out with Longwood students have been, in part, described in previous research as one of three empirical studies to explore supports and barriers for Longwood students with disabilities who were learning foreign languages (Scott, Hildebrandt, & Edwards, 2013).

STUDENT VOICES

This chapter examines student anxiety and attitudes toward target language use, highlighting pedagogical suggestions to make language teaching and learning more inclusive, through sixty- to ninety-minute interviews. The protocol for the interviews was developed with the purpose of exploring the experiences of students with disabilities while learning a second language in the classroom. Data were coded into eleven distinct categories: accommodations, advice for students, assessment, classroom environment, placement and dropping class, professor characteristics, study abroad, study strategies, group work, student anxiety and student affect, and speaking the target language. This study focused on data from the last three categories and highlights UDI Principles 4, 5, 8, and 9. At the close of the chapter, we will explain how these data, along with the literature above, informed pedagogical modifications made to a fifth-semester Spanish conversation class taught by the author in the spring of 2019.

To begin, learner anxiety was mentioned several times throughout these interviews, with some participants hesitant to use the target language in class at all. Ellie explained that she "didn't want to make mistakes," while Jamie confided that "when [she] didn't know the answer, that was overwhelming." Additionally, there were some misunderstandings of basic language course expectations and the need for target language use, expressed by participants when asked to give advice to foreign language instructors. For example, Paul recommended the following: "Don't immerse. One of my brothers who's taking Spanish has complained that . . . the professor speaks completely in Spanish. I think . . . that's a bad idea because you know, he's not doing it because he's interested in the language. He's doing it to satisfy that goal [course requirement] so don't make his life harder than it is. Don't make any student's life harder than it is." Marc advised, "Don't speak too much in the particular language you are teaching," while Samantha recommended that "maybe lower levels, no . . . automatically jump into like Spanish because it's hard." Those instances of anxiety and common language-learning misconceptions suggest that UDI could be helpful when teaching beginning-level language classes, particularly if instructors explain to students why using the target language during and outside of class time is critical to their success. Explicitly addressing the rationale for target language use can help students develop the metacognitive basis necessary to establish a firm foundation for their own continued linguistic development. That foundation can help them then focus on creating meaning in the target language rather than focusing exclusively on grammatical accuracy in their message.

Perceptible information (Principle 4) means that "instruction is designed so that necessary information is communicated effectively to the student, regardless of ambient conditions or the student's sensory abilities" (Scott, McGuire, & Foley, 2003, p. 44). Participants in this study explained that instructors can "rephrase [ideas] in so many different ways that if you don't understand one way, [they should] do it a different way so it kinda makes sense" (Jackie) and that they should be "willing to explain things in more than one way" (Jamie). Nonverbal means of communication, including visual aids (Marc), illustrations (Samantha), gestures (Samantha), and writing on the board (Jamie), were also highlighted by participants. Advance organizers, like a routine (Jackie), were also mentioned as a useful means of aiding in the comprehension of the second language: "[the effective language instructor] would give you forewarning of the subjects that she would probably bring up" (Morgan). Valerie pointed to the benefit of an organized schedule: "and maybe on the bottom of the syllabus along with the homework maybe say this is what we are discussing today, tomorrow we are studying this, you know. This is what we are studying tonight. I would study this and here is the homework assignment, that definitely helps."

Tolerance of errors (Principle 5) characterizes "instruction [that] anticipates variation in individual student learning pace and prerequisite skills" (Scott, McGuire, & Foley, 2003, p. 44). Participants in this study related thoughts about this tolerance of errors, pointing to the diversity of students in the classroom and their varying proficiency levels, time needed for tasks, and length of attention span: "You do have different levels of [language] proficiency even amongst the 101 . . . and just taking the placement test can only be so accurate" (Marc); "getting professors to understand that some students are gonna take more time than others and need more help" (Jamie); "not do PowerPoint the whole time. I would take breaks from it so if you were going to do activities I would change to the activity and take a break so that students are mentally awake" (Valerie). A piece of advice offered to instructors came from Lisa, who suggested that "instructors in general need to be aware that just because a student looks perfectly normal and can hold down a perfectly normal conversation, there might be something going on," while Morgan offered comfort to language students: "everyone makes mistakes, and no one is perfect."

Promoting a *community of learners* (Principle 8) entails an "instructional environment [that] promotes interaction and communication among students and between students and faculty" (Scott, McGuire, & Foley, 2003, p. 44). At the heart of the language learning endeavor, interaction and communication among people in the classroom underlies contemporary language learning. Jamie pointed to instances when a community of learners wasn't established in a language classroom and instructors "get impatient with students because they just don't get it" and lamented that "teachers don't have the time or the patience a lot of times." Ellie expressed a more nuanced view of participation in the language classroom, reasoning that "the more uncomfortable you are in a foreign language class probably the better it is for you because if you're comfortable with sitting in the back and never participating, you're never really gonna learn anything and if that's what you're there for, then that's what you're there for, that's your own thing but, um, from the aspect of really trying to grasp the language you're never really going to get it if they don't call on you and put you on the spot and make you uncomfortable, unfortunately."

John explained that instructor enthusiasm and interest in students' lives helps build community, "if you can somehow connect with them and talk about topics that affect them and what they are going through." Jackie asked for instructors who were "giving us more opportunities to speak in Spanish, whereas just don't have the two oral evaluations and that's it," while Abby reflected that "being forced to speak in the groups definitely helps you—helped me—grow within Spanish." Responsiveness to student concerns in person and via email was mentioned by several participants, with Melissa telling instructors that "responding to your emails" helps students buy into the language course. Ellie mentioned that "having a classroom feel that's really that comfortable and not feeling like you can't ask questions" helps students increase their participation in class and Paul advised that "humor works. . . . Every professor needs to have that."

Instructional climate (Principle 9) necessitates instruction [that] is designed to be welcoming and inclusive. High expectations are espoused for all students" (Scott, McGuire, & Foley, 2003, p. 44). A number of instructor characteristics mentioned in interviews with participants seemed to underscore the need for a welcoming and inclusive instructional climate. Jamie listed several instructor traits that would be beneficial: "Patience and good listening skills," "empathetic is good too . . . I don't know, just compassion," and "warm, inviting, patient." Jamie highlighted the flexibility necessary for instructors, being sure that they are "keeping in mind that the plan, or the lesson, or the way that [they] are teaching might need to completely be reconstructed." Marc cautioned that instructors "definitely have to define expectations," while Paul suggested that instructors can espouse high expectations by "speaking the language. It's flexing that muscle. It's not something you get when you're sitting there conjugating verbs all day on a piece of paper." An openness and acceptance of students with special needs was also mentioned by several participants, often with a need for confidentiality. Paul suggested that instructors "offer to say on the first day of class when you're going through the syllabus or something, point out if you have a disability please see me after class. Please swing by my office some time. Make it known that their disabilities should not be shunned from the class. That it's . . . that it should be an open knowledge to the professor and that student." Marc appreciated instructors who didn't make a big deal of accommodations: "The whole not making it feel like you have to explain yourself is the most important part for me." And Lisa explained that she preferred discretion and "the instructors that just kind of nod and are willing to keep it quiet rather than make a class announcement about it. I prefer that. I think most people do."

This section of the chapter documented what students with disabilities across two university contexts had to say about using the target language and the associated anxiety they felt at times during class. It used the four UDI principles to organize participant comments, which will inform the next section devoted to pedagogical implications.

INCLUSIVE PEDAGOGY AND WORLD LANGUAGES

UDI in language teaching is an exciting area of investigation, particularly as it relates to student target language use and anxiety. This final section of the chapter applies the suggestions from the literature explored above and from student participants to the context of a real class: a fifth-semester Spanish conversation course taught by the author during the spring of 2019. Using the same four UDI principles as above, this section will offer specific pedagogical steps undertaken to decrease all students' anxiety and, thereby, increase in-class inclusion and equity among all students.

PERCEPTIBLE INFORMATION (PRINCIPLE 4)

To design instruction "so that necessary information is communicated effectively to the student, regardless of ambient conditions or the student's sensory abilities" (Scott, McGuire, & Foley, 2003, p. 44), the author undertook a number of steps throughout the semester. To begin, she used the university's learning management system to upload copies of all PowerPoint presentations before each class, so that students were able to access them before, during, and after class as necessary. Students were also able to preview any videos presented during class and watch them again after class, since links were embedded in the presentations. Presentations included clear and large visuals to clarify and supplement the information offered in the slides, while maintaining as clear a presentation as possible. Videos used in class, as often as possible, included subtitles in Spanish so that students had both aural and visual linguistic input during viewing. Additionally, videos were viewed at least twice during class after students completed short, previewing activities to prime them for the new material being addressed in the videos.

During the first week of class, students were taught how to circumlocute; that is, they were taught how to explain their way out of having to use a particular word if they could not think of it. This communication strategy was reinforced with each new chapter, as students played a variation of Taboo with new vocabulary words in which students described the new words in Spanish to their partner who determined which word from the list was being described.

Routines were established early in the semester so that most classes had a similar schedule to enable students to follow along as easily as possible. Each slide presentation began with an agenda for the class period that listed the anticipated activities. Most days began with a warm-up in pairs, followed by a previewing or prereading activity and a video or short reading relevant to the theme of the day, and ending with several chances for students to create language related to the topic at hand. That informal practice, followed by a model communication created by native speakers and production by students, allowed for predictability that would minimize confusion for all students.

TOLERANCE FOR ERROR (PRINCIPLE 5)

Keeping in mind the need for "instruction [that] anticipates variation in individual student learning pace and prerequisite skills" (Scott, McGuire, & Foley, 2003, p. 44), the author took several measures during the Spanish conversation class to increase inclusion and equity among students. During the first day, she took ten minutes of class time to explain why using Spanish during and outside of class was important to the students' linguistic development, drawing parallels between learning to play a sport and musical instrument with learning to speak a second language, as suggested by Edwards (2011). As part of that ten-minute conversation in English, she pointed out that perfection is not expected and that errors are part of the learning process. She further explained that we all make mistakes even when speaking our native languages, so expecting perfection while using the second language for spontaneous communication is unrealistic, both for the professor and for themselves.

While evaluating students' work submitted for evaluation, her feedback focused on the linguistic functions and forms under study and gave less emphasis to those that were not the focus of instruction; that is, she commented on how students could improve their message related to the communication strategies and grammatical structures that were explicitly studied since the beginning of the semester, unless errors interfered with the clarity of the message. She did not point out each grammatical error, choosing to focus instead on the themes addressed within the course in order to focus students' attention and not overwhelm them with less critical details.

A COMMUNITY OF LEARNERS (PRINCIPLE 8)

To increase "interaction and communication among students and between students and faculty" (Scott, McGuire, & Foley, 2003, p. 44), the instructor implemented a number of pedagogical interventions, beginning with learning each student's name the very first day and repeating each student's name at the beginning of class for the first three weeks. She also asked three students to repeat the names of their classmates each day across those first weeks, explaining that they are all going to be spending the semester together and that they should know one another's names as members of the classroom community.

An additional means of increasing the sense of community among learners involved an assignment called "Day of the Expert," in which each student made a five- to seven-minute presentation to the class about something in which they were an expert so that all students could share a bit about themselves unrelated to Spanish with the class. In an effort to share a bit about herself, the author created a presentation to serve as a model for students and shared her hobby of knitting, how she learned, and the knitted monsters she has made for friends and family.

To enable students to get to know one another in a more informal way, many classes began with a "walk and talk" activity in which they paired up with someone from the class that they did not know very well to talk about a variety of topics, depending on the theme of the day. During that activity, they spent fifteen minutes walking inside the building in which class was held or outside if weather permitted. Those minutes at the beginning of class engaged in informal conversation set the stage for the rest of the class period, allowing students to ease into class first in informal conversation with a peer before focusing on more formal communication on the topic at hand.

INSTRUCTIONAL CLIMATE (PRINCIPLE 9)

The UDI principle related to instructional climate describes how "instruction is designed to be welcoming and inclusive" and how "high expectations are espoused for all students" (Scott, McGuire, & Foley, 2003, p. 44). During the Spanish conversation class in the spring of 2019, the author enacted several strategies to have an inclusive and equitable class with high expectations. To begin, the syllabus had sections concerning services offered by the on-campus Student Access and Accommodation Services office, Student Health Services, and the new student food pantry. As part of the discussion about Student Health Services, the author highlighted services related to mental health and briefly shared her own mental health challenges and current treatments, closing with the sentiment that it is a sign of strength to know when you need help. The syllabus also included descriptions of all assignments to be completed throughout the semester, along with the rubric that would be used to evaluate the students' performance and the dates on which the assignments would be due.

CONCLUSION

This chapter highlighted means through which instructors could leverage UDI principles 4 (perceptible information), 5 (tolerance for error), 8 (a community of learners), and 9 (instructional climate) to lower student anxiety and increase target language use, by referencing previous literature and by highlighting the voices of students with disabilities who took introductory language classes at the postsecondary level. It also outlined how the author implemented those UDI principles during a recent Spanish conversation class taught to undergraduate students.

Language teaching with UDI in mind holds great promise for the future as the language classroom becomes increasingly diverse and the need for equity and inclusion increases. Nearly all suggestions from the literature and participant comments addressed in this chapter, when put into practice, can benefit all students and not only those with disabilities and help them become better speakers of the language being studied. Much of what UDI proposes may be perceived as generally effective teaching practices; it is a proactive approach to teaching that supplements accommodations that students may receive through offices of student access or accommodations on campus with an effort to give all students the available supports.

By removing some of triggers that may provoke student anxiety, UDI principles and the accompanying pedagogical practices can help promote a culture of equity in the class and diminish the fear of students that they may be judged or continuously evaluated for their grammatical accuracy in the target language. Applying these principles and practices to the language classroom can also promote the instructor as a language learner themselves, instead of the "sage on the stage"; instructors can become conversational partners, rather than the sole expert in the room. These practices can aid students with and without disabilities, as well as students who speak the language at home or with extended family members. Those heritage language learners may experience language instruction that devalues their home language, while instructors who apply UDI principles can more aptly establish community in the classroom and improve instructional climate with the objective of respecting and empowering all learners. The time to include all students in the language classroom has come. Applying the principles and practices outlined in this chapter can decentralize the traditional role of the instructor as critic, while empowering students, no matter what their abilities, to communicate their thoughts, desires, and opinions in the target language.

REFERENCES

American Council on the Teaching of Foreign Languages (ACTFL). (2010). *Use of the target language in the classroom.* https://www.actfl.org/news/position-statements/use-the-target-language-the-classroom

Clementi, D., & Terrill, L. (2017). *The keys to planning for learning: Effective curriculum, unit, and lesson design.* American Council on the Teaching of Foreign Languages.

Edwards, H. (2011). *Examining target language use.* Project LINC. Longwood University, Farmville, VA. http://blogs.longwood.edu/projectlinc/files/2016/03/Module_TL_92011.pdf

Horwitz, E. K. (2000). It ain't over 'til it's over: On foreign language anxiety, first language deficits, and the confounding of variables. *Modern Language Journal, 84*(2), 256–259.

Horwitz, E. K., Horwitz, M. B., & Cope, J. (1986). Foreign language classroom anxiety. *Modern Language Journal, 70*(2), 125–132.

Illinois State University. (2019). *About.* https://illinoisstate.edu/about/

Krashen, S. (1982). *Principles and practice in second language acquisition.* Pergamon Press.

Longwood University. (n.d.) *About us.* http://www.longwood.edu/about/

McGuire, J. M., Scott, S. S., & Shaw, S. F. (2006). Universal Design and its applications in educational environments. *Remedial and Special Education, 27*(3), 166–175.

National Standards Collaborative Board. (2015). *World-readiness standards for learning languages* (4th ed.). National Standards Collaborative Board.

Rassaei, E. (2015). Oral corrective feedback, foreign language anxiety, and L2 development. *System, 49*(1), 98–109.

Scott, S. S., & Edwards, W. (2012). Project LINC: Supporting lecturers and adjunct instructors in foreign language classrooms. *Journal of Postsecondary Education and Disability, 25*, 253–258.

Scott, S. S., & Edwards, W. (2019). *Disability and world language learning: Inclusive teaching for diverse learners.* Rowman and Littlefield.

Scott, S. S., Hildebrandt, S. A., & Edwards, W. A. (2013). Second language learning as perceived by students with disabilities. In C. Sanz & B. Lado (Eds.), *Individual differences, L2 development, and language program administrators: From theory to application* (pp. 171–191). Heinle.

Scott, S. S., McGuire, J. M., & Foley, T. E. (2003). Universal Design for Instruction: A framework for anticipating and responding to disability and other diverse learning needs in the college classroom. *Equity & Excellence in Education, 36*(1), 40–49.

CHAPTER 7

Incorporating Equity and Inclusion in English Composition and Literature Courses

Brenda Refaei and Rita Kumar

Faculty wishing to promote equity and inclusion in their composition and literature classrooms need to examine both their pedagogy and curriculum. The curriculum needs to reflect the identities of the students in the class. At the same time, pedagogical approaches should be determined by the needs of the students in the classroom. This two-pronged approach ensures that faculty will develop a more robust approach to promoting equity while being inclusive in their classrooms. The pedagogical and curricular changes described in this chapter were developed to help students achieve the following outcomes based on the outcomes for diversity, equity, and inclusion at our institution:

- Students will recognize the need for a world that honors human difference and the importance of taking action to advance equity and inclusion.

- Students will learn the value of communicating in a manner that acknowledges and respects the differences of others. (University of Cincinnati Office of the Provost, n.d.)

Students in higher education need opportunities to think through issues of equity and inclusion in their college courses. English composition and literature courses provide an ideal opportunity to think through these issues as students work on developing their skills in writing and literary analysis.

ENGLISH COMPOSITION AS A KILLER COURSE

Often faculty and students may have different assumptions about what is appropriate college behavior. As Cox (2009) pointed out, "Sometimes the assumptions about appropriate social behavior and academic performance are class- or race-based, embodying norms and values that are not universally held or even acknowledged" (p. 11). Instructors may misinterpret student behaviors because they do not share cultural expectations for appropriate college behavior. In her research, Cox (2009) found that many writing classrooms use a "current-traditional rhetoric, [that] has its roots in a nineteenth-century theory of writing" (p. 11). This approach does not take into account students' lived experiences, and privileges one dialect of English associated with white, middle-class status. Inoue (2015) argued that writing courses reflect what he terms a "white racial habitus" that reifies White middle-class dialect as the normative standard by which all other English varieties are judged in the writing classroom, thereby reproducing the same social inequalities as the larger society. This inequality can be seen in Kynard's (2008) analysis of how students' use of "Black discourses" are penalized in institution-alized writing assessment. Because not all students speak the dialect promoted by the writing program, writing instructors wishing to promote inclusion must provide clear expectations and directions while also helping students to analyze how language varia-tion is used to reproduce inequality in society.

Similar to writing courses, the literature classroom has changed in response to the diversity that students bring in the form of different backgrounds in culture, language, economic status, race, ethnicity, and religion, to name just a few. In the face of such changing demographics, student needs, and realities in the last few decades, it has become imperative to provide students with a worldview reflective of many experiences and values. Choo (2018) described cosmopolitan literacy as necessary to prepare students for future workplaces since it is "the most fundamental . . . because it entails critical, aes-thetic, and empathetic skills and disposition needed to change with diverse values in our globalized world" (p. 7). She argued that literature provides an opportunity for students to learn and practice skills for evaluating diverse values, examining ethical dilemmas, and interacting with global injustice. Literature classrooms, even when the content is not global, need to be inclusive of the reality of the students who read and process it. For centuries, literature classrooms have been dominated by Eurocentric, patriarchal, and class-based biases that often perpetuate limited perspectives, stereotypes, and mar-ginalization and obstruct students' abilities to perceive concepts and issues from other perspectives.

ENGLISH COMPOSITION EQUITY CURRICULUM
CHANGING OUTCOMES
We take a two-pronged approach to equity and inclusion in our classes by using inclu-sive pedagogies and an equitable curriculum to meet the needs of our diverse student body. (See Chapter 4 of this volume for a description of our college demographics and mission.) In our approach to addressing the equity and inclusion outcomes listed above in our courses, we blend current research suggesting that composition courses should address transfer (Beaufort, 2012; Yancey, Taczak, & Robertson, 2014) with racial literacy described by Kareem (2019) and Sealey-Ruiz (2013). Sealey-Ruiz argued that composition courses should also facilitate the development of racial literacy. She defined racial literacy as involving "moral, political, and cultural decisions about how an English or writing classroom can be a catalyst for societal change" (p. 387).

She suggested that students develop racial literacy through discussing and writing about texts that address prejudice, discrimination, and racism. This blended approach enables us to best meet the needs of all students enrolled in our composition courses while ensuring they learn the writing content they will need for their academic and professional goals.

English Composition is required for all students at our institution. The course outcomes are aligned with the Council of Writing Program Administrators' (2014) first year outcomes statement. In our college, faculty design their own curricula to meet the outcomes. In our sections of English Composition, we follow a transfer curriculum outlined by Beaufort (2012) and informed by the work of Sealy-Ruiz (2013) and Kareem (2019). Kareem (2019) suggested that instructors "reflect on how race is related to rhetorical knowledge, research processes, and writing conventions" (p. 287). This reflection can open opportunities for students to examine how their own literacy practices are privileged or discouraged in the composition curriculum and more generally in other writing situations they encounter.

CHANGING CURRICULUM

Beaufort recommended that composition courses be designed to explore an essential question as described by Wiggens and McTighe (2005). In our course, the essential question is: How can we use language and literacy to promote equity and inclusion in our professional lives? This question guides the selection of readings, the development of writing activities, and the processes of assessment.

The first writing assignment students complete is a rhetorical analysis of a nonfiction text. The sources for this analysis examine equity in education, criminal justice, health, and economics, which are topics relevant to many students' majors. Students select the text and subject area they are most interested in reading and writing about. Examining the role of equity in these areas provides an opportunity to raise student awareness of issues they will encounter when they enter their professional lives. Analyzing these texts as a rhetorical activity allows the class to balance focusing on writing elements with addressing the content of their articles. Beaufort (2012) suggested the benefit of asking composition students to analyze a text is that they learn reading and analytical skills they will be able to transfer to other writing situations. Many of our students state that they have not ever engaged in this kind of analysis of a nonfiction text. Beaufort argued that students should engage in repeated analytical activities to develop their capacity to apply the skills to new situations.

The second assignment builds on the skills of the analysis as students write a research paper. Beaufort (2012) recommended students engage in an inquiry research project that "seeks to address an important question as yet without a definitive answer." Each student develops his or her own research question based on the reading and topics they analyzed in the first assignment. However, each research question must explore the relationship of equity and inclusion to their topic. The focus on equity and inclusion begins to address essential questions of the course—how we use language and literacy to better promote equity and inclusion. This research assignment incorporates the analytical activities of the previous assignment in that students must analyze each of the sources they find to answer their research question. Students can work collaboratively to find appropriate sources in the library. They discuss how these sources help them to answer their research question. This collaborative approach to researching their topics gives opportunities for students to support each other. Students often cite their groups as one of the essential factors in their ability to successfully complete their research projects. Another factor that leads to success is that they are able to research topics personally relevant to their own experience and interests. For instance, a White, male student majoring in criminal justice used the opportunity to learn about racial biases in sentencing. An African American female student noted that she was able to use the resources she discovered while researching mental health concerns in the African American community to address her own needs for mental health assistance.

Following the recommendations of Yancey, Taczak, and Robertson (2014), the third assignment requires students to communicate about their topic using a new genre with a specifically identified audience and purpose. This assignment provides an opportunity to think through how one can address equity and inclusion outside of one's professional community. Students consider the very specific needs of an audience who needs to hear about their research topic. They describe what those needs are and identify why their new audience will be interested in this topic. Then they identify a genre that is relevant for this audience and reframe the information from their research topic in the new genre. In the final assignment, students reflect on the intersection of social responsibility and their role as citizens and writers in promoting equity and inclusion.

INCLUSIVE COMPOSITION PEDAGOGY

FLEXIBILITY

If we are to meet our students where they are, we need to adopt an antiracist pedagogy that reframes outcomes and goals of composition (Kareem 2019). We suggest that instructors need to take into consideration the needs of students when developing course policies such as due dates for assignments. Our students are often overburdened with obligations outside of school, which necessitates having a flexible assignment policy. Our students are also often unfamiliar with the expectations for the genres of writing called for in the assignments. We address this need by utilizing a portfolio pedagogy, which allows us to provide guidance and support to students as they work to develop a final draft that will appear in their portfolio. Because they are unfamiliar with different writing genres, we also spend class time discussing how their work will be evaluated. We follow the advice of composition researchers like Inoue (2015), who suggests developing the grading criteria with students.

SCAFFOLDING

We begin our classes by meeting students where they are. We work with them to identify their current beliefs about writing and examine where those beliefs come from. By making explicit students' expectations for writing, we are able to identify areas of potential conflict and areas we can build upon. An activity that is particularly helpful for engaging students is one we have adapted from Sommers (2011) in which students write their belief statements about writing and then identify statements of writing they agree or disagree with using a Four Corners group discussion strategy. This activity allows students to build community as they can physically see who agrees and disagrees with their beliefs. Students are asked to share their reasoning for agreeing and disagreeing with the belief statements. These discussions allow students to voice concerns that are shared by others in the class. The instructor is able to address some concerns at this time and address others as the course progresses. It is a particularly useful activity for the first week of class.

Students come into first-year composition with a wide range of experiences with writing. Some students completed a strenuous high school English curriculum, while others are returning students who have forgotten what they learned in high school. Because of the wide range in preparation, it is important that we scaffold learning for our students. We use our course outcomes to develop major writing assignments. We analyze these assignments to determine the concepts and skills students will need to develop to successfully complete them. We use these concepts and skills to develop lessons where we introduce the concept/skill, and provide examples and opportunities to practice. Students are then asked to apply the concept/skill to the writing project with instructor feedback. This scaffolding structure allows us the opportunity to provide feedback as students work on their projects instead of waiting until they are completed.

STUDENT INVOLVEMENT

Another key element of our course design is providing opportunities for students to revise and resubmit their work. An essential part of antiracist pedagogy, according to Inoue (2015), is to involve students in the assessment of their work. We engage students in assessing their own work in a number of ways. First, we work with students to develop the criteria to be used to evaluate their work. Instructors and students begin by identifying the elements of the assignment that should be evaluated. Students work in teams to describe the levels of achievement for the elements. The entire class reviews the newly created rubric and discusses the criteria to see if they are described appropriately and in language everyone can understand. Once the rubric has been clarified, students are given papers from previous students to apply the rubric to. Students discuss how the rubric helps them to evaluate the writing. Then students apply the rubric to a peer's draft during a peer review activity. Students use this feedback from their peers to revise the paper for instructor feedback. Students are asked to use this feedback to revise the paper one more time before a grade is assigned. This process engages all students in developing a shared understanding of the standards against which their writing will be judged. More importantly, it gives them a voice in developing those standards. Students who do not share the instructors' expectations for writing are given the opportunity to examine those differences and to discuss them before their writing is assigned a grade.

ENGLISH LITERATURE EQUITY CURRICULUM
CHANGING OUTCOMES
Success in the required English composition courses frequently builds students' confidence to take the more challenging literature courses. However, unlike the composition courses, literature courses are not required for all students. A typical literature classroom at our college can include a wide range of majors besides English majors and all the demographic variations we see across the college. We offer literature courses that include a survey of American literature, British literature, and world literature in addition to ethnic literature, poetry, and creative fiction.

In the Survey of World literature course, the content of the course with its focus on non-Western literary traditions naturally lends itself to the development of cosmopolitan literacy in a world of increasing global connectedness. However, it challenges the worldview of students who are unable to conceptualize the world beyond the boundaries of the West. This was clearly evident when a student in the World Literature class declared at the beginning of the term that he did not see how African literature could possibly be intellectually stimulating or of any critical literary value. The same student, who had never been exposed to literary traditions beyond the Western canon, was thankful at the end of the term for the opportunity to interact with literature that made it possible for him to understand the world and the human condition from a different perspective.

CHANGING CURRICULUM
Such instances make it imperative that we intentionally think about equity and inclusion in both curriculum and pedagogy. We need to take into consideration the limited exposure of students to a secondary school literary curriculum that is still evolving from being largely reflective of Eurocentric values. A study by Skerrett (2010) examined two diverse secondary schools' (one in the United States and the other in Canada) selection and distribution of literary texts and concluded that at both schools, "Eurocentric and Anglo-centric literature dominated the curriculum of advanced courses" (p. 36). This curricular policy challenges the notion of equity, which supports the idea that all

students, irrespective of background, are "capable of engaging in, and entitled to, a rigorous and responsive education" (p. 56). Turner (2017) reported that academic activists have been demanding decolonization of curricula, beginning with English curricula that have been labeled as being "too white and Eurocentric in scope" (p. 18). Walder (2007) argued that the demand for literary studies globally is waning and that is partly because it is not situated in "real life situations" that reflect our evolving political history marked by mass migration and changing boundaries (p. 195). Therefore, in terms of course content, based on the type of literature course, literary selections are chosen carefully to include a broad range of authors, themes, and genres across gender, race, and social backgrounds. In courses such as World Literature the opportunity to build inclusive course content increases because of the nature of the course. However, irrespective of the type of literature, inclusive content can be integrated.

INCLUSIVE PEDAGOGY IN THE LITERATURE CLASSROOM

ESTABLISHING CONTEXT

Since a typical literature class for nonmajors consists of students from across disciplines, it is important not to make assumptions about their experience and skills with literary texts, terminology, and analysis. A useful way to introduce students to literary studies is to contextualize the readings for the term by providing students with an overall historical, cultural, social, and political background for the authors they will study, so they can understand the how, where, and when of the literary selections. This kind of an introduction emphasizes the role of context in reading a text. Students learn how a text is the product of complex and diverse contextual influences. It also encourages them to think about their own context and how it can influence the way they read a text. We demonstrate to the students how to situate a literary selection by researching its context and presenting it. Then each student is invited to take responsibility for researching and introducing a reading to the class through a short five- to eight-minute presentation. Each student also provides discussion questions for the designated reading on a discussion board of the learning management system (LMS) to guide the class discussion.

SCAFFOLDING

To scaffold student learning, the instructor models the presentation for the first reading of the term and provides the discussion questions. The instructor discusses the rubric for evaluating presentations and discussion questions with the students so they can understand how their work will be evaluated. Modeling of the presentation helps students with diverse skills understand how to research the context of a text and how to use it to understand the text better.

In class, after the student presentation, the readings are discussed first in small groups of four to five students, randomly assigned by the instructor. The groups change every class meeting, so students collaborate with different classmates and get to know all their peers over the course of the semester. The student groups use the discussion questions posted by the student presenter for the day to begin their discussion of the text. As the small groups engage in discussion, the instructor walks around, listening in and occasionally engaging in brief conversations with the groups. After the small group discussion, the groups are invited to share their responses to the questions with the class. As responses are shared, whole-class discussion ensues as new questions are raised. The instructor encourages students to comment and where needed, provides relevant insight. This pedagogical approach allows inclusion of students who are more comfortable speaking in small groups. Since the discussion begins with student-developed discussion questions, they feel more connected with the text and less intimidated. The instructor uses these questions as a springboard to more complex questioning of the text. As each student gets to lead a class discussion through a presentation and discussion questions, the exploration of the text becomes a shared experience. In the small groups, students share their perceptions and responses to the designated text, listen to their peers' views, and analyze the text from various perspectives to answer the question, how does this text function within its context?

STUDENT INVOLVEMENT

Students also write a short paper in response to the reading before they come to class. This approach allows validation of each student's interaction with the text based on their own experiences and background, before they share and hear other perspectives. The short papers allow the instructor to provide ongoing feedback to each student and helps establish dialogue between the instructor and student as the student works on analysis and writing skills.

When all students are involved in the process of introducing the text and write their responses before class discussion, it allows them to engage in the literary analysis process equally. Students actively participate in their own learning. Instead of lecturing, the instructor encourages students to read critically using the intersection of the literary text's context alongside their own identities and life experiences where applicable to engage in meaning making. During discussion, the instructor guides the students to see the text from several perspectives, which allows students to explore how implicit bias informs the way they understand the text. The small group discussion followed by the large group discussion allows for close probing of the text, uncovering assumptions and appreciation of how the text's own cultural, social, and historical context influences its meaning. Students are encouraged to identify evidence from the text to support their interpretations. This process helps students to understand their meaning-making processes and learn how to question and distinguish interpretations based solely on personal beliefs and values from those that are based on textual evidence.

In keeping with the goals of inclusion and equity, we have also revised our assignments to help students demonstrate their learning in a variety of ways. Students are assessed using short response papers, presentations, collaborative work, and literary analysis papers. Since students bring a broad spectrum of skills, we offer students a choice of prompts to select from for their literary analysis paper. The literary analysis assignment is broken down into four tasks. The first task for the student is to choose a prompt and propose a plan for how they will use the text to respond to the prompt. The second task is to write a skeletal draft of the essay in response to the instructor-provided prompts, which is submitted for feedback to the instructor. Based on the feedback, the students then develop a complete draft for peer review. The third task involves revision of the draft based on peer feedback. The fourth task requires students to submit the final draft with a checklist that helps them to make sure they have followed directions and completed all the steps for the final draft. By breaking the literary analysis paper into four tasks, students can think and reflect about their prompt choice, rationalize it meaningfully, and receive peer and instructor feedback before submitting a final draft. Students who have limited or no exposure to literary analysis find the scaffolding at different stages of the writing very helpful. This change in assignment design focuses on meeting the students where they are. It actively engages students in the process of literary analysis while making other perspectives available to them and helping them gain confidence in their writing.

CONCLUSION

In composition and literature, we created courses where students could learn to value communication in ways that acknowledge and respect the differences of others. This respect begins with awareness and recognition of the wide variety of English dialects and the discussion of why some are preferred over others. Furthermore, we reexamined our curriculum and pedagogy to help students honor human difference and see the importance of advancing equity and inclusion. In reexamining the curriculum, we saw ways we could promote equity by including the works of authors not part of the usual canon. We used an essential question to guide the reading and writing activities that focused students' attention on equity. In our continual self-exploration of how we can be more inclusive teachers, we employed pedagogical approaches to create interdependent groups and involved students in the design of their assignments and how they would be assessed while validating their experiences and perspectives. These pedagogical practices promote a more inclusive classroom for all students but are particularly helpful to students who have been traditionally underserved.

Students need opportunities to explore how their language, its literature, and literacy practices are reflected in the curriculum. They also need to examine how language and literacy can embody worldviews that are different from their own if they are to become more open to and more self-aware of their role in promoting equity and inclusion as an engaged professional and citizen. In this chapter we have illustrated how student groups, student experiences, varied and explicit assignments, and portfolio teaching create an inclusive learning environment for students. Thoughtfully designed groups help students build supportive classroom community. These groups not only help students understand course concepts but also can play an important role in helping students feel like they belong in the classroom. Students need multiple opportunities to bring in or build upon their own experiences with the course content. These experiences need to be validated in the class discussions. A variety of explicitly developed assignments gives students the opportunity to best showcase what they know about course concepts. Scaffolding assignments that build toward a final product allows instructors the opportunity to provide guidance before a final grade is assigned. Finally, portfolio teaching allows students to build their work over time. Having time to review their work and share it with others helps students revise their work so it better meets the criteria for evaluation. The portfolio's reflective practice encourages students to integrate new knowledge with what they previously knew about the topic. Inclusive practices in curriculum design and pedagogy as described in this chapter can be easily adopted in English composition and literature classes or adapted for other disciplines to build more equitable classrooms.

In both composition and literature, our aim is to infuse awareness of the role contexts—particularly sociocultural contexts—play in literacy. Although it may seem apparent that literature examines sociocultural contexts, when one culture's traditions are the default, it promotes a particular perspective as the standard, perpetuating myths about literary value and influence. This same issue arises in composition courses when one English dialect or one type of writing, such as the research paper, is accepted as the standard for academic writing. These approaches to literature and composition arise out of the White racial habitus most English faculty adopted throughout their education. As with most cultural values, faculty enact the hegemonies of their discipline. We must examine how our own perceptions and experiences influence our curricula and pedagogies if we are to create inclusive classrooms that achieve equitable outcomes for all students. English faculty play a central role in challenging the perception that one worldview or dialect is better than another.

REFERENCES

Beaufort, A. (2012). College writing and beyond: Five years later. *Composition Forum, 26*. http://compositionforum.com/issue/26/college-writing-beyond.php

Choo, S. S. (2018). The need for cosmopolitan literacy in a global age: Implications for teaching literature. *Journal of Adolescent & Adult Literacy, 62*(1), 7–12. https://doi.org/10.1002/jaal.755

Council of Writing Program Administrators. (2014). *WPA outcomes statement for first-year composition (3.0), approved July 17, 2014.* wpacouncil.org/positions/outcomes.html

Cox, R. (2009) *The college fear factor: How students and professors misunderstand one another.* Harvard University Press.

Inoue, A. (2015). *Antiracist writing assessment ecologies: Teaching and assessing writing for a socially just future.* Parlor Press.

Kareem, J. (2019). A critical race analysis of transition-level writing curriculum to support the racially diverse two-year college. *Teaching English in the Two-Year College, 46*(2), 271–296.

Kynard, C. (2008). Writing while Black: The colour line, Black discourses, and assessment in the institutionalization of writing instruction. *English Teaching: Practice and Critique, 7*(2), 4–34.

Sealey-Ruiz, Yolanda. (2013). Building racial literacy in first-year composition. *Teaching English in the Two-Year College, 40*(4), 384–398.

Skerrett, A. (2010). Of literary import: A case of cross-national similarities in the secondary English curriculum in the United States and Canada. *Research in the Teaching of English, 45*(1), 36–58.

Sommers, J. (2011). Reflection revisited: The class collage. *Journal of Basic Writing, 30*(1) 99–129.

Turner, C. (2017, October 26). Cambridge activists want more subjects "decolonised": Review at university will determine if more topics than English are too white and Eurocentric in scope. *London Daily Telegraph,* p. 5.

University of Cincinnati Office of the Provost. (n.d.). *Diversity, equity, and inclusion.* https://www.uc.edu/about/provost/colleges-and-offices/offices/undergraduate-affairs/gen-ed-core-rd/definitions.html

Walder, D. (2007). Decolonizing the (distance) curriculum. *Arts and Humanities in Higher Education, 6*(2), 187–196. https://doi.org/10.1177/1474022207076828

Wiggens, G., & McTighe, J. (2005). *Understanding by design* (2nd ed.). Pearson Prentice Hall.

Yancey, K., Taczak, K., & Robertson, L. (2014). *Writing across contexts: Transfer, composition, and sites of writing.* Utah State University Press.

REFLECTION ON
Inclusive Humanities

Humanities is often seen as a discipline where it is easy to address issues of equity and inclusion. However, educators still need to be intentional in integrating activities and assignments that incorporate equity and inclusion. The focus of these chapters is to make the courses inclusive and equitable to all students. The educators designed the course activities and assessments in order to be accessible to students. They use flexible course policies, scaffolding activities, and established routines that help create a community of learners. Moreover, they share the criteria used to evaluate student learning with students, so both students and educators have a similar understanding of how student learning will be evaluated.

INCLUSIVE PRACTITIONER BEHAVIOR

1. What language instructor practices helped most when you were learning another language? Why were they helpful? What language instructor practices impeded your learning of another language? Why were they barriers?

2. How do you value students' sociocultural backgrounds?

INCLUSIVE PEDAGOGY

1. How can you provide more scaffolding and establish routines to promote student success in your courses?

2. How can the practices outlined in this chapter and based on UDI inform teaching in other content areas?

INCLUSIVE CURRICULUM

1. How can you decolonize your curriculum so that it represents the diversity of those who contributed to the discipline's development?

INCLUSIVE ASSESSMENT

1. How can you work with students to develop a shared understanding of how their learning will be assessed?

2. How do you provide a variety of assessments that will allow students to best represent their learning?

PART IV
Inclusive STEM

Unlike humanities, STEM is often seen as a more challenging area in which to practice equity and inclusion due to the pragmatic nature of the content and the perceived inflexibility of the curriculum. Natalia Darling and her colleagues, who teach a wide range of mathematics courses, challenge the common perception of an inflexible curriculum and describe how mathematics instruction can be and should be more equitable and inclusive. Similar to English, mathematics is a gatekeeper course and failure in it creates academic challenges, especially among underrepresented students. To counteract mathematics anxiety and the perceptions of elitism associated with mathematics, instructors need to provide lessons and activities that are inclusive of students' backgrounds and values. The authors propose that by providing more meaningful and accessible contexts, mathematics education can be more engaging and inclusive. To that end, they provide specific mathematics modules and activities that can be adapted by instructors to meet the needs of inclusion and equity in their own classrooms.

STEM continues to be a disciplinary area that historically lacks appropriate representation across gender, race, ethnicity, and abilities. Higher education institutions can play a pivotal role in diversifying enrollment in STEM courses, by efforts in both recruitment and retention of students. To achieve this, diverse students need to have equity of access and experience in the science curriculum. Authors Mun Chun Chan, James Olsen, Michelle Ohnona, and Ester Sihite describe how STEM courses of Biological Chemistry and Molecular Gastronomy developed an intentionally inclusive pedagogy. The authors demonstrate how such inclusive goals can be integrated into the curriculum to enhance engagement and support the objective of increasing the number of underrepresented students, and their retention, in STEM education.

Emily Neimeyer and Michael Gesinski continue the conversation about the difficulty of retaining underrepresented students in STEM courses, which in the long run impacts workforce diversity in the fields of science and technology. They outline the development of a hybrid model for organic chemistry that uses varied pedagogical styles such as traditional lecture components woven with clicker questions, flipped classroom videos, and guided inquiry activities. As part of an initiative to integrate active learning, the hybrid model helped create inclusive and collaborative classrooms that both engage and encourage.

CHAPTER 8

Flexible Approaches for Equitable Mathematics for *All*

Natalia P. Darling, Eugene F. Kramer, Fabio Santos, Jordan Crabbe,
Adam Chekour, and Zekeriya Karatas

Often math courses are a high hurdle for students in their educational career. The traditional mathematics curriculum has a history of high failure and low retention issues for many groups, including underrepresented individuals (Basile & Lopez, 2015; Estrada et al., 2016; Moses & Cobb, 2001; Schoenfeld, 2004). Students who enter the classroom with math anxiety related to past experiences sometimes have perceptions that mathematics is not relevant to their lives. A common student stereotype is that math is for the elite, which opposes the potential of mathematics as a tool for social mobility (Moses & Cobb, 2001; Schoenfeld, 2004). To counter these detrimental mindsets and provide relevant and effective educational experiences, pedagogical strategies should embrace inclusive practices and equitable approaches for ethnically and socioeconomically diverse students (Parker, Bartell, & Novak, 2017; Wachira & Mburu, 2019). Mathematics instructors have a responsibility to provide meaningful lessons and activities that speak to students' backgrounds and encourage students to collaborate while developing quantitative reasoning and critical thinking skills. Meaningful lessons that connect with students should be created within the framework of supporting equity and promoting success for all. Meeting these goals requires addressing the various cultural perspectives and backgrounds of students. This includes incorporating strategies based on Universal Design for Learning (UDL)—a process that builds tools directly in the curriculum to maximize learning, and benefits all learners by addressing different learning styles and individual needs (Hunt & Andreasen, 2011).

The math modules and activities presented in this chapter address curriculum standards, are mindful of inclusive practice, and strive to provide context relevant to students. The materials were developed to address the needs of a suburban regional campus of the University of Cincinnati, UC Blue Ash College (UCBA). (See Chapter 4 this volume for more details about student demographics.) UCBA is an open access institution providing opportunities for a wide-ranging student population. The courses discussed include developmental and first-year college math courses. The modules provide a framework for delivering mathematical content that includes awareness of diversity issues in terms of gender, socioeconomic status, various learning styles, and English language learners.

Furthermore, we provide examples on how to integrate diverse cultural, racial, and ethnic historical contributions while also promoting a universal and accessible approach.

RATIONALE FOR EQUITY AND INCLUSION IN MATHEMATICS

Students' struggles with personal and academic factors contribute to underachievement. In this chapter, we deal with mathematical education; however, the concepts and hurdles presented are equally valid for many disciplines. As educators and institutions, we should be mindful of diversity and inclusion when setting educational and pedagogical goals. Educational decisions have a far-reaching impact on individual students and society. The National Council of Teachers of Mathematics (NCTM) has published position statements regarding access and equity in mathematics education to support high-quality mathematics programs. The first of six principles outlined by NCTM is equity. Excellence in mathematics education requires equity, high expectations, and strong support for all students. This speaks to students from underserved groups, which include those from low socioeconomic status, minority groups, females, and students who are not native speakers of English (NCTM, 2000).

Starting points to consider when addressing equity include math anxiety and negative mindsets related to learning. Past poor performance in math courses may cause math anxiety and requires not only addressing the math skills, but also presenting strategies for reducing anxiety (Ashcraft & Moore, 2009; Namkung, Peng, & Lin, 2019). The origins of mathematics anxiety include assumptions related to math concepts and approaches as a whole. For instance, many students' previous experience with math may not include flexible and creative reasoning in problem-solving, and frequently adhere to preset and rigid procedures, and the assumption that there is only one correct answer (Richland, Stigler, & Holyoak, 2012). This rigid approach, encountered in many mathematics classes, does not meet the needs of racially minoritized students and contributes to low motivation and performance in mathematics learning (Tate, 2013).

Other detrimental assumptions affecting motivation are related to mindsets. On the one hand, many students believe that individuals have an innate fixed trait that determines math ability and performance, and thus may not try difficult tasks. On the other hand, some students may develop a growth mindset that believes everyone has a malleable potential for developing math abilities and admits the value of hard work in developing strategies and skills (Haimovitz & Dweck, 2016; Hwang, Reyes, & Eccles, 2019; Sun, 2018a; 2018b). Low-achieving students who are struggling benefit from interventions supporting the view that math ability and intelligence are malleable traits (Hwang, Reyes, & Eccles, 2019). Teaching practices that embrace mistakes, struggles, and failures promote a growth mindset and potentially improve persistence and motivation. Math anxiety and growth mindsets are pertinent to all individuals in the classroom and in our global community.

Effective and inclusive classroom strategies can contribute to motivating students to explore mathematical applications beyond the classroom. An initial point in the development of the modules was to consider the traditional textbook approaches. Standard mathematical contexts rely on examples that fall short in terms of inclusion and diversity. A few exercises attempt to vary cultural names and gender pronouns; however, the examples arguably miss the mark on establishing contexts relevant to the diversity of learners the text is trying to reach. Conventional examples employ contexts such as investments of hundreds or tens of thousands of dollars (e.g., a home purchase or exercises referring to swimming pool maintenance costs), all contexts that may not always be relevant to the student population of the course. Reflecting on these contexts provides an opportunity to create thoughtful changes that can be addressed within lesson plans and activities.

Motivation and student engagement in the mathematics classroom can be addressed by providing new, meaningful, and current contexts, with realistic and accessible perspectives. To provide this context and model the alternative viewpoints for students, we created mathematical modules and corresponding activities that view key components of the curriculum through a diversity and inclusion lens. The modules and follow-up activities address three different mathematics courses (Fundamentals of Algebra, College Algebra, and Statistics), which are available for download on the open access companion site for this book. For most students in each of these courses, math anxiety is real, as is the need to develop successful study strategies and a growth mindset. For all modules, there is an in-class portion to introduce concepts and terminology, as well as the start of higher-level questions, and out-of-class activities where students are asked to refine skills and assess/evaluate their work. The modules acknowledge equity and inclusion by infusing cultural influences and empower both instructors and students to rehumanize mathematics (Morales & DiNapoli, 2018), making the material relevant to the students in their lives now. These strategies assist in developing student persistence and motivation and enable math to be a tool for students to reach their academic, professional, and personal goals.

DESCRIPTION OF MATHEMATICS MODULES AND ACTIVITIES

Course material and integrated diversity and inclusion principles are presented using the framework of cognitive learning and constructivist theories (which include traditional problem-solving learning based on trial and error and self-questioning and self-monitoring strategies) as well as Culturally Relevant/Responsive Pedagogy (CRP). Math pedagogy practices can integrate/develop social responsibility and awareness (Bandura, 1989; Bonner & Adams, 2012; Nezhnov et al., 2015; Steele, 2005; Ukpokodu, 2011; Wright, 2017). Ukpokodu (2011) referred to CRP as a sociocultural approach that uses students' life experiences and cultural knowledge to facilitate the learning and teaching process.

The modules presented in this chapter consist of two main sections. The first section provides a lesson plan and integrated collaborative work. Module contexts address mathematical procedures and critical thinking standards but are enhanced by including examples of diverse cultural and ethnic historical mathematics contributions to the mathematics field. The real-world topics discuss social challenges related to wage discrepancies and food insecurity to promote a more accessible and relevant approach. The mathematics lesson plan addresses student learning objectives by providing a framework for diversity in gender, socioeconomic status, and culture. For instance, the lesson plans use multiple communication modes such as written, visual, and video material references and content, followed up with student interaction and reaction prompts. In the multipronged prompts students are requested to reflect on ideas captured from the math lecture materials and create their own response. Allowing for work within groups and individual work respects individuals and their cultural strengths. Additionally, the prompts and lesson format target the goal to encourage student persistence and empower each student to critically examine mathematics as a learning opportunity about themselves and others.

A consideration that developed during the process of adapting the lessons and activities to adhere to socially responsive techniques is the need to provide instructors with as much guidance as possible. They need support related to expanding math objectives with specific diversity goals in order to ensure success in the implementation of learning objectives that embrace diversity, equity, and inclusion. The module lesson plan format was kept consistent with K–12 standards to provide both adjuncts and instructors a standard procedural document. Specific guidelines for interacting with students in order to become familiar with their interests and be considerate of the diverse backgrounds are listed for instructors. Allowing for a variety of response modes is encouraged to accommodate different learning styles. The interactive instruction and participation (and grading) remain consistent, while maintaining an emphasis on encouraging students to embrace a growth mindset and explore different approaches and viewpoints.

The follow-up section for each module continues to develop the material through activities and integrates core diversity and inclusion objectives. Activities associated with each module allow for multiple actions and expressions adhering to the UDL educational framework to promote a growth mindset and provide an opportunity to mirror diversity and inclusion in the development of the mathematical concepts. Ideally, the combination of modules and activities with references will enable instructors to model inclusive ideas and continue to build practices that will lead directly to deepening student understanding.

The math modules and activities presented here address both developmental and college level courses that 1) foster contextualized tasks that connect students and mathematics, 2) provide multiple methods of participation that engage students, and 3) develop a growth mindset.

MODULE 1 AND ACTIVITY 1 FOR FUNDAMENTALS OF ALGEBRA

Module 1 focuses on foundations of algebra, the first of the developmental courses at the college, which has no prerequisites. Over 60 percent of the incoming students at our college qualify for developmental mathematics courses and students struggle with the content as well as the minutiae related to being a college student. The content learning objectives include distinguishing counting numbers and applying arithmetic rules to add, subtract, multiply, and divide whole numbers and then signed numbers. Instruction requires scaffolding related to content objectives as well as attending to classroom management and developing student strategies for college success.

For teaching the content, as opposed to rote memorization, the objective in culturally responsive mathematics is to develop contexts that are pertinent to student lives and create meaning and purpose (Bonner & Adams, 2012; Nezhnov et al., 2015). To this end, on the first day of class a survey is provided with questions about students' values, interests, and study habits to determine individual interests and concerns. Themes related to siblings, family life, sports, languages spoken, and so forth are included. For example, if many students state that they have attention deficit issues and this is a concern, then when listing the class objectives of the day, we add a bulleted list of tips on how to keep focused in class and when studying. The particulars on listing the objectives and problem context are driven by students' needs.

When introducing math vocabulary and number classification, students are asked to consider how they count and what purpose numbers have other than counting. As they list ideas, instructors can segue to historical facts related to multiple cultures. The concept of none, one, and many from the view of Mayans, Aztecs, Sumerians, and Babylonians and the perspectives of traders, hunters, and families are considered. What might be deemed as "primitive" (such as using fingers and toes or slipknots or notches on sticks) is historically mathematically creative (Ifrah, 1985). Symbols from cultures associated with how they write numbers directly explain how mathematics has evolved within cultural contexts and each of us can learn these concepts and apply them to our lives. Handouts are created that contain culturally diverse contexts for addition and subtraction exercises (and if the survey results mentioned particular countries, then handout examples are adapted to add some recipes or facts related to those areas), but students are asked to provide additional countries and subtopics during class discussion for ongoing in-class activities. The resource "Fundamentals of Algebra Module 1," is available on the open access companion site for this book, refers to useful game websites (Math Trainer, n.d.; Zetamac, n.d.) that provide opportunities for alternative learning styles, and examples of activity sheets are in the resource "Fundamentals of Algebra

Activity 1," available on the open access companion site for this book. These student activity sheets contain organized subsections that include written vocabulary and are supplemented with visuals to help students who struggle with language, as well as to promote visual appeal for all students.

In our experience, students often take out their cell phones and are distracted from classroom work, but we take this opportunity to redirect them to search for recipe ingredients such as for Peruvian ceviche and map the location of the country (*On the World Map*, n.d.; Salgado et al., 2020). Student input is taken orally during class, as well as with provided index cards that they can fill out for instructor collection—allowing for multiple venues of participation. Interaction is encouraged and students are reminded that their voices matter. Instructors encourage group work, but students are allowed to work individually if they prefer. Regardless of the work mode for a particular handout, a whole-class discussion follows to ensure the numerical conclusions make sense. Papers are collected and any questions or inaccuracies are discussed without revealing student names. This discussion allows for both oral and written questions. When students do not have cell phones (from experience, this is a minimal number) to review websites, they can be partnered with someone who does have a phone or laptop. This is also an opportunity for the instructor to discuss the school resources related to laptops and future calculator use (our school has laptops and calculators available for daily checkout with student identification cards).

Follow-up activities encompass assignments based on websites that explore US salaries that vary with education, gender, and ethnicity (BLS, 2019; Phelps & Crabtree, 2013). Students are given example data details, prompts for interaction and reaction related to the meaning of the data, and the opportunity to co-create possible word problems that prompt for arithmetical operations (add or subtract, multiply or divide the whole numbers). They are also asked to consider references to Mexico's wage details (Ferri, 2016; Woody, 2017) and encouraged to find other websites if they choose. These activities simultaneously address social equity and global responsibility by raising awareness about inequities in our local and global communities. Practicing mathematics operations while creating unique objectives with no preset answers develops a growth mindset. The student-centered, socially responsible perspectives enable and empower students to create their own math problems and relate their community interests to a global community to develop creative viewpoints and critical reasoning skills.

By creating meaningful lessons and activities that include student interests, value their backgrounds, and respect differences in race/class/culture/gender/learning styles, students are able to understand the rationale of activities and appreciate authentic interaction that extends to global outlooks. The examples provide real-world context for students using realistic sums of money, data, and information related to a variety of countries within diverse cultural perspectives, exploration of gender and race issues, and acknowledgment of cultural contributions to the history of mathematics. The activities promote classroom participation that minimizes math anxiety by allowing for varying modes of interaction based on individual preferences, recognizes issues of inclusion through a selection of problems in different contexts, and accommodates alternative assessment opportunities for students to express their learning in different manners and modalities. Armed with new understanding, the students are better prepared to understand the relevance of math to make informed decisions in their lives.

MODULE 2 AND ACTIVITY 2 FOR COLLEGE ALGEBRA

Module 2 is concerned with College Algebra. This course is the traditional entry-level quantitative reasoning course for science, technology, engineering, and mathematics (STEM) majors and many business majors. The focus is on algebra concepts, critical thinking, and problem-solving skills. For many UCBA students, this is their first college-level math course. This module deals with exponential functions. These functions model many real-world, day-to-day applications. As previously mentioned, customary approaches to the material include dealing with bank accounts with tens of thousands of dollars or in mathematical constructs that appear irrelevant to any real-world applications. The module uses contexts to engage students and address inclusion, such as population growth of various countries, credit cards, and loans (CreditCards.com, n.d.; List of countries by average wage, n.d.; PBS LearningMedia, n.d.). Students are also asked to reflect on the economic implications of, for example, population growth, such as how the models inform government funding and types of loans/credit. To engage students, we have identified outside resources, such as websites that provide content regarding loans and credit card policies. Students are asked to complete worksheets as well as reflect via multiple venues (reflection opportunities include in-class written or oral explanations, or online blogs and journal entries) on implications presented in the materials. Other examples include saving for a used car as opposed to the amount of interest earned on $25,000. Examples and activities are accessible for students and provide opportunities to think critically about the global community. Additionally, students develop some new tools to becoming more fiscally aware.

The guided worksheets and presentation of new material have built in opportunities for group and collaborative work as well as reflection that helps promote a growth mindset. For example, students are directed to a website to look at a payment structure for a credit card when paying only the minimum payment requested by the credit card company. Students are asked to reflect on the implications of differing interest rates, initial balances, and time, both in the lecture and follow-up assignments. We point out that the same mathematical concepts work in their favor in earning interest—on any initial amount of money. The lecture portion and guided notes are also designed to allow time for individual and group reflection, discussion of mistakes or misconceptions. Two resources, "College Algebra Module 2" and "College Algebra Activity 2," are available on the open access companion site for this book.

MODULE 3 AND ACTIVITY 3 FOR STATISTICS

Module 3 focuses on business statistics. This course is an introduction to statistical methods and techniques from economic and business perspectives. It is required for several programs at the college including business administration, finance, marketing, and economics majors. Topics presented in the module and activity (Anderson et al., 2014; Camm et al., 2017) include the analysis of regression models when one or more predictor variables are categorical. For the analysis, binary indicator variables, with the values 0 and 1, are considered to represent categorical variables with two levels. We discuss the context of what should be assigned 0 or 1, as well as connotations associated with each assigned value. Specifically, an exploration of assigning a set of levels to gender as a predictor in a regression model invites the discussion of arbitrary assignment of the value 0 to either males or females. Students' ideas are valued and appreciated, and honest dialogue is encouraged so that participants express their feelings and experiences to each other (Bart, 2016). The examples and activities in the lesson were designed to show that the regression analysis results are independent of the coding scheme selected and that the decision regarding who to assign the value of 0 (or, the value of 1) is completely arbitrary. Students are guided to discover that regardless of choice in numerical value representation of categorical variables, there are no effects in the ultimate results of the analysis.

Students can complete several in-class activities (either individually or in self-chosen group settings based on preferences) that use technology to aid in the analysis of the regression models discussed. An out-of-class assignment allows for student flexibility in review time prior to collection of work by the next class meeting. The assignment structure recognizes issues of diversity and inclusion and promotes unbiasedness and making appropriate and sensitive statements when discussing data analysis results that involve gender, race, and ethnicity. Enabling students to participate in the choices between which gender gets assigned a 0 or 1 empowers students in the math process, and the discussion opens opportunities for conversation regarding topics in bias and equity. Two resources, "Statistics Module 3" and "Statistics Activity 3," are available on the open access companion site for this book.

CONCLUSION

To reach students and convince them that mathematics is relevant to them outside of the classroom, we need to employ real-world and culturally relevant examples. "Until recently, embedding mathematics pedagogy within social and political contexts was not a serious consideration in mathematics education. The act of counting was viewed as a neutral exercise, unconnected to politics or society. Yet when do we ever count just for the sake of counting? Only in school do we count without a social purpose of some kind. Outside of school, mathematics is used to advance or block a particular agenda" (Tate, 2013, p. 48). The examples in this chapter will help build a framework of problem solving and learning outside the classroom, which is a primary goal of higher education. For each of the modules, the overriding objective is to maintain standard math objectives while changing the framework to a culturally relevant context for students. This requires instructor flexibility and innovation to determine student concerns and address their interests. One way to address student concerns is by creating new math story problems that do not rely on standard textbook aids. Socially responsive topics may be uncomfortable for both instructors and students, but the pedagogical approach empowers students. There are no set of rules, just a guiding principle to make the class environment a safe haven for honest discussion regarding cultural relevance and math (Moses & Cobb, 2001). Although there are a variety of factors that may influence student perceptions, the implementation of these culturally relevant math activities is significant if we are to endorse transformation in the classroom to enable student persistence, motivation, and success.

According to Carter and Welner (2013, p. 217) some US students "run in the proverbial race of academic and economic success in lanes replete with hurdles," and this assignment of lanes can be predicted based on race, ethnicity, first language, and income. Ladson-Billings (2013) reframed existing achievement gap discussions to that of an opportunity gap that can be redressed by teachers who "are willing to meld academic demands with compassion" (p. 21). An NEA May 2020 report on ethnic studies advocated expanding educational opportunities, and states that strategies that enhance equity should be encouraged (NEA, 2020). The strategies shared in this chapter maintain high expectations of students by upholding standard learning objectives while integrating culturally responsive objectives. These strategies provide meaningful context that values student perspectives and diverse background, while striving both for positive academic outcomes and social, psychological, and cultural well-being. The concept of building bridges between existing standards and objectives and cultural backgrounds values every learner and cultivates critical and authentic mathematical knowledge (Ellis, 2019).

REFERENCES

Anderson, D. R., Sweeney, D. J., Williams, T. A., Camm, J. D., & Cochran, J. J. (2014). *Statistics for business and economics* (12th ed.). Cengage Learning.

Ashcraft, M. H., & Moore, A. M. (2009). Mathematics anxiety and the affective drop in performance. *Journal of Psychoeducational Assessment, 27*(3), 197–205. https://doi.org/10.1177/0734282908330580

Bandura, A. (1989). Human agency in social cognitive theory. *American Psychologist, 44*(9), 1175–1184. https://doi.org/10.1037/0003-066X.44.9.1175

Bart, M. (2016). *Diversity and inclusion in the college classroom. Faculty Focus Speciality Report.* http://provost.tufts.edu/celt/files/Diversity-and-Inclusion-Report.pdf

Basile, V., & Lopez, E. (2015). And still I see no changes: Enduring views of students of color in science and mathematics education policy reports. *Science Education, 99*(3), 519–548. https://doi.org/10.1002/sce.21156

Bonner, E. P., & Adams, T. L. (2012). Culturally responsive teaching in the context of mathematics: A grounded theory case study. *Journal of Mathematics Teacher Education, 15*(1), 25–38. https://doi.org/10.1007/s10857-011-9198-4

Bureau of Labor Statistics (BLS). (2019, January 17). Usual weekly earnings of wage and salary workers, fourth quarter 2018. *Bureau of Labor Statistics, US Department of Labor.* www.bls.gov/news.release/pdf/wkyeng.pdf

Camm, J. D., Cochran, J. J., Fry, M. J., Ohlmann, J. W., Anderson, D. R., Sweeney, D. J., & Williams, T. A. (2017). *Essentials of business analytics* (2nd ed.). Cengage Learning.

Carter, P. L., & Welner, K. G. (2013). *Closing the opportunity gap: What America must do to give every child an even chance.* Oxford University Press. https://doi.org/10.1093/acprof:oso/9780199982981.001.0001

CreditCards.com. (n.d.). *Credit card payment calculator: The true cost of paying the minimum.* www.creditcards.com/calculators/minimum-payment/

Ellis, M. (2019). *Knowing and valuing every learner: Culturally responsive mathematics teaching.* https://www.researchgate.net/publication/336314904_Knowing_and_Valuing_Every_Learner_Culturally_Responsive_Mathematics_Teaching

Estrada, M., Burnett, M., Campbell, A. G., Campbell, P. B., Denetclaw, W. F., Gutiérrez, C. G., Hurtado, S., John, G. H., Matsui, J., McGee, R., Okpodu, C. M., Robinson, T. J., Summers, M. F., Werner-Washburne, M., & Zavala, M. E. (2016). Improving underrepresented minority student persistence in STEM. *CBE Life Sciences Education, 15*(3), 1. https://doi.org/10.1187/cbe.16-01-0038

Ferri, P. (2016, December 9). El salario mínimo en México, uno de los más bajos de América, llega a la Suprema Corte de Justicia. *El País.* elpais.com/internacional/2016/12/08/mexico/1481224214_357441.html

Haimovitz, K., & Dweck, C. S. (2016). Parents' views of failure predict children's fixed and growth intelligence mind-sets. *Psychological Science, 27*(6), 859–869. https://doi.org/10.1177/0956797616639727

Hunt, J. H., & Andreasen, J. B. (2011). Making the most of universal design for learning. *Mathematics Teaching in the Middle School, 17*(3), 166–172. https://doi.org/10.5951/mathteacmiddscho.17.3.0166

Hwang, N., Reyes, M., & Eccles, J. S. (2019). Who holds a fixed mindset and whom does it harm in mathematics? *Youth & Society, 51*(2), 247–267. https://doi.org/10.1177/0044118X16670058

Ifrah, G. (1985). *From one to zero: A universal history of numbers.* Viking.

Ladson-Billings, G. (2013). Lack of achievement or loss of opportunity? In P. L. Carter & K. G. Welner (Eds.), *Closing the opportunity gap: What America must do to give every child an even chance* (pp. 11–24). Oxford University Press. https://doi.org/10.1093/acprof:oso/9780199982981.001.0001

List of countries by average wage. (2019, February 16). In *Wikipedia.* en.wikipedia.org/wiki/List_of_countries_by_average_wage

Math Trainer. (n.d.). *Math trainer: Mental fitness.* https://www.mathtrainer.org

Morales, H., & DiNapoli, J. (2018). Latinx bilingual "students" perseverance on a mathematical task: A rehumanizing perspective. *Journal of Research in Mathematics Education, 7*(3), 226–250. http://dx.doi.org/10.17583/redimat.2018.3274

Moses, R. P., & Cobb, C. E., Jr. (2001). *Radical equations: Math literacy and civil rights.* Beacon Press.

Namkung, J. M., Peng, P., & Lin, X. (2019). The relation between mathematics anxiety and mathematics performance among school-aged students: A meta-analysis. *Review of Educational Research, 89*(3), 459–496. https://doi.org/10.3102/0034654319843494

National Council of Teachers of Mathematics (NCTM). (2000). *Principles and standards for school mathematics.* National Council of Teachers of Mathematics.

National Education Association (NEA) (2020, May). *NEA report on ethnic studies.* https://ra.nea.org/wp-content/uploads/2020/06/NEA_Ethnic_Studies_Report_2020.pdf

Nezhnov, P., Kardanova, E., Vasilyeva, M., & Ludlow, L. (2015). Operationalizing levels of academic mastery based on Vygotsky's theory: The study of mathematical knowledge. *Educational and Psychological Measurement, 75*(2), 235–259. https://doi.org/10.1177/0013164414534068

On the World Map. (n.d.). Peru location on the South America map. http://ontheworldmap.com/peru/peru-location-on-the-south-america-map.html

Parker, F., Bartell, T. G., & Novak, J. D. (2017). Developing culturally responsive mathematics teachers: Secondary teachers' evolving conceptions of knowing students. *Journal of Mathematics Teacher Education, 20*(4), 385–407. https://doi.org/10.1007/s10857-015-9328-5

PBS Learning Media. (n.d.). *The lowdown: The math of credit cards* [Video]. www.pbslearningmedia.org/resource/mkqed-math-rp-creditcards/the-math-of-credit-cards/#.WzoKC9JKjIW

Phelps, G., & Crabtree, S. (2013, December 16). *Worldwide, median household income about $10,000.* Gallup. com. news.gallup.com/poll/166211/worldwide-median-household-income-000.aspx

Richland, L. E., Stigler, J. W., & Holyoak, K. J. (2012). Teaching the conceptual structure of mathematics. *Educational Psychologist, 47*(3), 189–203. https://doi.org/10.1080/00461520.2012.667065

Salgado, M. H., Dice, V., Dice:, J., & Dice:, D. (2020, April 2). 5 recetas de cocina peruana para hacer en casa: Recetas, saladas. *Sapos y Princesas.* https://saposyprincesas.elmundo.es/recetas/saladas/recetas-de-cocina-peruana-para-hacer-en-casa/

Schoenfeld, A. H. (2004). The math wars. *Educational Policy, 18*(1), 253–286. https://doi.org/10.1177/0895904803260042

Steele, M. M. (2005). Teaching students with learning disabilities: Constructivism or behaviorism? *Current Issues in Education, 8*(10), 9.

Sun, K. L. (2018a). Beyond rhetoric: Authentically supporting a growth mindset. *Teaching Children Mathematics, 24*(5), 280.

Sun, K. L. (2018b). The role of mathematics teaching in fostering student growth mindset. *Journal for Research in Mathematics Education, 49*(3), 330–355. https://doi.org/10.5951/jresematheduc.49.3.0330

Tate, W. F. (2013). Race, retrenchment, and the reform of school mathematics. In E. Gutstein & B. Peterson (Eds.), *Rethinking mathematics* (2nd ed., pp. 42–51). Rethinking Schools.

Ukpokodu, O. N. (2011). How do I teach mathematics in a culturally responsive way? Identifying empowering teaching practices. *Multicultural Education, 18*(3), 47.

Wachira, P., & Mburu, J. (2019). Culturally responsive mathematics teaching and constructivism: Preparing teachers for diverse classrooms. *Multicultural Learning and Teaching, 14*(1). DOI:10.1515/mlt-2016-0023

Woody, C. (2017, March 1). Mexico's wages are so paltry that human-rights and legal groups are sounding the alarm. *Business Insider.* www.businessinsider.com/mexico-wages-incomes-poverty-2017-2

Wright, P. (2017) Critical relationships between teachers and learners of school mathematics. *Pedagogy, Culture & Society, 25*(4), 515–530. https://doi.org/10.1080/14681366.2017.1285345

Zetamac. (n.d.). *Arithmetic game.* https://arithmetic.zetamac.com/

CHAPTER 9

Strategies for Incorporating Inclusive Pedagogy in STEM Courses

Mun Chun Chan, James Olsen, Michelle Ohnona, and Ester Sihite

The National Science Foundation (NSF, 2019) reported that there remains an underrepresentation of specific groups in STEM education and STEM workforce (classified as science and engineering fields [S&E] by the NSF) in the United States—particularly women, persons with disabilities, and people from racial and ethnic groups: Black, Hispanic, and American Indian or Alaska Native (hereafter referred to as underrepresented groups). Furthermore, a smaller percentage of members of these groups with STEM degrees are employed in STEM occupations compared to White men with similar degrees (NSF, 2019). The gap in STEM bachelor's degrees awarded to these underrepresented groups has narrowed unevenly, with some groups (including Black and American Indian or Alaska Native) seeing little gains in the last eighteen years, though other groups of students (such as Hispanic students) have seen modest growth. Still, the gap remains vast. Furthermore, retention of STEM majors in college (those who come into college planning to major in STEM, and still plan to do so three years later) is lower compared to other majors (82 percent in non-STEM, only 67 percent in science and engineering) (National Science Board, 2018).

Part of the solution to narrow these inequities must occur in institutions of higher learning, with institution-wide efforts to increase recruitment and retention of students in STEM, particularly underrepresented students. Institutional support for initiatives aimed at improving instructional outcomes in STEM courses needs to be more robust and occupy equal priority with research (Fairweather, 2005). As Packard (2016, introduction) summarized, underrepresented students are more likely to leave STEM fields. Most importantly, research indicates that they are often precisely the type of talented and competent students that should be actively retained in STEM because they are important for the pace of scientific advance in the future (Antonio et al., 2004; Packard, 2016; Page, 2007; Terenzini et al., 2001).

As an institution, Georgetown University is recruiting and providing financial and educational support to first-generation students whose academic interests are focused on the sciences, as part of the Regents STEM Scholars Program, instituted in 2016

(Regents, n.d.). The goal is to provide first-generation students with equity of access and experience in the science curriculum. Furthermore, Georgetown University is in the process of implementing core science requirements for all undergraduate students as part of its "Science for All" program (Groves, 2017). It is hoped that courses under this new program will positively impact non-STEM students, changing their feelings toward and engagement with scientific knowledge and processes. For Georgetown, the ethical impetus to put in place initiatives aimed at retaining underrepresented students is also rooted in our institution's Jesuit values. Beyond this ethical imperative lies the reality that diversity improves outcomes across a range of indicators, and, simply put, improves our practice as students and scholars (Rock & Grant, 2016). The success of these efforts requires faculty to develop innovative, inclusive courses that engage the increasingly diverse students in their classrooms.

REDESIGNING STEM COURSES

Over the course of the past decade, the Doyle Faculty Fellowship Program at Georgetown University's Center for New Designs in Learning and Scholarship (CNDLS) (Doyle, n.d.) has served to support faculty in the redesign of their courses to engage questions of social difference more deeply. The focus on pedagogy is intentional, as our experience working with faculty in this program has made evident that in the pursuit of meaningfully equitable learning contexts, teaching is of central importance. Efforts aimed at recruitment and retention of a diverse student body are important. Students must figure prominently in institutional responses to the challenges of diversifying their student body. We contend that the role of teaching, mentorship, and faculty-student relationship building must be privileged, valued, and explicitly supported in order for these attempts to be successful. Through their intensive and often protracted exposure to students, faculty can play an outsized role in supporting underrepresented students both during their studies and as they pursue opportunities after graduation.

The Doyle Faculty Fellowship Program uses an interdisciplinary model aimed at assisting faculty in enhancing themes of difference and diversity in their courses, while supporting faculty in identifying and employing inclusive pedagogical strategies in their teaching. Inclusive pedagogy (Hockings, 2010) refers to the manner in which pedagogy, assessment, power, climate, and content are aligned with the goal of creating a learning experience that is meaningful and accessible to all students. The Doyle program begins with participation in a four-day, inclusive pedagogy-oriented institute and intensive small-group course-design consultations over the summer, followed by monthly cohort meetings during the academic year. Faculty engage with pedagogical concepts and literature, discuss issues of identity and equity in higher education, and review and provide feedback on each other's course redesign projects. The growing community of program alumni offers continued support and contributes to creating a culture of inclusive teaching on campus.

Faculty fellows from STEM fields play an important and growing role in the Doyle Faculty Fellowship. STEM courses offer challenging opportunities in which to develop creative models for the infusion of inclusive pedagogical approaches in course design. The research on the value of inclusive pedagogical practice supports our contention that incorporating inclusive pedagogical goals, elements, and strategies is an effective means for the recruitment and retention of underrepresented students in STEM fields.

THE IMPACT ON UNDERREPRESENTED STUDENTS IN STEM

Individual faculty can play a key role in supporting and retaining not only underrepresented students but also a diverse student body. Included among the ways faculty can positively influence the retention of students in STEM majors are fostering a classroom climate in which students feel welcomed, well-supported by faculty, and can develop rapport with faculty (Brown et al., 2009). Faculty's affirmation of students' capabilities and intentional efforts to eliminate "stereotype threat" (Steele, 1999) help create an atmosphere of trust within the classroom (Brown et al., 2009).

Hurtado and colleagues (2010) also posited the importance of the *relevance* of science coursework to students' lives for facilitating academic and social adjustment among underrepresented groups in the sciences, underscoring the value of experiential and application-based learning. A similar finding and implication were echoed by Bonous-Hammarth (2000), whose study indicated that the more activist-oriented and socially engaged underrepresented students were, the less likely they were to persist in STEM. Therefore, it follows that STEM courses that are applicable, socially conscious, and relevant, and therefore inclusive of all members of the course, would better serve to retain underrepresented students (Sellers et al., 2007). Efforts to incorporate social justice elements and context to scientific knowledge have proven to be successful in engaging both underrepresented STEM majors (Chamany, Allen, & Tanner, 2008; Gilbert, 2003) and non-STEM majors (Chamany, 2006; Farrell, Moog, & Spencer, 1999).

Also, in terms of curriculum design and pedagogy, Brown and colleagues (2009) highlighted the positive contributions of inquiry-based learning, for example by "encouraging students to engage in the scientific method" (pp. 6–7). Adding active learning elements has been shown to be a successful strategy for improving student achievement in many different courses in different STEM fields (Freeman et al., 2014; Mervis, 2010), including among less academically prepared first-year students (Haak et al., 2011). Practices such as incorporating elements of inquiry-based labs (Prezler, 2009) and exposing students to real-world applications and STEM careers (Hurtado et al., 2010) have been shown to be effective at increasing the retention of students in STEM fields.

127

Table 9.1. Summary of STEM courses redesigned with inclusive pedagogy goals

DISCIPLINE	TITLE AND INSTRUCTOR	PROJECT DESCRIPTION
Biology	Developmental Neurobiology, Dr. Elena Silva	Upper-level biology majors examined the role of diversity in experiment design in the field, and considered disparities in scientific literacy and accessibility. Thus, they discussed the importance of diversity in science within the context of the topic.
Geoscience	Environmental Geoscience, Dr. Sarah Stewart Johnson	Students participated in a project to open up access to field studies of water quality for those with physical disabilities, allowing individuals to participate in these studies despite physical disabilities. Students helped to produce 360-degree, immersive videos. This encouraged students to engage in questions of who can participate in science.
Human Science	Physiological Adaptations, Dr. Jason Tilan	Prehealth students examined the role of social diversity in creating or exacerbating conditions that led to the physiological adaptations under study, thus expanding their definitions of "scientific explanations" for phenomena.
Mathematics & Statistics	Introduction to Mathematical Statistics, Dr. Nicole Meyer	Students assessed and critiqued the myriad ways in which statistics are used to describe difference both between and within groups of people, using historical illustrations of the impact of statistics on justice and equity.
Biology	Teaching Assistant Training, Dr. Youngeun (Kaitlyn) Choi	Course was meant for students who would teach for the first time. Students were asked to devise active learning tools to explain foundational concepts in biology, and examined issues at the interface between science and society.

INCLUSIVE PEDAGOGY STEM COURSES

Table 9.1 offers an overview of Doyle courses from STEM fields in recent years. We have chosen to highlight two additional courses, discussing each in detail. Though each case study draws on experiences in specific courses, both highlight the fact that with institutional support and faculty interest, an intentional approach to promoting equity in STEM classrooms can result in impactful outcomes for students and faculty alike. Crucially, the outcomes reported in each of the case studies correlates to the literature summarized above.

CASE STUDY: BIOLOGICAL CHEMISTRY

In a mid-level majors and prehealth biochemistry course, Mun Chun Chan incorporated lessons on the importance of diversity in science by privileging a framework that encouraged students to view scientific knowledge as a form of situated knowledge (Haraway, 1988). The instructor discussed nine different case studies on important biochemical research work, incorporating narratives on scientific discovery and the scientists involved. The link was made to the importance of diversity within science. By providing historical and individual context to the scientific content, the hope is to deepen students' understanding and improve their ability to learn and remember the material (Chamany, Allen, & Tanner, 2008; Gilbert, 2003)

Biological Chemistry is a prerequisite class for students majoring in biology, or completing prehealth requirements. About three-quarters of the students are majors in a STEM discipline. About 10 percent of students are postbaccalaureates, college graduates returning to complete required prehealth courses. Due to different foundational courses and preparation, there is a diversity of student prior knowledge in the class. Furthermore, many first-generation Regents Scholars (see above) are premed, and therefore, a majority take this course.

The syllabus of Biological Chemistry is content heavy, but the course was developed (by Dr. Anne Rosenwald, Biology Department, Georgetown University) to incorporate inclusive pedagogy elements, emphasizing active learning and application of content. The course has changed in order to promote equity of experience for students with different academic training, preparation, learning styles, and needs. Assessments are varied; evidence of mastery is shown via exams that focus on application of knowledge, along with lab performance, literature research, and oral and written delivery of scientific information. A nightly study space supervised by trained undergraduate teaching assistants is widely utilized and has improved student retention. A course and lecture guide providing clear structure and content expectations is distributed and adhered to throughout the semester.

Achieving Course Goals. As they advance, students gain power to decide who is welcome in the scientific and health fields (Harding, 1993, introduction), influencing the diversity, inclusivity, and the direction of their respective fields. One important part of providing equity of experience is to show students that they "belong" in the department and field. By discussing the diversity of scientists in biochemistry, the instructor hoped to illustrate that not only is the field diverse, but that diversity leads to strength in the field.

The instructor presented nine case studies available on the open access companion site for this book, each focused on a particular moment in biochemistry history, or a particular scientist. Each case emphasizes one or more main points of the framework detailed in Table 9.2, meant to cohesively argue for the importance of diversity in science. Primary data from scientific papers is also studied, providing a link between the

Table 9.2. Framework for introducing inclusive pedagogy content in biochemistry course

1. Science is a conflict of ideas.	In order for science to advance, new ideas are generated, tested, and resolved. Therefore, there is a constant conflict of different ideas within science.
2. Science is done by individuals.	Individual scientists working alone or as part of groups do the research and discovery.
3. Individual scientists have their own characteristics.	Individual scientists come from a certain period of history, specific places within a specific society, with different personal histories and personalities. They have different expertise.
4. The characteristics of an individual scientist affects the science they do.	The scientist's characteristics affects the science they produce.
5. Diversity of scientists improves science.	Therefore, in order to advance and improve science, we need a diversity of scientific ideas, which means we need a diversity of scientists. What does diversity mean in the context of scientists? In our society, who gets to be a scientist? It is beyond the scope of this course to dive deeply into the uneven distribution of resources (education, financial support, opportunity) that changes the likelihood that someone gets to be a scientist. Nor is it within the scope of this course to discuss all discrimination (blatant and subtle, individual and institutional) that promotes certain individuals and not others. However, we acknowledge these injustices exist and that they change the answer to who gets to be a scientist. If a diversity of scientists improves science, *a lack of diversity impoverishes science.*
6. What is our response to this narrative?	As you proceed down your individual career paths, you will find that your agency will grow, and your ability and power to either support or challenge the status quo will increase. What is to be expected of us, of you?

scientific "facts" and circumstances of the scientific production. This approach is similar to that introduced by Chamany (2006). While Chamany uses case studies to capture the interest of non-STEM students, here case studies are used to teach STEM students that the scientific knowledge they are learning is intimately linked to society and can be a tool for social justice.

It was important that the individual cases could be placed into the context of a larger framework or argument about the nature of science and the importance of diversity in science.

A brief summary of the case studies presented and a link to the framework and course content are available on the open access companion site for this book.

Results and Response from Students. Most students found the introduced case studies to be interesting and relevant, and they welcomed the change in focus and perspective. In one particularly memorable exchange, a postbaccalaureate relayed that she shared the cases with her young daughter, in the hope of inspiring her daughter. In an ungraded reflection, many students expressed interest in greater incorporation of the themes of diversity in other STEM courses. Still, we met with some resistance; at least one student responded that the cases were a waste of time since the material would not be tested. We believe that engaging in metacognitive discussions on the importance of these case studies will help mediate this opinion.

Since the first semester when these case studies were adopted, other faculty and graduate students tasked with teaching sections of this course have adopted the case studies in their own classrooms and have responded positively to the change. Michael Hickey, who is the current lab director of the course, commented that he enjoyed the process of learning more about the scientists, and adapting the cases to suit his style, interests, and positionality as a first-generation college graduate. The case studies are now fully incorporated in all sections of the course.

CASE STUDY: MOLECULAR GASTRONOMY

In a chemistry course for nonmajors, Jennifer Swift taught chemistry within the context of cooking and food, showing the practical use of scientific knowledge, the scientific method, and a laboratory experience via recipes. By teaching science in a specific context, she hoped to change preconceptions of who "belongs" in a science course and to emphasize the importance of scientific knowledge for all. This course also incorporated elements of social justice as it pertains to food insecurity and the diversity of foods within immigrant and culturally diverse communities . McGee's *On Food and Cooking: The Science and Lore of the Kitchen* (2004) was the reference textbook.

This course is designed for non-STEM majors and assumes no prior chemistry knowledge. The class was designed for about twenty students but is scalable to about sixty. Students came with a diversity of chemistry backgrounds, from no high school chemistry to college-level chemistry. Students were an even mix of freshmen, sophomores, juniors, and seniors. Similarly, there was a diversity of race and ethnic groups among students. The attitude of students to STEM varied, but many came with negative preconceptions (or misconceptions) of the content and structure of STEM courses. Importantly, students also came with different experiences in the kitchen. Because part of the course is focused on small group lab work within the home kitchen, the experience of students depended on forming groups with a range of different skills and experiences.

Courses designed under the "Science for All" program are meant to emphasize the scientific process, application of the scientific process, and context for scientific knowledge. In addition, faculty are encouraged to incorporate elements of social justice and the social implications of science within their courses. It is hoped that these courses will positively impact the affective domain of non-STEM students, changing their feelings toward scientific knowledge and process. Though this course was developed before these requirements were adopted, they reflect the best intentions and goals of the requirements and continues to be offered.

This course examined the interconnected relationship between food and chemistry. It activated inner curiosity to find answers for observed kitchen phenomena, including why an egg solidifies when you cook it, why fruit turns brown when it's cut, or why recipes have the ingredient lists they do. These questions are all rooted in the science of the food's components and the chemical reactions and phase changes that occur during their preparation. Relevant concepts and language surrounding the chemistry behind proteins, fats, carbohydrates, water, salt, and other foods were taught during the semester, using actual recipes to illustrate key points when applicable.

Achieving Course Goals. The Molecular Gastronomy course sought to teach the skills of acquisition and use of scientific knowledge within a specific context—cooking and food. The hope was that with the practice of these skills, students' preconceptions of the esoteric or intimidating nature of science would be transformed. The application of scientific knowledge was a second goal for the course. This course requires the practice of the scientific process within the context of a home kitchen, using recipes in order to illustrate key concepts learned in class.

Studies have shown that engaging and talking about issues surrounding social justice as it pertains to STEM is an effective way to engage non-STEM students in a STEM-related discipline (Chamany, 2006). Toward that end this course incorporated discussions on food security and the cultural importance of specific foods for various communities.

For classes that require group work, group composition is an important factor. Students self-reported on their prior cooking and chemistry knowledge. Groups of students were then assigned with members at different and complementary skill levels. It was also important to have groups with diverse genders and class years, as the instructor has found that diverse groups are best able to complete the unsupervised laboratories successfully and cohesively. Interestingly, the instructor reported that though the groups were mostly racially mixed, this was more by default than design. Research has also shown that diverse groups are more successful in solving complicated tasks as long as all members feel empowered to contribute to the group (Rock & Grant, 2016).

The instructor believed that the lab/scientific process component should be an integral part of a nonmajors' STEM course. For this course, assigned groups had to complete three or four different recipes during the semester. Each recipe illustrated key concepts of the course. Choosing the correct recipes/labs was important for the success of the course. Recipes used relatively inexpensive, easy-to-find ingredients and common kitchen equipment, as the "experiments" were to be performed in student apartments and dormitory kitchens. Recipes grew in complexity as the semester progressed.

As one example of a lab, students were asked to make lollipops. As the sugar and water lollipop mix boils, students can observe water evaporation and monitor the temperature of the solution. As the ratio of water to sugar decreases, the temperature of the boiling mixture increases (compared to the boiling temperature of water). The correct temperature for making hard candy is a tight range; this temperature corresponds to a precise ratio of water to sugar. Even in the absence of a candy thermometer, students can determine the ratio of water to sugar by taking a teaspoonful of the mixture and dropping into ice water. Depending on the ratio, the cooled mixture has different textures.

Another important aspect of the design of the laboratory component of this course is that it can be scaled. A class of sixty students could be divided into more initial groups. Since each group works independently within their own "laboratories," the class could accommodate the higher number.

Assignments for the course were designed to encourage students to forge connections with one another by working in groups. One assignment required students to conduct a comparative analysis of food staples at grocery stores in communities with two different zip codes (zip codes were used as rough surrogates for communities). Students had to locate and examine common ingredients and foods in these stores, such as flour, milk, and tomatoes. Students were asked to list where food items were found (i.e., which section/aisle). They also had to list the varieties of foods that they came across; for example, milk is found not only as fresh milk, but also as canned, ultrapasteurized boxed, or powdered. This encouraged students to think about the impact of the development of food science and chemical processing on the food available to consumers, thus allowing for a common starting point when these chemical processes were discussed.

Another important purpose of the exercise was to encourage students to look at the relationship between available ingredients in the grocery stores of different communities in DC. This encouraged students to understand the relationship between the availability and variety of common cooking ingredients and the characteristics of the community the grocery stores serve, both in terms of culture and wealth. Additionally, students learned about food insecurity by reading excerpts from the USDA food insecurity report, and had a guest lecture by Michael Curtin Jr., the CEO from DC Central Kitchen, a charity organization fighting food insecurity in DC.

As a final assignment, students had to design a menu from a single culinary tradition. They needed to provide the recipes for their menu, and to annotate the science that occurs in each step of the recipe. This allowed them to demonstrate their newly gained chemistry knowledge. For example, the technique of making a sauce can be an illustration of the concept of emulsion. Students presented their menu to the class orally and submitted chemically annotated recipes for their final assignment. By the end of the semester, the assignments take students through Benjamin Bloom's taxonomy of learning domains from remembering and understanding scientific facts to applying and analyzing those facts.

Results and Response from Students. Overall, the response from students to the class was positive. Many of the positive comments on the class focused on how much they learned, both chemistry and food/cooking knowledge. Students enjoyed the group work, and forming diverse groups allowed individuals with different skill levels to work together, ensuring relatively even success of the unsupervised experiments. Students who had a positive experience in this course came in with a desire to learn more about cooking and chemistry. However, students who did not have a positive experience mostly reported taking the course to fulfill their STEM requirement. This illustrates a need for activating intrinsic motivators.

At its best, STEM courses for non-STEM majors not only deliver fundamental scientific knowledge, but also change affinity for STEM knowledge and encourage the practice of scientific processes. However, if STEM courses are mandated, it is crucial that the individual intrinsic motivations of each student be activated in their chosen courses. Thus, providing context that resonates with an individual student is important in the process (Sellers et al., 2007).

CONCLUSIONS AND AVENUES FOR FUTURE INNOVATION

The primary goal of this chapter is to emphasize the need for institutional support for faculty seeking to diversify STEM courses and to offer concrete examples of how inclusive pedagogy can be incorporated in a wide variety of STEM courses. Such efforts are effective in increasing engagement of students and support the larger goal of increasing retention of underrepresented groups in STEM majors or engaged with scientific knowledge.

We believe that an important part of the successful implementation in the courses discussed above is the guidance of education experts at CNDLS, and the support of the community of Doyle Faculty Fellows each academic year. There is a growing effort at Georgetown to build a stronger community of STEM faculty who are interested in the work and mission of equitable STEM education. We encourage all STEM faculty to engage with this work and engage with their students.

Guides that we have found to be useful for STEM faculty who are looking to begin this work include materials from the Center for the Integration of Research, Teaching, and Learning (CITRL) (Sellers et al., 2007), Becky Wai-Ling Packard's guide to mentorship (Packard, 2016), and resources at the National Center for Case Study Teaching in Science (2021).

ACKNOWLEDGEMENTS

The authors would like to thank Professor Jennifer Swift (Chemistry Department, Georgetown University) for sharing her course design with us.

REFERENCES

Alger, J. R. (1997). The educational value of diversity. *Academe, 83*(1), 20–23.

Antonio, A. L., Chang, M. J., Hakuta, K., Kenny, D. A., Levin, S., & Milem, J. F. (2004). Effects of racial diversity on complex thinking in college students. *Psychological Science, 15*(8), 507–510.

Bonous-Hammarth, M. (2000). Pathways to success: Affirming opportunities for science, mathematics, and engineering majors. *Journal of Negro Education, 69*(1/2), 92–111.

Brown, M. K., Hershock, C., Finelli, C. J., & O'Neal, C. (2009). *Teaching for retention in science, engineering, and math disciplines: A guide for faculty* (Occasional paper, no. 25). https://ag.purdue.edu/omp/Documents/Teaching%20Resources/Teaching%20for%20Retention%20in%20Science-Engineering-Math%20Disciplines.pdf

Chamany, K. (2006). Science and social justice: Making the case for case studies. *Journal of College Science Teaching, 36*(2), 54.

Chamany, K., Allen, D., & Tanner, K. (2008). Making biology learning relevant to students: Integrating people, history, and context into college biology teaching. *CBE Life Sciences Education, 7*(1), 267–278.

Doyle *Engaging Difference Program*. (2019). Berkley Center for Religion, Peace, & World Affairs, Georgetown University. http://doyle.georgetown.edu/

Fairweather, J. S. (2005). Beyond the rhetoric, trends in the relative value of teaching and research in faculty salaries. *Journal of Higher Education, 76*(4), 401–422.

Farrell, J. J., Moog, R. S., & Spencer, J. N. (1999). A guided inquiry general chemistry course. *Journal of Chemical Education, 76*(4), 570–574.

Freeman, S., Eddy, S. L., McDonough, M., Smith, M. K., Okoroafor, N., Jordt, H., & Wenderoth, M. P. (2014). Active learning increases student performance in science, engineering, and mathematics. *Proceedings of the National Academy of Sciences, 111*(23), 8410–8415.

Gilbert, S. F. (2003). Educating for social responsibility: Changing the syllabus of developmental biology. *International Journal of Developmental Biology, 47*(2–3), 237–244.

Groves, R. (2017). Science for all. *Provost's Blog*, Georgetown University.

Haak, D. C., HilleRisLambers, J., Pitre, E., & Freeman, S. (2011). Increased structure and active learning reduce the achievement gap in introductory biology. *Science, 332*(6034), 1213–1216.

Haraway, D. (1988). Situated knowledges: The science question in feminism and the privilege of partial perspective. *Feminist Studies, 14*(3), 575–599.

Harding, S. (1993). *The racial economy of science: Toward a democratic future (race, gender & science).* Indiana University Press.

Hockings, C. (2010). *Inclusive learning and teaching in higher education: A synthesis of research.* Higher Education Academy.

Hurtado, S., Newman, C. B., Tran, M. C., & Chang, M. J. (2010). Improving the rate of success for underrepresented racial minorities in STEM fields: Insights from a national project. *New Directions for Institutional Research, 2010*(148), 5–15.

McGee, H. (2004). *On food and cooking: The science and lore of the kitchen* (Rev. ed.). Scribner.

Mervis, J. (2010). Better intro courses seen as key to reducing attrition of STEM majors. *Science 330*(6002), 306.

National Center for Case Study Teaching in Science. (2021). http://sciencecases.lib.buffalo.edu/

National Science Board. (2018). *Science and engineering indicators 2018 digest* (Publication no. NSB-2018-2). https://www.nsf.gov/statistics/2018/nsb20181/digest/

National Science Foundation (NSF). (2019). *Women, minorities, and persons with disabilities in science and engineering* (Publication No. 19-304).

Packard, B. W. L. (2016). *Successful STEM mentoring initiatives for underrepresented students: A research-based guide for faculty and administrators.* Stylus Publishing.

Page, S. (2007). *The difference: How the power of diversity creates better groups, firms, schools, and societies.* Princeton University Press.

Prezler, R. W. (2009). Replacing lecture with peer-led workshops improves student learning. *CBE Live Sciences Education, 8*(3), 182–192.

Regents STEM Scholars Program, Georgetown University. (2019). https://futures.georgetown.edu/regents-science/

Rock, D., & Grant H. (2016, November 4). Why diverse teams are smarter. *Harvard Business Review.* https://hbr.org/2016/11/why-diverse-teams-are-smarter

Sellers, S. L., Roberts, J., Giovanetto, L., Friedrigh, K., & Hammargren, C. (2007). *Reaching all students: A resource for teaching in science, technology, engineering & mathematics* (2nd ed.). Center for the Integration of Research, Teaching, and Learning, Madison, WI. https://wmich.edu/sites/default/files/attachments/reachingallstudents.pdf

Steele, C. M. (1999). Thin ice: "Stereotype threat" and black college students. *Atlantic Monthly, 284*(2), 44–54.

Terenzini, P. T., Cabrera, A. F., Colbeck, C. L., Bjorklund, S. A., & Parente, J. M. (2001). Racial and ethnic diversity in the classroom: Does it promote student learning? *Journal of Higher Education, 72*(5), 509–531.

CHAPTER 10

Increasing Student Persistence through Active Learning Pedagogies in the Chemistry Curriculum

Emily D. Niemeyer and Michael R. Gesinski

Student persistence within STEM (science, technology, engineering, and mathematics) fields is a well-known issue in higher education. Of the students who enter college intending to pursue a major in science or math, less than 40 percent eventually earn a STEM degree (PCAST, 2012). Furthermore, research shows that students leaving STEM majors—often referred to as the "leaky pipeline"—is an even greater problem for those from underrepresented groups. Although underrepresented minority (URM) students—defined as Latinx, Black/African American, American Indian or Alaska Native, or Native Hawaiian or other Pacific Islander—enroll in science and math majors in the same proportion as their white peers, they leave STEM fields at much higher rates than their white counterparts (Riegle-Crumb, King, & Irizarry, 2019). This attrition of underrepresented students from college STEM programs ultimately affects the vibrancy and diversity of the science and technology workforce.

Undergraduate education in the first two years of college has become an important focus for improving STEM student persistence (Graham et al., 2013). Evidence widely supports the benefits of active, student-centered learning in the introductory scientific curriculum over traditional lecture-based instruction (PCAST, 2012). For example, students in introductory STEM courses that utilize active learning strategies have improved exam scores and are less likely to fail (Freeman et al., 2014). Active learning also increases the success of URM students in the sciences, with implementation of such pedagogies reducing achievement gaps for students from diverse backgrounds (Theobald et al., 2020). Moreover, the self-confidence and feeling of social belonging of underrepresented students is increased by active learning (Ballen et al., 2017), indicating that use of this pedagogy is critical to fostering inclusion and supporting equity for students in STEM fields.

Active learning is often defined broadly to encompass any pedagogical approach that emphasizes student participation and engagement in the learning process. In contrast to a traditional lecture where students passively receive knowledge from the instructor, active learning classrooms are student-centered and more inclusive of a wider range of abilities and learning styles (Moriarty, 2007). Many active learning pedagogical strategies exist within the sciences (Eberlein et al., 2008), and there is great variation in their implementation across disciplines and at different curricular levels. Common elements include small group discussion and problem solving, increased peer-to-peer interactions, and a focus on student engagement rather than instructor-transmitted information.

As part of a comprehensive grant-funded initiative at our institution, Southwestern University in Georgetown, Texas, we developed active learning methodologies for general and organic chemistry. Together, these courses span the first two years of our chemistry curriculum and have high enrollments relative to other courses at our college (thirty-five to forty-five for general chemistry; thirty to eighty for organic chemistry). STEM majors are a popular option at our residential liberal arts college, which enrolls about fourteen hundred students, of whom approximately one-third are from underrepresented groups. Students across a range of STEM disciplines commonly take general and organic chemistry, either as a requirement for their majors or because of their interest in pursuing a graduate degree in a health profession. Nationally, these courses are viewed as playing a central role in discouraging students from pursuing STEM degrees and have been identified as particularly deleterious to the persistence and success of URM students (Bayer Corporation, 2012).

We integrated active learning into our introductory chemistry courses because of a larger institutional goal to increase the persistence of STEM students—particularly women and those from underrepresented groups—at our university. Our pedagogical changes coincided with a transition to active learning in other introductory science and math classes as well as to inquiry- and project-based learning within science laboratory courses. Our general chemistry sequence now utilizes a flipped classroom format, which allows content to be delivered outside the classroom, freeing class time for application of concepts and higher-level cognitive activities. Our second-year organic chemistry courses employ a hybrid pedagogical model combining active learning techniques with a traditional lecture class. Implementation of these pedagogical strategies has led to increased student success within the first two years of our chemistry curriculum, greater classroom equity, and an increase in the persistence of students earning STEM degrees, with more pronounced improvements observed for students from underrepresented and low socioeconomic groups.

GENERAL CHEMISTRY—THE FLIPPED CLASSROOM

Implementation of the flipped classroom model varies greatly (Bishop & Verleger, 2013), but the term "flipped" is used to denote a pedagogical approach in which activities that typically take place in the classroom, such as lecturing on course content, instead occur at home. Individual computer-based instruction is the most common method for content delivery, allowing class time to be used for student-centered learning activities. Increased student access to web-based content via mobile devices paired with advances in instructional technology for faculty have fueled the popularity of the flipped classroom.

In our general chemistry course, students gain first exposure to new material outside of the classroom by watching a video lecture or completing a smart-book reading assignment on a web-based platform (figure 10.1). Video lectures were created for fifteen topics per semester (about one lesson per week) using the apps Doceri or Explain Everything on an iPad. Doceri, for example, makes a video as the instructor writes on the iPad like a chalkboard while also recording voice content. The videos contain material created from previous lecture notes and usually combine basic introductory information on a particular topic, a conceptual overview, and example problem-solving. Videos are five to seven minutes in length and are uploaded to YouTube, then linked through the university course management system, Moodle, for student access. Students also complete assigned readings on a web-based platform. The textbook for the course allows instructors to assign ongoing knowledge assessments that use adaptive technology to identify topics that students may not understand as they read and prepare for class.

Students are required to complete a video quiz or reading assessment prior to each class and these low-stakes assignments contribute a small percentage to their overall grade. Incentivizing out-of-class preparation is an important component of the flipped classroom (Seery, 2016) because it ensures students acquire a basic understanding of the assigned material prior to arriving in class. As one of our general chemistry students noted in a 2014 survey, the flipped classroom improved her learning because she came to class "ready with questions and already familiar with the topic for the day." This advance preparation helps to "spread out" the learning process for students, which can reduce cognitive loading and improve outcomes (Karaca & Ocak, 2017). Furthermore, flipped classrooms allow students to watch video lectures at their own pace—and rewatch sections that they may not understand—which can foster more inclusive classrooms by supporting a range of student expertise levels and learning styles (Abeysekera & Dawson, 2015).

When students arrive to class, they engage in a variety of activities that are centered around small-group learning. Groups of four students each are assigned at the beginning

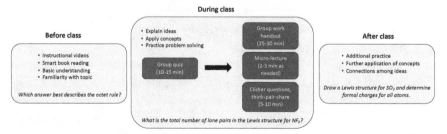

Figure 10.1. Summary of the flipped classroom in general chemistry. Example questions on the topic of Lewis structures posed to students before, during, and after class are included.

of the semester and each member signs a contract outlining expectations for group participation and behavior. Additionally, group members have the opportunity to evaluate their peers' contributions via a short survey at the conclusion of the semester and that information is used to determine student participation grades in the course. Each group is provided with a whiteboard at the beginning of the class period for use in collaborative problem-solving and to display their answers for discussion with other students and the instructor. Small-group work within the flipped classroom fosters a cooperative learning environment and therefore creates a more inclusive classroom for underrepresented students (Lage, Platt, & Treglia, 2000). The importance of peer interactions in our general chemistry class is evident: in a 2014 survey, 94 percent of students strongly agreed or agreed that the flipped classroom gave them greater opportunities to communicate with other students. One student noted that "peers are very helpful and [engaging] with them encouraged us to form study groups outside of class," while another said the flipped classroom "made it fun to be with your friends and figure things out instead of snoozing in class."

Frequent low-stakes assessments are central to the flipped classroom, and our general chemistry students take weekly in-class group quizzes (Figure 10.1) using immediate feedback assessment technique (IF-AT) cards. IF-AT cards provide affirmative or corrective feedback on multiple-choice answers using a scratch-off system. The cards offer a novel way for students to submit their answers, learn from mistakes, and receive partial credit for their work. Each class, students also work in their groups to complete a handout that is designed to encourage discussion and promote collaborative problem-solving (Figure 10.1). These worksheets include a mixture of conceptual and higher-level application problems, which helps students build upon the knowledge foundation that they acquired prior to class. Questions are selected based on desired student learning outcomes for the day and utilize a variety of active learning strategies, such as concept mapping and strip sequencing (Handelsman, Miller, & Pfund, 2006). After a question on the handout is introduced, groups must come to a collective answer and report it using their whiteboards while the instructor circulates around the classroom, answering individual and group questions. At the conclusion, one group is asked to report out on its answer and the instructor facilitates further discussion. The instructor may also provide a micro-lecture of two or three minutes (McLaughlin et al., 2014) to emphasize key points related to the question (Figure 10.1).

In addition to group problem-solving, our general chemistry students also answer individual clicker questions during class (Figure 10.1). Clickers are electronic response systems that allow students to anonymously answer questions posed by the instructor, with the results collected using a receiver and then displayed graphically. Depending on the platform chosen by the instructor, students can respond either using a purchased remote or through a free polling app on their smartphone, tablet, or laptop. Clicker questions have the benefit of providing immediate feedback to the instructor on student understanding of a particular topic. Think-pair-share activities may also be designed around clicker questions, which can help students identify their own misconceptions. Research also shows that women perceive that clickers improve their classroom experience, encourage them to be more engaged, and help them learn chemistry (Niemeyer & Zewail-Foote, 2018), so clickers may further contribute to the creation of an inclusive classroom environment.

Homework assignments are used to encourage students to review concepts, practice additional problem solving, and make further connections among ideas once they leave the classroom (Figure 10.1). In our general chemistry course, students complete five to seven problems using an online homework platform within one day following their class meeting. They also submit a homework assignment at the conclusion of each week that provides a summary review of topics and includes more challenging questions. These homework assignments allow students to assess their learning and gauge their understanding of particular concepts as introduced while also contributing a small percentage to their overall course grade.

Our students have very positive perceptions of learning within a flipped classroom. In a 2014 survey, 88 percent of students agreed or strongly agreed that the flipped classroom is more engaging than traditional lecture. Additionally, 75 percent of students agreed or strongly agreed that the flipped classroom helped them feel more motivated to learn chemistry while 81 percent said that it improved their learning of chemistry. Because the flipped classroom uses a variety of pedagogical approaches—such as small-group work, online instruction, microlectures, and clicker questions—it can meet the educational needs of students with different learning styles. Additionally, flipped pedagogy encourages greater interaction between individual students and among students and the instructor, creating an inclusive classroom environment that fosters more personalized learning (Altemueller & Lindquist, 2017).

ORGANIC CHEMISTRY—A HYBRID MODEL

At Southwestern University, organic chemistry has traditionally had a reputation for weeding out potential science majors. This issue is not unique to Southwestern; the national attrition rate typically ranges from 30 percent to 50 percent over the two-semester course (Grove, Hershberger, & Bretz, 2008). These high failure rates have a disproportionate impact on student success since organic chemistry is a gateway class, serving as a prerequisite for advanced courses necessary for STEM degree attainment. This problem has gained widespread attention, with a session at the 2016 American Chemical Society national meeting labeling this deficit in student understanding and retention within organic chemistry as a "crisis" (Halford, 2016).

This crisis can be partially attributed to the manner in which organic chemistry is taught. Traditional lecture models emphasize the dissemination of facts, implying that science is an exercise in memorization. This instructor-centered method of teaching focuses on lower-level student cognitive skills, in hopes that "remembering" will lead to the development of higher-level abilities such as "analyzing" and "creating" (Anderson & Krathwohl, 2001; Bloom, 1956). Recent evidence has indicated that student-centered pedagogies focused on higher-order cognitive skills are more effective at improving student understanding and retention (Freeman et al., 2014). Moreover, these strategies have been shown to create more inclusive classroom environments, thus improving success of students from underrepresented groups (Theobald et al., 2020).

With this in mind, we have developed a hybrid model for organic chemistry that presents students with multiple pedagogical styles by integrating traditional lecture components with clicker questions, flipped classroom videos, and guided inquiry activities. Student response devices (clickers) are combined with short lectures to test student misconceptions and allow students to develop new knowledge. Active participation in the learning process is incentivized by assigning a small percentage of students' overall grades to their answers; an incorrect answer is worth partial credit while no answer garners no credit. This low-stakes motivation has been shown to improve engagement in similar classroom activities (Niemeyer & Zewail-Foote, 2018).

Typically, students are introduced to a concept through a ten-minute lecture. Specific content is often intentionally omitted from this portion, forcing students to create their own knowledge during the activity. They are then presented with two types of questions that are generated by the instructor. First, they are asked to simply apply the concept to a situation they have never seen before (Figure 10.2: Application Clicker). This affords students the opportunity to demonstrate their understanding of the material and gain confidence in their abilities. Subsequently, students are presented with more difficult questions that require exploration and revision with the intention of creating new knowledge (Figure 10.2: Creation Clicker). With multiple-choice questions it is important to provide appropriate distractor/wrong answers that specifically address common misconceptions. These problems also provide ample opportunity to participate in metacognitive reflection to encourage awareness of the learning process, improving retention and supporting good study skills (Arslantas, Wood, & MacNeil, 2018). This workflow is exemplified in Figure 10.2 by a classroom module used to introduce the concept of induction.

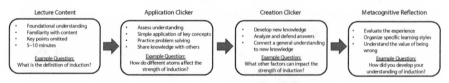

Figure 10.2. Workflow of a clicker learning activity. Examples of expected learning goals are included.

The role of the instructor in leading these activities is imperative and is greatly assisted by the immediate feedback provided by the clickers. Students are first allowed to respond individually to questions, giving a baseline for assessment of the initial lecture. Depending on the distribution of results, the instructor may choose to end the activity if most students answered correctly, provide a cryptic hint to sway students away from an incorrect answer, or employ a think-pair-share strategy if the class is split. The last is particularly valuable as it encourages the class to actively engage in discussion to defend, evaluate, and analyze their results regardless of their background. The dynamic nature of these activities further serves to engage the students and can create a cooperative and equitable atmosphere where everyone in the class is working toward the same answer (Niemeyer & Zewail-Foote, 2018).

Student perceptions of using the clicker have been overwhelmingly positive during the six years it has been implemented. In a 2014 survey, students rated this class structure an average of 4.43 out of a maximum of 5. There is a general appreciation of the balance that it creates in a large classroom setting, as one student commented: "The balance between clicker questions and lecture helps to break the monotony" of organic chemistry. Initially we were concerned that the difficulty of some questions would frustrate students. From their comments, it appears that the metacognitive reflections employed after particularly difficult experiences as well of the low-stakes nature of the grading alleviates much of this stress. As one student explained, "I learn from failure."

Video lectures have also been incorporated into the organic chemistry series to flip classrooms using many of the same strategies described above for the general chemistry class. The videos are created using a high-resolution document camera and video editing software (Camtasia) that allows the students to see the instructor's face while speaking. This provides a level of personalization that the students often comment on in class. Students are then required to take a brief online content quiz to confirm their comprehension. They are given three chances to take the quiz and afforded the highest grade of their attempts. Class time is then used for application of these concepts through higher-level cognitive activities, which would traditionally take place while performing homework assignments (Lage, Platt, & Treglia, 2000).

This technique works best for topics where a large amount of content dissemination is necessary. For example, lecturing on spectroscopy can be tedious as students are expected to commit a series of numbers and patterns to memory. By moving this content to a short video, students are able to spend classroom time with the instructor applying this knowledge to structure elucidation problems. Students often comment on the usefulness of these instructor-generated videos because it slows down the pace of the course by allowing students to replay the content. Therefore, these video lectures accommodate a variety of learning styles, creating an inclusive environment where all students' needs are being met (Abeysekera & Dawson, 2015).

In addition to attending three fifty-minute lectures a week, students are required to attend one fifty-minute discussion session. These sessions range in size from ten to twenty students and give the instructor a chance to work with students in a more intimate setting, allowing them to feel comfortable asking questions. Typically, students are randomly assigned to groups of three or four and are required to work together, thus providing an opportunity for students with disparate backgrounds to interact and form relationships.

Worksheets have been generated that encourage students to create their own knowledge under the guidance of the instructor. These activities utilize a strategy similar to Process-Oriented Guided Inquiry Learning (POGIL) although applied less rigidly (Moog & Spencer, 2008). The topics of these worksheets are either not explicitly covered in lecture or are extensions of covered material. The most impactful exercises are applied to concepts that require a copious amount of writing because it allows students time to slow down and learn the material at their own pace instead of simply copying notes from a lecture. It has been demonstrated that these sorts of process-oriented learning activities improve persistence rates of URM students in STEM majors (Dirks & Cunningham, 2016).

Most of these guided inquiry activities give students some foundational understanding of material through traditional lectures, video lectures, a reading assignment, or some combination of all three. The worksheet then challenges the students to work together to develop new knowledge by applying this foundation to new content. For example, when teaching reversible reactions of aldehydes and ketones, time is spent in the lecture exploring the mechanism of hydrate formation with a focus on connections to other transformations. During the discussion session, students are given the structures of other similar molecules and prompted to develop mechanisms for the other reversible reactions (acetal, imine, and enamine formation).

This method requires a significant investment of time and energy by the instructor as students get frustrated and often require guidance and reassurance. Continuous reinforcement is necessary to explain that they are not expected to get the correct answer without assistance. It also gives the instructor an opportunity to create personal relationships with individual students and to gauge their progress, ensuring no student is falling behind. Students tend to appreciate the intimate and challenging nature of these sessions. As one enthusiastic student commented in 2015: "Discussion is life. It's the reason I understand this class. I would like another discussion period to be honest. It's beautiful."

EVIDENCE OF SUCCESS

Previous research has shown that students perform better on examinations and are less likely to fail introductory science and math courses that use active learning strategies (Freeman et al., 2014). Since our transition to an active learning curriculum within our general and organic chemistry courses, D/F/W rates (the percentage of students earning a D or F grade or withdrawing, W, from the course) have declined and student grades are better. Most notably, the greatest improvements occurred for underrepresented and low socioeconomic status (SES) students. For example, Figure 10.3A provides a comparison of average D/F/W rates in general chemistry from 2003 to 2007 when the course was taught using a traditional lecture method and 2013 to 2017 when the course used flipped pedagogy. The D/F/W rate decreased for all students when general chemistry was taught using active learning methodologies, indicating fewer students were receiving D or F grades or withdrawing from the course. Moreover, the greatest declines were observed for underrepresented and Pell-eligible students, with D/F/W rates decreasing from 35 percent to 28 percent for URM students and 35 percent to 20 percent for Pell-eligible students. (Pell grant eligibility is a common way to identify students with high levels of financial need.) Similar trends occurred within organic chemistry (Figure 10.3B) with D/F/W rates decreasing for all students when the course was taught using active learning (2013–2017) instead of lecture (2003–2007). The largest declines occurred for URM students (from 53 to 35 percent) and Pell-eligible students (D/F/W rates decreased from 51 to 35 percent).

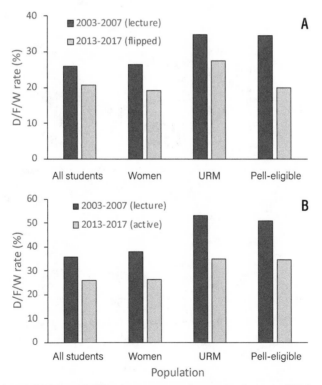

Figure 10.3. Average D/F/W rates for all students, women, underrepresented minority (URM) students, and Pell-eligible students in the first semester of general (**A**) and organic (**B**) chemistry.

When active learning pedagogies were used in the general and organic chemistry classrooms, our students were also more successful and earned higher grades overall. Grades were converted to a numerical scale (e.g., 4.0 = A, 3.0 = B, etc.) and average grades were calculated for students in general chemistry (Figure 10.4A) and organic chemistry (Figure 10.4B) when the courses were taught using active learning (2013–2017) and lecture (2003–2007). In both courses, grades were higher for students in active learning classrooms but the greatest increases occurred for underrepresented and Pell-eligible students in general chemistry and women taking organic chemistry. For example, the average grades of Pell-eligible students in general chemistry increased from a C+ (2.4) to a B– (2.7). Higher grades in introductory science and math courses are correlated with increased student confidence and greater STEM persistence (Toven-Lindsey et al., 2015).

STEM graduation rates are also a key indicator of our success in creating more inclusive classrooms that support the success of all students. Graduation rates were determined by tracking if a student went on to earn a STEM degree after enrolling in general chemistry during their first semester at Southwestern University. For comparison, we

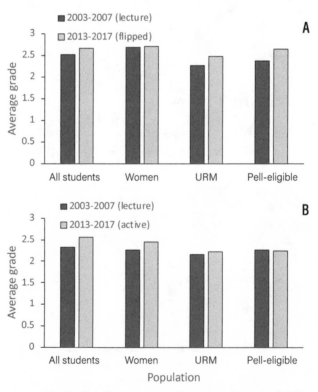

Figure 10.4. Average grades for all students, women, underrepresented minority (URM) students, and Pell-eligible students in the first semester of general (A) and organic (B) chemistry.

determined graduation rates during two years when general chemistry was taught primarily by lecture (2003 and 2004) and after the integration of active learning (2013 and 2014). The results are presented in Figure 10.5. STEM graduation rates were uniformly higher for students who were enrolled in general chemistry taught using flipped pedagogy compared to traditional lecture. The greatest gains were made by underrepresented and Pell-eligible students, with graduation rates more than double for those in active learning classrooms compared to lecture. The STEM graduation rates for underrepresented students in the 2003 and 2004 cohorts show that these students were much less likely to graduate with a STEM degree when compared to the total group of all students. STEM graduation rates for underrepresented students achieved parity with the total student population for the 2013 and 2014 cohorts and interestingly, graduation rates for women and Pell-eligible students in those cohorts exceeded the rate for all students. These results are particularly notable within the context of a national study showing that underrepresented students who enter college intending to major in the sciences have much higher probabilities of completing degrees in non-STEM fields compared to their white peers (Riegle-Crumb, King, & Irizarry, 2019). It is important to note that, while we observed gains in STEM student success, persistence, and graduation rates, our aggregated data may mask inequities in outcomes that exist across racial and ethnic categories (McNair, Bensimon, & Malcom-Piqueux, 2020).

Research suggests that active learning pedagogies improve outcomes for marginalized students in STEM courses by providing increased opportunities for "deliberate

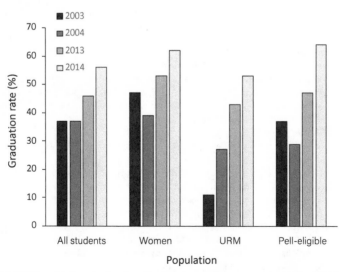

Figure 10.5. STEM graduation rates for all students, women, underrepresented minority (URM) students, and Pell-eligible students who took general chemistry in their first year at Southwestern University in 2003, 2004, 2013, and 2014.

practice" and fostering a "culture of inclusion" (Theobald et al., 2020). Improving student learning is a central tenet of the active learning classroom, and results in the use of evidence-based pedagogical methods such as scaffolded learning, repetition of concepts, and frequent opportunities for feedback. Additionally, the collaborative nature of active learning classrooms communicates that the instructor cares about students and their success, which also promotes an inclusive environment (Theobald et al., 2020). Although a variety of factors affect student persistence within STEM fields (Toven-Lindsey et al., 2015), the results we have observed—lower D/F/W rates and higher grades in our courses along with increased STEM graduation rates for URM and low SES students—highlight the importance of using active learning within introductory chemistry courses. These pedagogical changes have increased STEM student success and persistence by creating inclusive, collaborative, and welcoming classrooms that provide a more supportive and equitable learning experience for our students.

ACKNOWLEDGMENTS

This work was supported by the Howard Hughes Medical Institute through the Undergraduate Science Education Program (52007558). We also wish to thank Dr. Natasha Williams, director of Institutional Research and Effectiveness at Southwestern University, for her assistance with obtaining and analyzing institutional data sets.

REFERENCES

Abeysekera, L. & Dawson, P. (2015). Motivation and cognitive load in the flipped classroom: Definition, rationale, and a call for research. *Higher Education Research & Development, 34*(1), 1–14.

Altemueller, L., & Lindquist, C. (2017). Flipped classroom instruction for inclusive learning. *British Journal of Special Education, 44*(3), 341–358.

Anderson, L. W., & Krathwohl, D. R. (Eds.) (2001). *Taxonomy for learning, teaching, and assessing: A revision of Bloom's taxonomy of educational objectives*. Longman Publishing Group.

Arslantas, F., Wood, E., & MacNeil, S. (2018). Metacognitive foundations in higher education chemistry. In C. Cox & W. E. Shatzberg (Eds.), *International perspectives on chemistry education research and practice* (Vol. 1293, pp. 57–77). American Chemical Society.

Ballen, C. J., Wieman, C., Salehi, S., Searle, J. B., & Zamudio, K. R. (2017). Enhancing diversity in undergraduate science: Self-efficacy drives performance gains with active learning. *CBE—Life Sciences Education, 16*(56), 1–6.

Bayer Corporation. (2012). Bayer facts of science education XV: A view from the gatekeepers—STEM department chairs at America's top 200 research universities on female and underrepresented minority undergraduate STEM students. *Journal of Science Education and Technology, 21*(3), 317–324.

Bishop, J. L., & Verleger, M. A. (2013). The flipped classroom: A survey of the research. *120th ASEE Annual Conference and Exposition*, Atlanta, GA, paper #6219.

Bloom, B. S. (Ed.) (1956) *Taxonomy of educational objectives*. Longman Publishing Group.

Dirks, C., & Cunningham, M. (2016) Enhancing diversity in science: Is teaching science process skills the answer? *CBE—Life Sciences Education, 5*(3), 218–226.

Eberlein, T., Kampmeier, J., Minderhout, V., Moog, R. S., Platt, T., Varma-Nelson, P., & White, H. B. (2008). Pedagogies of engagement in science. *Biochemistry and Molecular Biology Education, 36*(4), 262–273.

Freeman, S., Eddy, S. L., McDonough, M., Smith, M. K., Okoroafor, N., Jordt, H., & Wenderoth, M. P. (2014). Active learning increases student performance in science, engineering, and mathematics. *Proceedings of the National Academy of Sciences, 111*(23), 8410–8415.

Graham, M. J., Frederick, J., Byars-Winston, A., Hunter, A.-B., & Handelsman, J. (2013). Increasing persistence of college students in STEM. *Science, 341*(6153), 1455–1456.

Grove, N. P., Hershberger, J. W., & Bretz, S. L. (2008). Impact of a spiral organic curriculum on student attrition and learning. *Chemistry Education Research and Practice, 9*, 157–162.

Halford, B. (2016, March 12). Is there a crisis in organic chemistry education? *Chemical & Engineering News, 94*(11), 24–25.

Handelsman, J., Miller, S., & Pfund, C. (2006). *Scientific teaching.* W. H. Freeman.

Karaca, C., & Ocak, M. A. (2017). Effect of flipped learning on cognitive load: A higher education research. *Journal of Learning and Teaching in Digital Age, 2*(1), 20–27.

Lage, M. J., Platt, G. J., & Treglia, M. (2000). Inverting the classroom: A gateway to creating an inclusive learning environment. *Journal of Economic Education, 31*(1), 30–43.

McLaughlin, J. E., Roth, M. T., Glatt, D. M., Gharkholonarehe, N., Davidson, C. A., Griffin, L. M., Esserman, D. A., & Mumper, R. J. (2014). The flipped classroom: A course redesign to foster learning and engagement in a health professions school. *Academic Medicine 89*(2), 236–243.

McNair, T. B., Bensimon, E. M., & Malcom-Piqueux, L. (2020). *From equity talk to equity walk: Expanding practitioner knowledge for racial justice in higher education.* Jossey-Bass.

Moog, R. S., & Spencer, J. M. (2008). *Process-oriented guided inquiry learning (POGIL).* American Chemical Society.

Moriarty, M. A. (2007). Inclusive pedagogy: Teaching methodologies to reach diverse learners in science instruction. *Equity & Excellence in Education, 40*(3), 252–265.

Niemeyer, E. D., & Zewail-Foote, M. (2018). Investigating the influence of gender on student perceptions of the clicker in a small undergraduate general chemistry course. *Journal of Chemical Education, 95*(2), 218–223.

President's Council of Advisors on Science and Technology (PCAST). (2012). *Report to the president. Engage to excel: Producing one million additional college graduates with degrees in science, technology, engineering, and mathematics.* PCAST.

Riegle-Crumb, C., King, B., & Irizarry, Y. (2019). Does STEM stand out? Examining racial/ethnic gaps in persistence across postsecondary fields. *Educational Researcher.* https://doi.org/10.3102/0013189X19831006

Seery, M. (2016). Flipped learning in higher education chemistry: Emerging trends and potential directions. *Chemistry Education Research and Practice, 16*(4), 758–768.

Theobald, E. J., Hill, M. J., Tran, E., Agrawal, S., Arroyo, E. N., Behling, S., et al. (2020). Active learning narrows achievement gaps for underrepresented students in undergraduate science, technology, engineering, and math. *Proceedings of the National Academy of Sciences, 117*(12), 6476–6483.

Toven-Lindsey, B., Levis-Fitzgerald, M., Barber, P. H., & Hasson, T. (2015). Increasing persistence in undergraduate science majors: A model for institutional support of underrepresented students. *CBE—Life Sciences Education, 14*(2), 1–12.

REFLECTION ON
Inclusive STEM

The authors in this section illustrate how others can adopt inclusive strategies that "rehumanize" STEM courses. These instructors began with reexamining their position within their courses. They acknowledged the variety of ways of knowing as they redesigned their pedagogy, curriculum, and assessment practices. They worked to understand who their students were so they could create a classroom that is welcoming, supportive, and affirming. Drawing upon inclusive practices of UDL and CRP, the authors used a variety of techniques in introducing course content. They presented several ways faculty can implement student interaction in STEM courses. The authors critically evaluated their existing curriculum to intentionally redesign it for inclusivity, seeking to make it relevant to and representative of the students in the class. Their attention to inclusivity encompassed their assessment practices. They provided a variety of assignments and activities for students to demonstrate their knowledge. The educators provided frequent, formative feedback so students could monitor their learning.

The following questions are designed to help readers consider how they might adopt some of the strategies and approaches described in the preceding chapters.

PRACTITIONER BEHAVIORS

1. How can we create, encourage, and sustain educator interest for meaningful diversity and inclusion in the classroom? How can we build a sustainable model for educators to be inclusive in the STEM classroom?

2. What kind of measures can be taken in a classroom to create a safe environment for inclusion?

3. What are current perceptions of diversity and inclusion in the STEM classroom? In what ways do our personal histories and views of the world affect our teaching approaches and methods?

4. Faculty can encounter barriers such as student resistance, time commitment, and institutional constraints when incorporating inquiry-based pedagogies into their classrooms. Reflect on the barriers that you may encounter for your class. What resources can you leverage to address these issues?

PEDAGOGY

1. Like other aspects of an intentionally designed course, the first step in incorporating inclusive pedagogy elements into your course is to write out one or more teaching/learning goals. A good strategy might be to start with considering the students you are going to teach. What are the main goals you hope students will meet from this element of the course? Which inequities are you trying to overcome in your cohort?

2. How often do we modify our teaching approach in response to the analysis and reflection of our teaching or in reaction to current research on inclusive pedagogy?

3. Identify two topics within your introductory STEM course that you currently teach by lecturing. Which active learning pedagogies do you think best align with your desired student learning outcomes for these topics? What steps are necessary to teach these topics through active learning the next time you offer the course?

4. What challenges do you see in terms of equity and inclusion in STEM classes at your institution? How do you envision changing your pedagogical approach may address these issues?

CURRICULUM

1. To what extent do you critically question and revise the effectiveness of your curriculum and teaching practice to promote diversity, inclusion, and engagement? How much do you involve your students in this process?

2. How relevant are your curriculum materials and classroom activities to the experience of your students?

3. Inclusive teaching methodologies have the greatest impact when they are integrated throughout all levels of the STEM curriculum. How can you work with your colleagues to create a scientific curriculum that improves student persistence and success, specifically for underrepresented students?

ASSESSMENT

1. Iteration is of course the secret to improved teaching and course design. The question is what to change and how to improve. How will you assess if your course goals are met, or that the new element is successful? Consider assessment strategies that are transparent to students and allow them to have a stake in the current and future iterations of the course. For example, a mid-semester survey on how they feel this element of the course is going; or a chance for them to suggest other topics they might want to incorporate into the course in the second half. A good assessment strategy should serve not only to assess student learning, but also to advance the goals of the course.

2. How can we design, create, review, and adapt assessments to be authentic and meaningful to students from an equity and diversity and inclusion point of view?

PART V
Inclusive Professional Practice

In addition to the traditional disciplines, higher education institutions offer programs that directly lead to licensing and professional practice. Some disciplines, like business, span academic and professional practice. Like disciplinary instruction, the professional practice curriculum and its delivery require intentional attention to principles of equity and inclusion. In these courses, educators promote cultural competence required to create professionals who employ social justice practices in their careers.

Brent Oliver, Becky Van Tassel, and Roseline Carter address the systemic discrimination that LGBTQ2S+ clients experience in health and social care environments. They argue that barriers to adequate healthcare and essential services in the LGBQT2S+ community are real and can be changed if medical and human service professionals are educated about gender and sexual identity as well as how to communicate sensitively about sexual health. They describe how a curriculum developed within a framework of adult education and transformative learning theory needs to be integrated into the course curriculum of health and social service students so they can be prepared to address unconscious bias, privilege, and oppression.

Beth Monnin and Shawna Staud expand on the need to include cultural competence to address diversity in the professional practice curriculum with their chapter on a dental hygiene program. They explore and explain the benefits of several immersion and role-playing activities that enhance the cultural awareness of dental hygiene students. Based on the experiences of their students, they claim that such activities are crucial to the cultural competence of future dental hygienists who will interact with a diverse population.

Lizzie Ngwenya-Scoburgh and Patrice Gillespie hone in on the interdisciplinary context of the business world, which has become a global society. Business has changed in a shrinking world and it is imperative that educators respond to this by preparing individuals to enter a world where they can become agents of social change. They speak to the importance of teaching students that equity and inclusion in business practices lead to a competitive advantage. They describe specific class activities that incorporate discussion and reflection that connects students both at the academic and social levels for understand differences and practice inclusion.

CHAPTER 11

Creating a Culture of Respect

Utilizing Transformative Learning Theory in Developing a Gender and Sexual Diversity Curriculum

Brent Oliver, Becky Van Tassel, and Roseline Carter

Access to the best possible medical care and social support is a fundamental human right. Unfortunately, lesbian, gay, bisexual, transgender, queer/questioning, and two spirit (LGBTQ2S+) individuals in Canada have twice the level of unmet health and social needs as the general population. LGBTQ2S+ individuals confront numerous barriers to accessing health and social services including structural discrimination, substandard care, heteronormative assumptions, and a lack of knowledge among professional caregivers. Homophobia and heterosexism are root causes of health and social inequities for LGBTQ2S+ populations in North America. The systemic discrimination perpetrated by the health and human service systems, and the individual prejudices of the workers within those systems, lead to essential services being perceived as unsafe by LGBTQ2S+ individuals. Consequently, health and social care environments must demonstrate cultural awareness and respect for LGBTQ2S+ clients in order to be considered accessible (McNair & Hegarty, 2010).

Medical and human service professionals often receive little professional training or instruction on the unique health issues of LGBTQ2S+ populations and commonly report discomfort when talking about sexuality, a lack of information about gender and sexual identity, and a lack of skill to communicate about sexual health (Barr et al., 2014; Shindel & Parish, 2013). Additionally, students in professional degree programs frequently express discomfort speaking about sexuality and tend to problematize any group that fails to fit within normative cultural constructions of gender or sexuality (Dixon-Woods et al., 2002; Jeyasingham, 2008; Trotter et al., 2006).

The goal of adult education in a professional context is to support students to attain the capabilities, skills, and insights that are essential for their emerging practice (Mezirow, 2003). This involves a process that helps students to become socially responsible and autonomous learners. Professional decision-making requires an awareness of the source and context of one's knowledge and critical reflection on the validity of one's assumptions (Mezirow, 2012). In preparation for effective practice in the helping professions, students must learn to reason for themselves as well as to negotiate and act on their own values, beliefs, feelings, and judgments rather than those assimilated from others (Mezirow, 2009). Across North America students in the helping professions are not receiving adequate preservice training to create increased awareness of sexual and gender diversity and to separate personal from professional values about sexuality .

This chapter discusses a collaborative scholarship of teaching and learning (SoTL) project between the Department of Child Studies and Social Work at Mount Royal University (MRU) and the Centre for Sexuality (CFS) in Calgary, Alberta. The objectives of this project were to evaluate the effectiveness of a workshop that utilized transformative learning principles in providing introductory training on gender and sexual diversity. The workshop, entitled "Creating a Culture of Respect," was delivered to first-year students enrolled in the social work, nursing, midwifery, and child studies programs at MRU.

TRANSFORMATIVE LEARNING

Based on constructivist approaches to adult education, transformative learning theory draws from multiple theoretical frameworks including humanism and critical social theory. It is consistent with the objectives of professional training related to sexual and gender diversity. Mezirow (2009) defined transformative learning as an approach to adult education that enables students to "recognize, reassess, and modify structures of assumptions and expectations that frame tacit points of view and influence thinking, beliefs, and actions" (p. 18). In higher education, transformative learning can be distinguished through an explicit focus on reflective discourse, inclusive processes, supportive learning environments, and social change.

Transformative learning involves reflective discourse, which is the process through which we communicate with others to better understand the meaning of an experience. It requires openness to other points of view and empathy for how others think and feel. As defined by Mezirow (2003), reflective discourse involves the examination of one's established beliefs, feelings, and values to arrive at a best (professional) judgement. At its core, reflective discourse involves welcoming difference and diverse points of view, important factors when addressing the socially charged topic of sexual and gender diversity (Mezirow, 2003).

Inclusive learning processes are central to effective transformative learning. Mezirow (2009) envisioned a reciprocal process that allows learners to become more "inclusive, discriminating, reflective, open, and emotionally able to change" (p. 22). Within a safe space, he theorized a learning process initiated by a disorienting dilemma that causes learners to reflect on their existing assumptions. Steps in this model involve self-examination, building competence and self-confidence, exploring new relationships, and considering options for new roles (among others) (Mezirow, 2009; 2012).

155

Given this imperative for change, transformative learning can be perceived by students as a threatening emotional experience (Mezirow, 2012). Consequently, facilitating safe and supportive learning environments is a critical prerequisite to transformative learning. Environments that allow for personal and professional growth are a required condition for transformative learning processes as are trusting relationships that allow for dialogue, questioning, and sharing (Taylor & Snyder, 2012). In this context, the role of the educator is critical, and instructors are viewed as facilitators committed to reflective discourse and greater agency for learners (Mezirow, 2012). Transformative learning has been widely adopted as an effective approach for working toward social change in a community context (Trisdell, 2012). Consequently, social action is widely considered as an important product arising from transformative learning processes.

CREATING A CULTURE OF RESPECT

The act of education is highly political (Carpenter, 2012). The environment in which one operates and educates will influence and be influenced by politics and systems of inequity and oppression. Mullaly and West (2017) posit that oppression is perpetuated by unconscious thoughts leading to corresponding beliefs and actions. Consequently, the role of adult education is to provide transformative experiences to learners that allow them to become aware of their own unconscious thoughts, attitudes, and beliefs (Glowacki-Duda et al., 2012). Unconscious thoughts and beliefs are learned over a period of time and this learning itself can be understood as "unintended and frequently unnoticed" (Jarvis, 2006, p. 53). Homophobia, transphobia, sexism, and misogyny are often ingrained in our unconsciously held beliefs imparted through socialization. Accordingly, it is necessary for health and social service providers to be aware of their own positionality and privilege so that they don't perpetuate inequity and exclusion in their professional practice.

Since 2015, trainers from the Centre for Sexuality have partnered with instructors within the Faculty of Health, Community, and Education at MRU to provide Creating a Culture of Respect workshops for preservice professionals studying to be social workers, child and youth care counselors, nurses, and midwives in Canada. During this time, students registered in fifteen sections of a first-year university course (Fundamentals of Professional Communication) participated in a ninety-minute in-class workshop aimed at increasing their knowledge, comfort level, and skill in working professionally with LGBTQ2S+ clients. Facilitators from the Centre for Sexuality worked with over five hundred students in these interdisciplinary classrooms. These sessions were collaboratively designed to align with established curriculum outcomes and professional accreditation guidelines.

The Centre for Sexuality envisions inclusion as a sense of safety and belonging that is represented structurally throughout organizations, communities, systems, and societies. Centre facilitators intentionally engage in curriculum design that is built on adult learning best practices. MacKeracher (2004) highlighted that adults require educational content that is timely, focused, practical, and builds on their prior knowledge and experiences. The curriculum for this introductory training on gender and sexual diversity was created to be both a transformative experience and a skill-building opportunity for students. The workshop design focused not only on the actual content of the curriculum but also on the characteristics of the facilitator and the facilitation process. Because the workshop was one module within a larger university course, time constraints meant that only ninety minutes could be allocated. Facilitators were tasked with the intense job of building rapport, engaging in experiential activities, and providing practical tools that can be applied in the field within a very tight timeline. It is important to note that it is impossible to create safety for all students at all times. The notion of safety is very important to address, as it is not the responsibility of LGBTQ2S+ participants to make their straight peers feel safe to explore these topics. Rather, it is the role of the facilitator to intentionally curate a learning environment that does not force LGBTQ2S+ students to educate their peers. Since safety is so paramount to this topic, it is discussed throughout this chapter.

Necessary components of a transformational learning experience include: safety for participants to share and process, content conveyed through dialogue, the sharing of thoughts and experiences, equity created in the group, and power being shared between the facilitator and the participants (Nemec, 2012). These concepts are crucial for allowing students to engage with activities that are designed to create a sense of discomfort and challenge their previously held beliefs about LGBTQ2S+ individuals.

Each Creating a Culture of Respect session began with the construction of group "bill of rights" and it is through this open conversation that a sense of safety and rapport were built. Toward creating this sense of safety, the facilitators intentionally worked with participants to co-create the groups' rights or norms for each session. There are five areas that must be addressed when discussing the rights: participation, pass, privacy, respect, and fun. The facilitator began by openly acknowledging that topics related to sexuality, sexual orientation, and gender identity are highly personal and each person will have different values and lived experiences when it comes to this topic. It is due to the highly personal nature of this content that we make the time for individuals to feel safe enough to experience a sense of discomfort. We then opened dialogue with each group to ask, "Why is it important to feel discomfort in this session?" A typical group response included comments such as, "we may notice that the content has touched on our values"; "we may feel uncomfortable in our professional practice and we need to learn how to deal with this"; or "we can then critically reflect on those feelings." Following this open conversation, we then moved through the bill of rights and asked participants to describe how they can participate, pass, respect privacy, recognize when respect is not being shown, and engage in the materials in a comfortable and safe manner.

There are many common and key responses that we needed to prompt the group to contribute. For example, under "participate" it was important that all agreed to participate with curiosity, ask questions, and engage with the material in a manner that acknowledges that there are LGBTQ2S+ individuals in the room. This meant that it was okay to ask questions rooted in a desire to learn, but not okay to express values or viewpoints that would be harmful to LGBTQ2S+ participants. It was also necessary to articulate that participants have the right to not engage in the activities and to take the time to care for themselves. Lastly, it was important when privacy was discussed to be explicit that LGBTQ2S+ participants did not have to feel the need to out themselves in the sessions to educate their peers, while simultaneously stating that they could choose to do so if they desired.

It was in this moment of dialogue that facilitators hoped to address the multiplicity of truths in the room. This allowed the facilitator to recognize that preservice professionals come with prior thoughts and knowledge about this topic, and to dig into the differences between personal values versus professional ethics. This facilitation technique also served to create and hold space for those students from LGBTQ2S+ communities to share, while simultaneously feeling supported by the facilitator. Safer engagement for LGBTQ2S+ individuals was paramount, as discourse among participants can be useful in addressing homophobia, transphobia, and biphobia, but this discourse can also be potentially harmful for those who have experienced this form of oppression.

The content of the sessions focused on providing information that allowed participants to understand the differences among sex, gender, and sexual orientation; the artful facilitation of an activity designed to create a "disorientating" experience; and providing clear examples and tools that can contribute to a greater sense of inclusion. Examples of these tools aimed at a greater sense of inclusion include a "see," "hear," and "feel" model that allowed individuals to reflect on the physical, emotional, and social space in which they practice. This tool encouraged participants to think about how health and social service systems can perpetuate inequity and oppression through the use of policies, practices, forms, language, and the creation of services that do not include the voices of those from LGBTQ2S+ communities.

Within successful transformative learning spaces, it is common to have varied experiences and reactions among participants. Truly transformative learning settings will challenge participants to question their unconscious bias, feel a sense of discomfort, and engage actively in grappling with new concepts. For both participants and facilitators, this can be an unsettling experience. Signs of discomfort should not be entirely unfavorable, as they are possible indicators that participants are experiencing a "disorientating event" where they are integrating new concepts or beliefs. However, the true test for facilitation is to ensure that participants do not venture beyond experiencing the discomfort that leads to learning versus discomfort that feels unsafe and where learning is no longer possible. For facilitators it was required that they read the room for subtle signs that participants were feeling unsafe. These signs may include defensiveness, lack of concentration on the topic, disengagement, fidgeting, and leaving the space. These potentially tense situations can be alleviated by the artful and intentional curation of safer spaces through the "rights" activity at the beginning of the session.

EVALUATING SUCCESS

In order to determine the impact of the Creating a Culture of Respect initiative, a SoTL study was conducted simultaneous to delivery of the workshops. This mixed methods study evaluated to what extent students reported a measured change in their knowledge, skill, and comfort level related to communicating about sexuality with clients as a result of participating in the workshop, and what learning, if any, students were able to apply in their professional work with clients in the field. Additionally, project investigators were also interested in students' feedback and insights on the workshop curriculum.

Data collection tools included surveys and one focus group. Students who participated in the training were recruited to complete an evaluation questionnaire featuring both open- and closed-ended questions (n=409). The survey instrument included pre- and posttest measures and was administered by the Centre for Sexuality trainers immediately prior to and immediately following the workshops. Following collection of the survey data, interested students were invited to participate in one focus group (n = 5), which was facilitated by a trained peer facilitator. During the focus group students were asked a series of open-ended questions regarding their knowledge, skill, and comfort level related to working with LGBTQ2S+ populations and their ability moving forward to apply this in their professional work with clients. Data analysis was conducted of the pre- and postworkshop survey questionnaires and qualitative data from the surveys and focus group. Qualitative responses were analyzed using methods of constant comparison and content analysis.

Findings from the quantitative data (published in detail elsewhere) validated the effectiveness of the workshop curriculum in meeting core objectives. In summary, students reported significant changes in their knowledge and comfort level related to communicating about sexuality with LGBTQ2S+ clients as a result of participating in the workshop and a majority of students reported that the material presented in the workshops would be applicable in their future work with clients.

Results from the qualitative data highlighted the learning students experienced in the workshops and its relevance to their future work in the helping professions. Here, students described learning processes consistent with adult education and transformative learning theory. Generally, students felt that the material presented in the workshop would be applicable in their future professional work with clients because it taught them how to better understand LGBTQ2S+ individuals and the complex realities many face in accessing health and social services. Students commonly reported that the workshop better prepared them to work with members from LGBTQ2S+ communities and that they were able to relate this to their emerging clinical practice.

Additionally, the workshop reinforced the importance of awareness and understanding regarding sexuality and gender in professional practice. In particular, students valued learning about the distinctions among sex, gender, sexual orientation, and gender expression. As discussed earlier, the workshop included an exercise identifying key concepts and initiated a discussion about how they are distinguished. For a majority of participants this was a simple but powerful message that challenged earlier information. Consequently, students appreciated the concrete teaching strategies employed in the workshops, including this student, who commented, "I liked that the presenter drew on the board in a way that was easy to understand. The presenter clarified questions well." Another student captured the learning reported by many in explaining, "I now know the difference between sex and gender as well as all the different ways to identify within those categories." Numerous students connected this practical learning to broader concepts of inclusion and equity, suggesting that "knowing terminology and how to interact appropriately with LGBTQ2S+ communities to create an anti-oppressive space will be a great asset." Additionally, many felt it would be a valuable tool for use with their clients in the field.

For many students these were new insights that validated the importance of being nonjudgmental in their approach to practice. Learning to recognize their unconscious bias, and to separate this in their professional practice, was a connected strategy many students took away from the training. For instance, one student nurse commented, "I will be more aware and make sure not to make assumptions based on looks or gender expression. . . . People who may appear to be one identity may be different from what I was expecting." This learning was shared across disciplines. A student in child and youth care reported that she had learned, "When working with children, do not assume their gender; let them express themselves freely and let them have their choice." Again, connecting this learning to their responsibility for equity and inclusion was mindful for many participants, including this student who affirmed a commitment to acting on these new insights by stating, "I will be an advocate for this to make a positive change."

As part of providing feedback on their learning, students who participated in the workshops highlighted aspects of the training that supported their development. Critical within this space was the role of the facilitator and the pedagogy employed. The need to create an open, respectful environment free of judgment was an important factor raised by many students. The role of the facilitator was foundational in this effort. Numerous participants credited the workshop facilitators with creating a supportive learning environment. One student reported, "The presenter was very open and accepting of all answers contributing to the discussions and all the topics were presented respectfully."

Others commented on "how approachable and knowledgeable the presenter was" and "the inclusive approach" adopted in the training. Additionally, students commented on the instructor's ability to make the topic a comfortable one for them to discuss with their peers in the classroom.

Equally important to students' learning was the opportunity to discuss gender and sexuality in an environment free of judgment. Participants valued the openness of their peers in sharing ideas, perspectives, and views on gender and sexuality as part of the workshop. Given how stigmatized these topics are in contemporary discourse, connecting with their peers in an open, respectful, facilitated forum was seen as valuable by many students. When asked about the strengths of the workshop one student indicated that "how open everyone was in talking about it" was a highlight; while another agreed that "the time given for group discussion allowed us to create our own ideas and reflect on them." The ability to connect with their peers in an open discussion was reported by numerous students as important to the curriculum for the workshop.

Reflecting the importance of transformative learning spaces, many students offered that the workshop provided them with an opportunity to build self-awareness through dialogue with classmates. This was the case for a nursing student who commented that the workshop contributed to her understanding of "the importance of being self-aware and not putting your values on others." As part of the study, students also stressed the importance of open conversations, where "all opinions were validated and heard." Some students reported learning from their classmates' perspectives. Others appreciated open conversations that also focused on strengths in addition to the challenges faced by LGBTQ2S+ communities.

Feedback about the workshops were also provided by some students who felt challenged by the transformative pedagogy/approach to the workshops. Several students reported feeling uncomfortable both with the topic as well as the classroom discussion. While this was a minority of students, it does speak to the challenges associated with a transformative learning approach. For instance, some participants were uncomfortable with the format, reporting that they did not like small group discussions. A few students were not open to hearing other perspectives and suggested that at times, "questions and stories from classmates dragged on." Numerous students reported a general discomfort with the topic of gender and sexuality while others struggled with the negative conditions faced by LGBTQ2S+ communities. Some students reported feeling very sensitive to the stories they heard during the workshop and did not like hearing about experiences of exclusion and discrimination. This was the case for one childcare student who remarked, "Thinking about youth struggles affects me emotionally. I don't like to cry at school."

In some workshops there was a clash of values among students, causing some to feel offended both by the discussion and the topic itself. Some students were intolerant of the views of their peers or struggled with perspectives shared during the workshop.

Students offended by the workshop curriculum included those who felt unable to express their opinions, did not like their views challenged, felt defensive, or did not agree with workshop content. For example, one student reported that "I felt like my beliefs in prolife were under attack." Another student remarked, "It was a lot of information bombarded against me." It was also not uncommon for students to describe a sense of tension (or fear). This student describes both the tension she felt as well as the perceived response of the facilitator: "I did feel a little bit of tension at times, because sometimes people would ask questions and it is almost like the facilitator was so determined to give a polite answer that made it clearly respectful to the LGBTQ community, that like, she didn't really answer the question that the person was asking. . . . As much as I was impressed, I will admit part of the time I was a little bit nervous and a bit feeling defensive."

One challenge for facilitators is to address the complex and often conflicting emotions of the participants. It can be useful to affirm that this is a normal response to learning. Further, facilitators would at times "call in" participants to reflect that while this content may be difficult to hear or uncomfortable, this was an opportunity to cultivate empathy for individuals from this community. In situations where personal values and beliefs were cited as reasons to not engage with the notion of inclusion, facilitators would identify elements of their professional code of ethics and how the basic premise of a code of ethics is to do no harm. Facilitators would then venture into discourse about the relationship between harm and an active refusal to not respect pronouns, use preferred names, acknowledge partners, or use inclusive language in their approaches.

Concern came not only from those opposed to the content of the curriculum but also some students from within LGBTQ2S+ communities who reported finding the discussion upsetting. This was the case for one focus group participant who commented, "I wanted to jump on some people the way they were phrasing questions. I know it is also about communication, so I am sure some people, because they don't have the knowledge, don't know how to ask it in the polite or correct way." In future sessions we have allocated additional time to be spent on the "bill of rights" and worked on enhanced training for our facilitators to address harmful comments in a more direct manner. We are also hoping to get "allies" in the room more engaged in the process of "calling in" their peers and upholding the group's rights. Ideally, if all individuals are committed to the creation of safety there will higher levels of accountability to respect the rights.

In transformative approaches, this tension (related to a disorienting dilemma) is core to the learning process. Feeling uncomfortable was not uncommon, an experience met with hostility by some students and resolved (even embraced) by others. In the focus group, students discussed the generative nature of this tension and discomfort, including this social work student: "I am ironically less comfortable the more I learn. The more I learn about it the more I feel uncomfortable. . . . I feel like I am, you know, on a road trying to get to the ultimate end of being a hundred percent comfortable, even though I don't know that is possible, you know?" Acknowledging the need for open conversations about gender and sexual equity beyond the classroom, many students discussed their increased awareness of the need for safe spaces and their responsibility in carrying this into professional practice. One participant reported wanting to provide safe spaces for LGBTQ2S+ individuals as a healthcare professional and felt this curriculum better equipped her to do so. "I found that it was helpful to discuss further how to create a safe space and how to portray that as well in the hospital setting or different settings anywhere, like how can we make that a safe place where people can feel okay to be where they are and who they are in it." This was a view shared by a participant in the focus group who shared, "It is not even so much about exactly what you say, but making sure your first message is, 'I am a part of the safe space. You are safe in this space and I want to contribute to that.'"

Additionally, many workshop participants used this new knowledge as a catalyst for making commitments beyond professional practice to include advocacy and change-making. This was the case for one student who discussed how the workshop both raised awareness and provided a call to action: "So by me taking the first step it can create change, and I think that is what the workshop did, like pointing out those first steps to take." This also resonated for one focus group participant who commented, "It really lit a fire under me, this is something that needs to change, and I think the knowledge through the workshop kind of helped light that fire . . . like, "What can I be doing better? . . . How can I make myself more available? What are the small things that I can do that will have a big impact?"

IMPLICATIONS FOR TRAINING OF PRESERVICE PROFESSIONALS

Strengthening the ability of preservice professionals to offer responsive care is an important objective related to postsecondary education in professional faculties. This project addressed this need through a unique partnership involving MRU and the Centre for Sexuality in Calgary, Alberta. Curriculum grounded in the principles of adult education and transformative learning theory empowered students to feel more comfortable discussing sexuality with diverse client groups and taught them how to better understand the needs of LGBTQ2S+ communities.

The Centre for Sexuality believes that learning about unconscious bias, privilege, and oppression will lead to a more just and inclusive society for the LGBTQ2S+ community. It is difficult to truly measure an intangible like inclusion, as the feeling of inclusion is subjective and ever evolving. In order for inclusive pedagogy to be truly successful, it must be integrated into the course curriculum well beyond this ninety-minute session. Inclusion will ideally continue to be a topic of discussion in the course and will continue to be considered independently as the participants become fully employed health and social service providers. We endeavor to spark a passion and curiosity in participants to continue this conversation and learning well beyond the classroom and to be champions for inclusion as individuals, service providers, and community members.

Beyond student impact, project partners anticipate that findings from this community-engaged study will lead to increased health equity for LGBTQ2S+ clients and will support emerging practitioners to provide effective care and services. Thus, the project will directly impact local service provision and contribute to an emerging national discourse on providing better health and wellness services for LGBTQ2S+ clients.

REFERENCES

Barr, E., Goldfarb, E., Russell, S., Seabert, D., Wallen, M., & Wilson, K. (2014). Improving sexuality education: The development of teacher-preparation standards. *Journal of School Health, 84*(6), 396–414.

Carpenter, S. (2012). Centering Marxist-feminist theory in adult learning. *Adult Education Quarterly, 62*, 19–35. https://doi.org/10.1177/0741713610392767

Dixon-Woods, M., Regan, J., Robertson, N., Young, B., Cordle, C., & Tobin, C. (2002). Teaching and learning about human sexuality in undergraduate medical education. *Medical Education, 36*(5), 432–440.

Glowacki-Duda, M., Jones, D., Flynn, T., Frakenburger, W., Kissick-Kelly, D., Rediger, J., & Smith, K. (2012). A case study of radical adult education and transformative learning through a diverse adult learning workshop. *Journal of Transformative Education, 10*(2), 108–134.

Jarvis, P. (2006). *The lifelong learning and the learning society: Towards a comprehensive theory of human learning* (vol. 1). Routledge.

Jeyasingham, D. (2008). Knowledge ignorance and the construction of sexuality in social work education. *Social Work Education, 27*(2), 138–151.

MacKeracher, D. (2004). *Making sense of adult learning* (2nd ed.). University of Toronto Press.

McNair, R. P., & Hegarty, K. (2010). Guidelines for the primary care of lesbian, gay, and bisexual people: A systematic review. *Annals of Family Medicine, 8*(6), 533–541.

Mezirow, J. (2003). Transformative learning as discourse. *Journal of Transformative Education, 1*(1), 58–63.

Mezirow, J. (2009). Transformative learning theory. In J. Mezirow & E. W. Taylor (Eds.), *Transformative learning in practice: Insights from community, workplace, and higher education* (pp. 18–31). Jossey-Bass

Mezirow, J. (2012). Learning to think like an adult: Core concepts of transformation theory. In E. W. Taylor & P. Cranton (Eds.), *The handbook of transformative learning: Theory, research, and practice* (1st ed., pp. 73–95). Jossey-Bass.

Mullaly, B., & West, J. (2017). *Challenging oppression and confronting privilege* (3rd ed.). Oxford University Press.

Nemec, P. B. (2012). Transformative learning. *Psychiatric Rehabilitation Journal, 35*(6), 478–479. https://doi.org/10.1037/h0094585

Shindel, A., & Parish, S. (2013). Sexuality education in North American medical schools: Current status and future directions. *Society for Sexual Medicine, 10*(3), 3–18.

Taylor, E. W., & Snyder, M. J. (2012). A critical review of research on transformative learning theory, 2006–2010. In E. W. Taylor & P. Cranton (Eds.), *The handbook of transformative learning: Theory, research, and practice* (1st ed., pp. 37–56). Jossey-Bass.

Trisdell, E. (2012). Themes and variations of transformational learning: Interdisciplinary perspectives on forms that transform. In E. W. Taylor & P. Cranton (Eds.), *The handbook of transformative learning: Theory, research, and practice* (1st ed., pp. 21–37). Jossey-Bass.

Trotter, J., Brogatzi, L., Duggan, L., Foster, E., & Levie, J. (2006). Revealing disagreement and discomfort through auto-ethnography and personal narrative: Sexuality in social work education and practice. *Qualitative Social Work, 5*(3), 369–388.

CHAPTER 12
Cultivating Cultural Awareness in the Dental Hygiene Classroom

Beth Monnin and Shawna Staud

Today's dental hygiene curriculum typically consists of various types of modules, including discussions or assignments on cultural competence and diversity that teach basic information about cultures and communication. The information that students truly learn or understand about diversity is primarily assessed during clinical practice through the observation of students' interactions with diverse clientele. Standard 2.15 of the Commission on Dental Accreditation (2019) states that "*The ability to communicate effectively verbally and in written form is basic to the safe and effective provision of oral health services for diverse populations*" (italics in original). This requirement alone provides a fundamental reason to incorporate high-quality cultural diversity training into the dental hygiene curriculum. It is widely accepted knowledge that higher education pedagogies that incorporate experiences, as opposed to or in addition to lectures, provide a better learning experience. As will be described in this chapter, incorporating cultural immersion and role-playing activities has proven to be an effective way to develop more culturally competent dental hygienists.

HISTORY OF TEACHING CULTURE IN THE DENTAL HYGIENE CURRICULUM
Cultural competency is a lifelong process of increasing awareness, knowledge, and skills that involves valuing diversity, learning about cultures, avoiding stereotypes, gaining experience, and engaging with the community. According to the US Department of Health and Human Services (2016), culture can be described as a set of beliefs, values, attitudes, and behaviors that are common within a group. These may be generational, learned patterns of beliefs and behaviors or created in a current environment due to circumstances or actions of people within a group. A culturally competent person is able to respond to different groups with behaviors and attitudes that facilitate proficient treatment and communication. Another important aspect of cultural competency is cultural sensitivity, which involves making an effort to understand the different culture(s) that are encountered. Understanding diverse cultures is the first step in providing optimal patient care in oral healthcare settings. It is not expected that oral healthcare providers

necessarily become fluent in multiple languages to enhance communication, but rather that they become proactive in using tools to enhance communication and understanding of the different communities they serve.

To guide students through the process of becoming more culturally competent individuals, we incorporated activities that helped them progress through the Intercultural Development Continuum (IDI, 2021). This process involves developing a more diverse mindset by going through the steps of denial, polarization, minimization, acceptance, and finally adaptation (IDI, 2021). The first two levels, denial and polarization, are on the monocultural spectrum. Denial consists of uninterest in other cultures and polarization is when the person recognizes differences but does not accept them as normal (IDI, 2021). Minimization is the bridge between monocultural and intercultural mindsets. At this point, the embracing of other belief systems begins by understanding other cultures, which leads to acceptance. Acceptance of other cultures leads to adaptation, which is when behavior changes take place (IDI, 2021). The activities in this course encouraged students to move from the monocultural mindset to the higher levels of acceptance and adaptation (IDI, 2021).

There has been minimal research on the impact of current dental hygiene cultural competency curricula. Flynn and Sarkarati (2018), in a study at the University of Minnesota, demonstrated mixed results about the effectiveness of cultural competency curriculum. Again, this study did not involve cultural immersion or direct contact with other cultures. Most of the current curricula consist of preconstructed modules from external resources. In a literature review conducted by Govere and Govere (2016), several studies were found that assessed the cultural competency of healthcare providers in a hospital setting. The researchers used Boolean phrases of cultural competence, competency, sensitivity, awareness, and training in different search engines to find relevant studies. This search yielded seven relevant studies. Six of the seven relevant studies they discovered proved to be effective training tools. Those tools include: a cultural competence assessment process; standardized patient scenarios; nonverbal communication that included facial expressions and vocal tones; Inventory to Assess the Process of Cultural Competence among Healthcare Professionals; Patient-Reported Physician Cultural Competency (PRPCC) scale; Self-Assessment of Cultural Awareness questionnaire; Spanish proficiency clinical scenarios and questionnaires; and a healthcare provider questionnaire on a cultural competence training module. The training also appeared to have a positive effect on patient satisfaction. Govere and Govere (2016) found that five out of the seven aforementioned studies indicated an increase in patient satisfaction of care after cultural competency training took place. This research indicates the need for a more rigorous assessment of cultural competency training in the dental hygiene curriculum.

Assessment tools are available to measure students' cultural diversity knowledge and skills. Daughtery and Kearney (2017) examined an assessment tool from the US Department of Health and Human Services (HHS) Office of Minority Health (OMH), a Cultural Competency Program for Oral Health Professionals that proved to be effective for students. This government-designed tool contains several modules with situations that involve communication and treatment planning, but it does not involve direct patient contact and assessment. DeWald and Solomon (2009) showed similar results with the Cross-Cultural Adaptability Inventory completed by dental hygiene students. This external tool provided little evidence to indicate a positive assessment of cultural competence in dental hygiene students. These studies utilized question-and-answer systems of measurement to determine cultural competency. Due to the lack of effective assessment, the need for broader interactive measures was recognized.

The dental hygiene program at University of Cincinnati Blue Ash (UCBA) accepts forty-one students into each yearly cohort. Since the inception of selective admission in 2016, approximately 90 percent of those students have graduated with an associate of applied science degree in dental hygiene. Although the demographics of the program fluctuates slightly every year, it is still a predominantly White female group of students. Nationally this is comparable as approximately 82.2 percent of dental hygienists are White (Non-Hispanic) with White (Hispanic) following at 6.64 percent as the second most common race or ethnicity (Deloitte, 2017).

The cultural competency and diversity portion of the curriculum has always been delivered to second-year students during the final, spring semester. The pedagogy has primarily been a two-hour, lecture-based classroom discussion. During the 2018–2019 academic year, delivery of the information started in the fall semester of the second year and was distributed over the final two semesters of the students' dental hygiene education. UCBA dental hygiene students begin to treat patients in the middle of the spring semester of their first year. These appointments are typically friends and family members and the diversity training does not seem to be quite as imperative. We felt that students should start receiving cultural diversity information earlier and repeatedly, so they could apply what was learned into practice while treating community patients of diverse backgrounds.

Although race and ethnicity are predominantly what is thought of when one speaks of diversity, there are many other factors that are involved with cultural competency. We must consider sexual orientation, sex, age, socioeconomic backgrounds, religion, and the so often overlooked healthcare literacy. As we assess needs and develop treatment plans for our patients, all aspects of the person must be considered, which may involve asking personal questions and venturing outside of a personal comfort zone. To be comfortable with diverse populations and delivering culturally competent care, one must first learn to overcome the feeling of being uncomfortable. This can be accomplished by exposing oneself to other cultures and learning to accept differences.

DESCRIPTION OF PEDAGOGY

Currently, the project involves collaboration between two members in the dental hygiene department. Qualitative data consisted of students' journal and reading reflections. Students were asked to journal on projects and experiences, demonstrating any feelings or observations after the activities. Assessment to measure outcomes consisted of a final project presentation and a Likert-scale questionnaire (strongly disagree to strongly agree) to collect quantitative data about behavior changes and learning subsequent to experiencing inclusive pedagogy. An intercultural framework was established to gradually assess the attitudes, knowledge, and skills of diversity and inclusion over the course of two semesters. Students were informed that the activities may be sensitive in nature and feelings of discomfort are normal. The intention was to start with activities familiar to students, such as stereotypes, to get them acquainted with bias and start to raise awareness that discrimination is not just about race, class, and gender. Due to the sensitivity of some of these activities it is was important to not further marginalize underrepresented students. This was accomplished by initially demonstrating that everyone can identify with a unique trait or quality but these are not often easily recognizable.

Several activities were conducted throughout the academic year, as well as a book reading to enhance the cultural experience of the students. Students participated in two activities in the fall semester, starting with student orientation the first week of the semester. The activities were adapted from a *Diversity Activities Resource Guide*, developed by the University of Houston (n.d.). Given that our student population is predominately White, this exercise helps them understand what it feels like to be the target of stereotyping. The first activity was the Target/Non-Target one. This is a stereotype activity where students were asked to self-identify when groups are called out. The facilitator states a "group" that is often stereotyped, such as vegetarians. When students identified with this group, they stood up to indicate their inclusion in this group. The facilitator then read about typical stereotypes related to vegetarians and a discussion occurred about the unfairness and wrongness of these stereotypes. This was completed several times until every student had identified with at least one group. Sensitive areas such as race, religion, and socioeconomic status were intentionally avoided to prevent further marginalization of underrepresented students. To facilitate a positive classroom climate during this activity, the perspectives of individuals are respected by asking students not to speak until the activity is completed. This activity was voluntary, and any student could choose to not participate. The purpose of this activity was for students to understand how it feels (in a safe environment) to be stereotyped by others. At the end the students were asked the question, "How did this make you feel to be singled out?" This activity is a very basic step to acquaint students with the concept of implicit bias and facilitated a reflection on how they could move from a polarizing mindset on the intercultural framework to a more inclusive mindset. These realizations were especially effective for students who are not accustomed to being singled out or marginalized.

The next activity we used to develop students' cultural competency, Lemonheads and Whoppers, developed by the University of Houston, was completed early in the middle of fall semester. During this activity, students indicated groups they associate with by dropping a Lemonhead or a Whopper into cups. One candy represented the agent (with whom they identify—i.e., White female) group and the other candy represented a group outside of the student's culture. The purpose of this activity was for students to understand how many different cultures they do not associate with outside of their own identity. Through this activity they realize "people stick with their own." Both Target/Non-Target and Lemonheads and Whoppers activities relate to how it feels to be stereotyped and the reality of why stereotypes happen. Lemonheads and Whoppers further enhanced students' understanding of implicit bias and raised awareness of how they unconsciously choose groups and associates that are more like them. This implicit bias is often due to demographics and familial upbringings. The activity included a debrief at the end that consisted of asking students to assess their choice of candy, and helped raise students' awareness of how easily differences arise and the importance of examining their monocultural mindset to adopt an intercultural mindset and cross the bridge of minimization toward acceptance.

In an effort to increase students' awareness of the oral health crisis in America, the book *Teeth* by Mary Otto (2017) was lent to every student. This book discusses the oral healthcare system and the problems that arise, primarily in low-income populations, due to the lack of proper oral health. This project included in-class and/or online discussions, discussion board journaling, and reflective writing. Question prompts, such as the following, were used to initiate thought-provoking discussions:

- How do you feel about the initial actions of the emergency room in [a case discussed in the book]?
- As a professional how can you help prevent more of these cases?

These prompts were used for individual journaling and then discussed as a group in the classroom. Allowing students to respond privately to just the professors prompted more in-depth reflection that probably would not have happened in an open classroom discussion. The incorporation of this book provided students with real-life events caused by social class discrimination. The fact that these events really happened heightened the students' awareness of inequalities because it put names to the stories. This book assignment potentially increased students' understanding of disparities in the United States, which would help move them to the acceptance of others as part of the intercultural development continuum (IDC).

In the spring semester, another activity, the Game of Life, developed at the University of Houston, was implemented in the dental hygiene program. In this activity, designed to raise students' awareness of privilege, students were given an identification based on status or cultural group (identified as A, B, C, D, E). Letters were randomly distributed in order to provide all students with equal opportunity to be in each group. Students wore their letters on their shirts so others could understand what group they belonged to without unintentionally marginalizing anyone. Each student was given money and visited different departments (education, housing, banking, employment, judicial). Faculty assisted in this activity and were the moderators of the departments. Students were treated based on letter status and only given a certain amount of money and resources. For instance: Group A was the highest privileged group, treated with a lot of respect and given the most money and resources; in contrast Group E treated in a completely opposite manner. For example, when a student from Group A arrived at the bank to ask for money, they were immediately granted first place in line and all groups under them had to wait until that person was served. As a facilitator it was important to make the A and B groups feel more superior. Often a person in Group E was never served and simply walked away. Even though this was role playing, the students in Groups C–E became very frustrated at the unexplainable priority treatment given to Groups A and B. At the end, a debrief and a reflective writing paper were completed. Reflective papers were incorporated to provide students an outlet to openly express themselves without feeling judged. This reflection allowed them to think through and express feelings about privilege. With better awareness of their own privilege students may move into the adaptation phase of the IDC. Some of the reflection questions included:

- What are common challenges that your group faced?
- What are some behaviors that you noticed?
- What lessons from this activity can be applied to life?

The following comments were taken from students' reflection paper submissions. These comments also came up in a debriefing class discussion. Allowing students to document their feelings in writing helped support a good discussion, as many of their feelings may not have surfaced in an open discussion. One of the students mentioned, "I liked cutting in front of Groups D and E because I was always cut off by A and B." This student's comment suggests this artificial society can illustrate social inequality so students can see it, but they need help in thinking through how to address these social inequities. There was a large group discussion about how each person can be more tolerant of every person whom they encounter. This activity demonstrated to students how so many people are marginalized, which helped strengthen their awareness of this complex, implicitly biased society. One other student commented that this activity simulated the real world and stated, "We cannot change our parents or where we grow up but as we become adults we are given the opportunity to make choices." This activity increased the understanding of social class disparities. For some in the activity who were discriminated against due to their randomly assigned social class, they developed empathy as part of the intercultural framework. The empathy experienced by many demonstrates the adaptation step on the IDC.

For the final experience, the Cultural Dip, each student, as part of a group of two or three students, immersed themselves in a group that was unlike their own. Although students may have had some implicit bias or conscious stereotypes, they were to choose a group that felt safe but different from them. The experience was meant to make students feel slightly uncomfortable but not threatened or unsafe in any way. Such experiences were church services, PRIDE events, health centers, or any other place or event in which the student would be a minority and may feel uncomfortable. Students had two semesters to complete this pivotal project and a final PowerPoint presentation on the experience at the end of spring semester. To become comfortable with people who are not like oneself, it is important to first feel uncomfortable (safe but uneasy). The feeling of discomfort is a powerful tool to help one understand what minorities feel and experience on a daily basis. This immersive activity on the intercultural framework was designed to help support students in becoming more comfortable in a different environment, knowing that groups are just unique and different, not wrong. Most students reached the adaptation phase, which was demonstrated in their presentations along with indications of potential behavioral changes they will make. Furthermore, the project helped students not only understand what it is like to be in the minority of a group but also to experience feelings of being judged and marginalized. The aim of this experience is to encourage students to be more inclusive in their career and practice as dental hygienists.

EVIDENCE OF SUCCESS

To gather an understanding of the effectiveness of these diversity activities, a survey was distributed at the end of the semester. This was a Likert-scale survey that was distributed to all participating students to assess their general opinion of the project. The fifteen-question survey (see "Survey of Student Perceptions of Diversity Activities" on the open access companion site for this book) was completed by a sample size of thirty-four. Students were given an Institutional Review Board (IRB)–approved consent form and participation in the survey was completely optional. Overall the reactions to the experiences were positive and the students seemed to believe that these experiences helped them become better, more culturally aware people

The survey responses were divided into four categories. In the first category, students rated the course activities according to how helpful they were in understanding equity and inclusion (see Figure 12.1). When asked about the activities on the survey, 65 percent of the students agreed or strongly agreed that the book readings provided them with

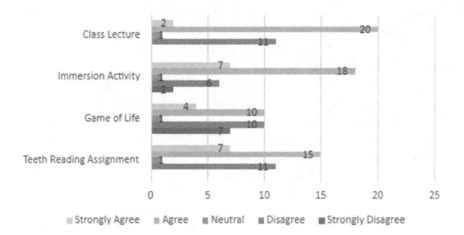

Figure 12.1. Diversity-focused course activities

the largest awareness of diversity and prepared them for a career as a dental hygienist. Sixty-five percent agreed or strongly agreed that the Game of Life activity provided the largest awareness of diversity and prepared them for a career as a dental hygienist. Around 74 percent agreed or strongly agreed that the Cultural Dip (Immersion) activity provided the largest awareness of diversity and prepared them for a career as a dental hygienist. Lastly, 65 percent agreed or strongly agreed that an interactive lecture focused on health literacy and culture provided in the classroom (not discussed in the chapter) increased their awareness of diversity and prepared them for a career as a dental hygienist. It appears that most students agreed or strongly agreed that these activities were a positive influence on their learning.

In the second category, students rated the course activities according to how effective they were in raising awareness related to diversity and inclusion (see Figure 12.2). Students were asked questions about whether they enjoyed the activities and if the activities and experiences altered their attitudes. An overwhelming 97 percent of students believed that because of these diversity activities, they gained a greater understanding and appreciation for people of backgrounds that are not their own. When asked about a change of attitude, 82 percent felt their attitude toward people with other belief systems had changed for the better. Although some students may not have really liked all of the activities, 70 percent agreed or strongly agreed they felt like a more culturally competent person, and 76 percent agreed or strongly agreed that it was a rewarding experience and they are a better person because of it. Seventy-nine percent of the students agreed or strongly agreed that they gained a higher appreciation of diversity, and 76 percent recommended these types of activities in other healthcare and dental hygiene programs.

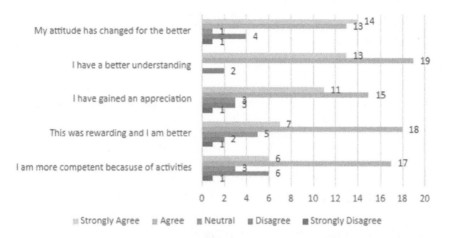

Figure 12.2. Course activities that raised awareness of diversity and inclusion

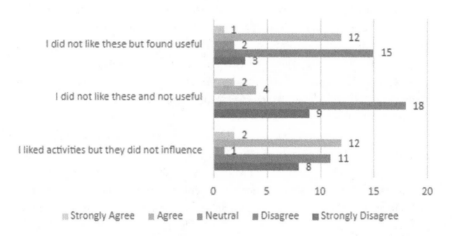

Figure 12.3. Students' perceptions of effectiveness of activities

Lastly, students rated the perceptions of the effectiveness of the activities as they relate to equity in dental hygiene (see Figure 12.3). Only 56 percent liked the activities but felt their attitude was not changed. Eighteen percent neither liked the activities nor found them useful, and 53 percent did not like the activities but found their education was enhanced.

However, 91 percent felt that they better recognized that the value of dental hygiene treatment and other medical treatments vary greatly among cultures, and

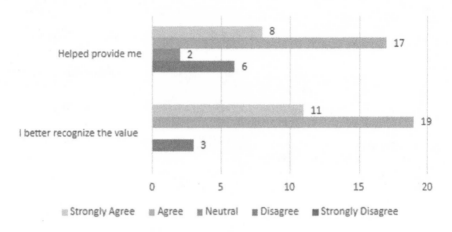

Figure 12.4. Students' perceptions of equity in dental hygiene

76 percent found that the activities helped prepare them to more effectively provide equitable treatment, such as listening to patients' concerns and proving individualized care that coordinated with beliefs, traditions, and resources of patients in the dental hygiene clinic (see Figure 12.4). Examples of equitable individualized care would be listening to patients and treating everyone as a human as well as suggesting or providing treatment that can be free or inexpensive to those who cannot afford dental treatment.

Throughout the semesters, various reflections were assigned relating to the activities. Regarding the Game of Life activity, students that were in the privileged groups recognized the unequal treatment and one student stated, "People were either bragging or complaining about money." A student in the middle-class group related, "I had to wait on Group A and B, so it felt good to make others below me wait." These two statements exemplify how easily power can lead to systemic ways to hold onto power so that individuals from lower groups are not able to advance socially or economically. During this activity, students (especially those in groups C, D, and E) perhaps recognized their attitudes and behaviors about their beliefs and how power is used to maintain existing social structures that marginalize some while privileging others.

The immersion experience, as described previously, seemed to be very successful and impactful as well. One particular student described the feelings of his experience exactly the way it was anticipated. This particular student, Lou (not his real name) attended an all-Black church in a religious, southern US town. Lou, who identifies as a White gay man, said he felt like everyone was staring at him, but were they staring because he was White, gay, or both? He further indicated that he felt very uncomfortable and that anxiety increased as the service started. He went on to state, "I finally felt a little more at ease and realized no one was glaring at me." He indicated that he did not feel uncomfortable because of his race but because of his sexuality: "Even though no one knew me, I understood that this religion viewed homosexuality as a sin." He said, "It was a humbling experience to submerge myself into a culture that I am not a part of." To become comfortable with others and recognize their humanity, students must first feel uncomfortable. This experience provided that level of emotional discomfort for this student when he immersed himself into a group in which he initially felt uncomfortable. These feelings of discomfort can be rectified by immersing oneself into new experiences. These new experiences may lead to better understanding and acceptance of cultures and social classes unlike their own.

FUTURE DIRECTION

Due to the predominantly positive feedback on the survey, we plan to continue with the book readings and activities. A pretest and posttest will be completed with the next cohort of students, which will provide statistical evidence of the success of the curriculum changes.

In addition to the final presentation of immersion experiences to their classmates, the goal is to integrate the presentation of student projects to the community, perhaps beginning with the local dental hygiene association. Currently these activities are introduced only to the second-year dental hygiene students with the hope to incorporate activities into the first-year dental hygiene curriculum as well to capture their opinions, growth, and changes as they progress through the program and expand their care to a variety of patients. We believe the continuous implementation of immersion and role-playing activities in college curricula are critical to the cultural acceptance and awareness of future healthcare providers.

REFERENCES

Commission on Dental Accreditation. (2019). *Accreditation standards for dental hygiene education programs.* https://www.ada.org/~/media/CODA/Files/dental_hygiene_standards.pdf?la=en

Daughtery, H. N., & Kearney, R. C. (2017). Measuring the impact of cultural competency training for dental hygiene students. *Journal of Dental Hygiene, 91*(5), 48–54. http://jdh.adha.org/content/91/5/48/

Deloitte. (2017). *Dental hygienists: Diversity.* https://datausa.io/profile/soc/dental-hygienists#:~:text=Demographic%20information%20on%20Dental%20hygienists,White%20(Non%2DHispanic)

DeWald, J. P., & Solomon, E. S. (2009). Use of cross-cultural adaptability inventory to measure competence in a dental hygiene program. *Journal of Dental Hygiene, 83*(3), 106–110. http://jdh.adha.org/content/83/3/106

Flynn, P., & Sarkarati, N. (2018). Improving evaluation of dental hygiene students' cultural competence with a mixed-methods approach. *Journal of Dental Education, 82*(2), 103–111.

Govere, L., & Govere, E. M. (2016). How effective is cultural competence training of healthcare providers on improving patient satisfaction of minority groups? *Sigma Global Nursing Excellence.* https://sigmapubs. onlinelibrary.wiley.com/doi/full/10.1111/wvn.12176

Intercultural Development Inventory (IDI). (2021). Intercultural development continuum. https://idiinventory .com/generalinformation/the-intercultural-development-continuum-idc/

Ocegueda, D. R., Van Ness, C. J., Hanson, C. L., & Holt, L. A. (2016). Cultural competency in dental hygiene curricula. *Journal of Dental Hygiene, 90*(1), supplement.

Otto, M. (2017). *Teeth: The story of beauty, inequality, and the struggle for oral health in America.* New Press.

Center for Diversity and Inclusion. (2019). *University of Houston.* https://www.uh.edu/cdi/diversity_education /resources/_files/_activities/diversity-activities-resource-guide.pdf

US Department of Health and Human Services. Office of Minority Health. (2016). *Cultural competency program for oral health professionals.* https://oralhealth.thinkculturalhealth.hhs.gov/Content/Course1 /Module1/Module1_1_2.asp

CHAPTER 13

Teaching the Concepts of Diversity and Inclusion in Business Classes

Lizzie Ngwenya-Scoburgh and Patrice Gillespie

As business professionals who transitioned into teaching, we understand the importance of helping students develop the cultural competence they will need for success in their professional lives. Cultural competence is about our will and actions to create understanding between people, to be respectful and open to different cultural perspectives, to strengthen cultural security, and to work toward equality in opportunity. Relationship-building is fundamental to cultural competence, calling upon the knowledge of a wide range of community members and resources to lay a foundation of understanding and acceptance (Livingstone, 2020, para. 1). Wang (2003) underlined the importance of intercultural competence in both global and domestic business contexts. As college business faculty, we searched for activities for business students to explore cultural competency that would be right for introductory business classes like Introduction to Business or Fundamentals of Management. We found the Bag of Inclusion, Diversity, and Empathy (Shaw, 2016) and the BARNGA (University of Michigan, 2017) game activities helpful in developing our students' cultural competency.

The activities described in this chapter were designed to address the needs of a suburban regional campus of the University of Cincinnati Blue Ash (UCBA). UCBA is an open access institution providing opportunities for a wide-ranging student population and addressing demands of the UCBA population for first-year college business courses like Introduction to Business, Survey of Business, or Fundamentals of Management. (See chapter 4 of this volume for more details about student demographics.) Business educators have continuously tried to find practical teaching approaches for the skills and operations of the business industry. The activities we introduce in this chapter provide a framework for delivering real-world experiences and include awareness of diversity issues in terms of gender, socioeconomic status, various learning styles, and the needs of English language learners.

In addition to promoting inclusion, the activities address curriculum standards and departmental objectives and complement the learning objectives of business communication. Specifically, cultural competence is essential in business where parties from diverse backgrounds often need to communicate to achieve their purpose. These activities also support the learning objectives for decision-making, problem-solving, and change management. The Business and Economics Department aspires to prepare students "for a professional career with a professional certificate or associate degree, pursue further study in our Bachelor of Applied and Technical Studies program, or transfer to the UC Lindner College of Business or other business/economics programs at most colleges." We believe by incorporating cultural competency activities in these introductory courses, students will be better prepared for more in-depth lessons in future business courses, and better prepared for a diverse workplace.

Cultural competence is developed over time and includes experience, guidance, self-awareness, and training, so business courses must address it in first-year classes. Teaching cultural competency can help all students become respectful of the cultures and people that they will interact with in and out of the educational setting (Lambert, 2012). Embracing cultural competency means appreciating the differences in individuals from a variety of cultural and ethnic groups within an organization (Hammer, Bennett, & Wiseman, 2003). Raising students' awareness of diverse cultural and ethnic groups' ways of knowing and operating is a crucial first step in helping them appreciate the differences they will meet in the business world.

Preparing our students for their professional life can begin in the educational culture that celebrates cultural diversity in the classroom so that all students feel like they belong. Students must feel valued, respected, and unafraid to bring their backgrounds and perspectives to light. Bennett (1993) proposed a framework for conceptualizing dimensions of intercultural competence. His developmental model of intercultural sensitivity (DMIS) was created as a basic outline to explain the reactions that people have to cultural differences. The stages of DMIS are on a continuum that ranges from ethnocentric to highly ethno relative (Cushner, McClelland, & Safford, 2015).

The DMIS was based on the theory that cultural awareness is accompanied by improved cognitive sophistication (Cushner, McClelland, & Safford, 2015). This model, which consists of six different stages, is applicable for both children and adults. These stages are denial, defense, minimization, acceptance, adaptation, and integration (Cushner, McClelland, & Safford, 2015). Each stage describes a cognitive structure that is communicated through attitudes and behaviors (Bennett, 1993). There are three ethnocentric orientations (denial, defense, minimization) and three ethno relative orientations (acceptance, adaptation, integration). The three ethno relative orientations are needed for cultural competence. Instructors can use the DMIS model to facilitate learning by recognizing a student's cognitive stage and helping the student progress into the next stage.

The following two activities demonstrate the practical use of the DMIS model. We strive to move the student along the DMIS continuum throughout the semester, using real-world examples to illustrate the denial-to-integration stages of cultural competence development in a safe environment for exploration and experience. The DMIS model facilitates easy assessment of the individual's cultural competence. As the activities progress, the students move from denying their biases to becoming defensive and even minimizing their biases. The students' journal assignments reveal development from acceptance to adaptation, which is the integration stage of cultural competency.

These activities can be incorporated in or adapted to align with the faculty's existing teaching methods. We have used these activities in both entry-level and upper-level management courses. The key is to incorporate them at the beginning of the course to create a sense of community and understanding. Teachers should repeat the activities mid-semester to assess whether a climate of inclusiveness persists. An inclusive classroom is one that is a safe and comfortable environment for student learning. An inclusive climate in the real world can also help employees find common ground, have open communication about diversity and inclusion, learn how to recognize and correct stereotypes, and work with and celebrate differences. Students demonstrate cultural competency when they are cultivated, supported, and reinforced.

The activities we use illustrate how employees can work inclusively in a diverse workforce even when faced with challenges. These efforts are proving to be a necessity as business environments become increasingly diverse with more and more business leaders seeing that cultural competency is crucial for business success. The demand for skilled workers is higher than ever, but availability is in short supply. Businesses need to cast their hiring net wide. A talent shortage exists, and management is always looking for the right people to run and grow businesses (Hammer, Bennett, & Wiseman 2003). The US Chamber of Commerce Foundation (2020) found that 74 percent of hiring managers agree that there is a skills gap in the current labor market, with 48 percent saying that candidates lack the skills needed to fill open jobs. According to Rock and Grant (2016), increasing the level of female employment could help raise Gross Domestic Product (GDP) by 5 percent. Rock and Grant's (2016) work also shows that 86 percent of females and 74 percent of male Millennials consider policies on diversity, equality, and inclusion when choosing employment. Cultural competency helps employees work and learn from each other. Cultural competency has the potential to alter behavior that leads to improved and more accurate group thinking.

The question is, how do we connect the classroom to future career opportunities for our business students? This is an important question to address given that the world is infinitely more complex and diverse than the microcosmic environment that the student inhabits. It can be a daunting task. For this reason, it is necessary to raise awareness of cultural diversity and teach cultural competence skills, so students will find success in their careers.

HOW TO CREATE CULTURAL COMPETENCY IN THE BUSINESS CLASSROOM

Educators can promote cultural competency over time by doing some self-reflective work on their own cultural competency while being aware of the cultures represented in their classrooms. Suggestions for inclusive educator behavior include some of the following actions:

- Being patient and understanding with beliefs
- Boosting your cultural competence by attending conferences, taking courses, or reading current material on cultural issues
- Encouraging discussion, not debate
- Facilitating religious practices and needs
- Giving attention to the nuances of each culture
- Implementing the Platinum Rule that says, "Treat others the way they want to be treated"
- Responding to students with respect, tolerance, and compassion
- Working on getting every name right by writing down the pronunciations and practicing if necessary

Furthermore, for our introductory business courses, it was important for us not only to use activities for business students to explore and practice cultural competency but also to make sure the course objectives presented below were addressed:

- Explore the communication process and how it affects you individually as well as its impact on the organization
- Distinguish between decision making and problem solving as well as the various approaches to decision making
- Explain the value and need for diversity in the workplace
- Examine the significant barriers to managing change

The two activities we chose to help students develop cultural competence were Bag of Inclusion, Diversity, and Empathy and the BARNGA game. Both of these activities teach students how to identify and challenge their cultural assumptions. The activities place students in scenarios where their attitudes, skills, and knowledge are consistently challenged. They are encouraged to build bridges in order to successfully complete the tasks at hand. These activities occur within the context of the course objectives.

ACTIVITY #1: INDIVIDUAL LEVEL OF CULTURAL COMPETENCY

Cultural competency requires more than becoming culturally aware or practicing tolerance. Rather, it is the ability to "identify and challenge one's own cultural assumptions, values, and beliefs, and to make a commitment to communicating at the cultural interface" (Livingstone, 2020, para. 4). Cultural competence is not static, and the level of cultural competence changes in response to new situations, experiences, and relationships. The three elements of cultural competence, attitudes, skills, and knowledge, are introduced through the Bag of Inclusion, Diversity, and Empathy and BARNGA game.

Bag of Inclusion, Diversity, and Empathy (Shaw, 2016) can teach empathy and acceptance of personal challenges. It is one of the activities that Shaw uses to help students recognize that "we all have different strengths and weaknesses, but this fact does not decrease our value as people" (para. 2). The purpose of this activity is to get the participants to realize strengths and weaknesses are contextual. All groups seem to be given the same instructions to complete the activity, but because of the differences in the materials given, some groups experience more challenges than others in completing the task.

For this activity, we split the students into five groups (Shaw uses six, but five works better in our classroom), then we give each group a box of materials and say that the supplies are all the same. However, unknown to the students, the supplies are not the same. Only one group will receive all the materials and instructions needed to successfully complete the activity. Students are told that it is a simple assignment and can be completed in about a minute. Next, teachers tell students that they are going to have a contest to see which group can finish first. The students believe the setup is fair until they see the limitations imposed on the different groups through the unequal distribution of needed supplies to complete the activity. The team with all the supplies usually finishes first. To emphasize the unfairness of the situation, instructors ask for the class to give that group an enthusiastic round of applause. After just a few minutes, the class will begin to talk about how "unfair" this activity was and how it does not make the "winning" team necessarily smarter.

DISCUSSION QUESTIONS

To help students reflect on how this activity connects to the goal of recognizing how a person's strengths and weaknesses do not define them, we developed discussion questions and a reflective writing assignment to focus students' attention on how resources affect performance. The discussion questions have the greatest impact when they are conducted right after the activity. If time allows, we present the discussion questions, which are answered with the groups. After the groups have compiled their answers, there is a large group discussion that considers the following questions:

1. For those who did not have an advantage, why did you not ask those who had a lead for help?

2. For those who won or who had an advantage, why did you not help those who did not have the same benefits?

3. How does this activity relate to people who have limitations?

4. How has this activity influenced you going forward?

5. Was the winning group the best? Why or why not?

6. What issues came up for you during the activity?

Students have responded with various observations. The following are typical student responses raised during the discussion:

- "I thought it was enough to be tolerant, but as we went through the exercise, I noticed I was impatient that all the groups were dumb and couldn't figure it out. Then I discovered there may be reasons for it."

- "We need to open up to understand others. I thought I was, but now I know I wasn't."

- "Language is important. I think I might take Sign Language to help deaf people communicate."

- "I have always liked having different people around me. I think that will help me in business."

CLOSING COMMENTS TO THE CLASS

After the discussion, instructors need to help students understand the connection of the activity to the business environment students will enter upon graduation. Instructors should note that organizations and workplaces come in many assorted sizes and have employees of many different backgrounds and ability levels. People in business have an enormous task ahead to honor others' identities, affirm others' successes, and be more mindful and inclusive moving forward.

REFLECTION JOURNAL ASSIGNMENT

As an after-class assignment, students write journal entries with their thoughts about what they have learned from this activity. Using their ideas from the discussion, instructors ask them to expand upon their thoughts and feelings. This activity has made a significant impact on the culture of our classrooms—we have seen students become more accepting of each other.

ACTIVITY #2: LEARNING TO COMMUNICATE EFFECTIVELY ACROSS CULTURAL GROUPS

As we stated earlier, cultural competency requires more than becoming culturally aware or practicing tolerance. It also requires assessing your own cultural viewpoints and biases. Individuals typically tend to make many assumptions about other groups based on their own biases. This activity creates a platform for students to assess and communicate their own cultural viewpoints and biases as they integrate into a group. Therefore, this activity can be good for developing cultural competence among students who are transitioning to the university with new norms and rules that are different from what they are used to. The activity can be a lesson for business students to help them realize that organizational cultures have their own rules that may not be initially apparent. Further, the activity can demonstrate to students the adaptability needed to overcome their biases. Through the activity, students learn that they need to develop better communication processes in order to build an inclusive environment.

The BARNGA activity supports the course learning objectives in two ways. First, the activity illustrates the importance of the communication process among individuals for problem solving and decision making. Secondly, the course objective of managing change in environments where possible cultural barriers may exist in work teams is also addressed. This activity is a card game called BARNGA, named for a West African town. The University of Michigan (2017) Inclusive Teaching Initiative defines BARNGA as a simulation game that encourages participants to critically consider normative assumptions and their own cultural expectations. Goldstein (2016) asserted that BARNGA can initiate the critical analysis of structural discrimination as well as empathy for those who struggle with it. The game challenges participants to develop coping behaviors and practices to help them succeed (win) in an environment where the rules keep changing but the participants are unaware that there are different specific rules (cultural expectations or norms) required at each table (diverse workforce) in order to succeed. The intricacies of this simulation can be used to introduce intercultural communication.

The only slight modification to the simulation we suggest from the original BARNGA game is the use of only three sets of tournament games in order to keep the tournament moving faster as students move from one table to the next. This allows the tournament to be completed in a shorter class session. The original card game has about ten different rules, which can be a little challenging for some students and time consuming to explain in one class period. The modification that we have incorporated specifically uses standard card decks as suggested by McNeely (2009) that can be purchased from any store versus the original BARNGA cards. Using standard cards does not alter the objective of teaching cultural competency. However, it reduces the frustration of trying to learn too many rules before engaging as a group and keeps the tournament moving faster as winners keep their momentum. The modification of using common household cards also gives students a sense of familiarity and initial equity as teams are instructed to shuffle the card deck provided and distribute an equal number of cards to each player—very similar to the beginning of many common card games.

DISCUSSION QUESTIONS

Using these discussion questions after the game can help students better understand how new norms and rules can be confusing when they are first encountered, especially when some individuals are deliberately excluded or not privy to the rules of the game.

1. What was going through your mind when . . .
   ■ the card game was introduced?
   ■ the card game first began?
   ■ the rules were taken away?
   ■ you had to move or did not have a chance to move?
   ■ playing with those from another table?

2. Did what you were thinking and feeling change during play?

3. What were your greatest successes and frustrations?

REFLECTION

Students write a reflection on their perspective of the game interaction—addressing these areas:

■ What happened during the game/tournament and how did you feel during this process?

■ What does the game suggest about what to do when you are in a similar situation in the real world? When you feel excluded? When you feel included and successful?

■ How does this game focus your attention on the hidden aspects of culture?

The common student responses suggest that they all initially assumed each table was playing the same game until they had moved to at least two other tables. During the game, individuals are prohibited from verbally communicating and from helping each other with the expected rules at each table (the constant change and limitation of cultural competency components), yet expected to function as an effective team (to win the game). The winners were initially happy that they had won until they realized that there were no losers at the second table. This was very discouraging and frustrating for them. Some students indicated that they felt neglected, while some felt like other team members were trying to help them, but the rules restricted how much they could help each other. The students that kept winning felt empowered because they thought they figured out early in the tournament that the team rules were all different. They said that the lack of verbal communication limited assistance in the completion of their task.

The activity helped them achieve the course objective: the importance of the communication process among individuals for problem solving and decision making. Eventually their reflections do help them realize that the premise of the activity is to teach them that not all organizational cultures are the same nor should employees assume that new or existing departments have the same culture. This activity supports the course objective of understanding business communication processes by encouraging students to explore potential barriers to managing change in environments where such barriers may exist.

THE DEBRIEF

This simulation helps students realize that when groups begin a task knowing the rules and with good communication, the process moves smoothly. However, team members who are not familiar with the rules are more likely to fail because they were not equipped with the rules of the game, so they did not begin with the same level of knowledge as the other team members. As the students keep changing teams, some eventually realize that each table has its own set of rules (this could be the assumed organizational culture). In cultural competency, we call this a set of behaviors, attitudes, and practices that equip individuals with the knowledge for working with others.

The point of the game is to help students make the connection that if individuals have biases, limited communication, and limited knowledge about the behaviors and expectations of others, the work environment will not be productive. Organizations need to create equitable structures and equip employees with knowledge that supports a productive work environment.

CONCLUSION

After using these simulations for the past few years, students have articulated an awareness of acceptance and incorporation of diversity. They developed a knowledge of how their own preconceived ideas are limiting. However, when they learn to include others, they realize that they can attain the team's goals more effectively and efficiently. This realization has the potential to transfer to an organizational environment where diverse teams have shown increased productivity (Vaccaro, 2014). We have observed this feedback through the reflection exercises after each activity. Students have verbally shared how connected they felt to others in the class as the semester progressed. They shared how group work has become less stressful as they increase their understanding of their differences. They have learned to view their differences as opportunities, not as hindrances, which has made them more aware of the need for cultural competence in business.

These activities have also helped us achieve core business course objectives. One cannot assume that organizational cultures are the same nor that departmental rules and cultures are the same. These activities support team-building concepts, as the work-teams need to be more open and inclusive in order to accomplish the organizational goals. The activities also help students recognize and analyze the differences and similarities between cultures. The different cultures in these exercises are represented by the different rules for each game. The deliberate challenge of limited resources and knowledge to work effectively to accomplish their tasks provides a safe environment to practice cultural competency. The awareness gained through the activities can be applied to the organizational rules of businesses throughout the world. Ultimately, these activities accomplish the course objectives of teaching students how to work on diverse, multicultural teams and encourages willingness to learn more about themselves and their own biases.

REFERENCES

Bennett, M. J. (1993). Towards ethnorelativism: A developmental model of intercultural sensitivity. In R. M. Paige (Ed.), *Education for the intercultural experience* (pp. 21–71). Intercultural Press.

Berardo, K. (2012) *Building cultural competence: Innovative activities and models.* Stylus Publishing.

Cushner, K., McClelland, A., & Safford, P. (2015). *Human diversity in education: An intercultural approach* (8th ed.). McGraw-Hill.

Gabriel, K. (2018). Five ways to promote a more inclusive classroom. *Faculty Focus.* https://www.facultyfocus .com/articles/teaching-and-learning/five-ways-to-promote-a-more-inclusive-classroom/

Goldstein, D. S. (2016). Using the BARNGA card game simulation to develop cross-cultural thinking and empathy. In F. Tuitt, C. Haynes, & S. Stewart (Eds.), *Race, equity, and the learning environment: The global relevance of critical pedagogies in higher education.* (pp. 83–95). Stylus Publishing.

Hammer, M. R., Bennett, M. J., and Wiseman, R. (2003). Measuring intercultural sensitivity: The intercultural development inventory. *International Journal of Intercultural Relations, 27*(4), 421–443.

Lambert, J. (2012). *The diversity training activity book: 50 activities for promoting communication and understanding.* American Management Association Publishing.

Livingstone, R. (2020). *What does it mean to be culturally competent?* Western Centre for Research & Education on Violence against Women and Children. http://makeitourbusiness.ca/blog/what-does-it -mean-be-culturally-competent

McNeely, S. (2009). *Ultimate book of card games: The comprehensive guide to more than 350 games.* Chronicle Books.

Mikhaylov, N. (2016). Curiosity and its role in cross-cultural knowledge creation. *International Journal of Emotional Education, 8*(1).

Rock, D., & Grant, H. (2016, November 4). Why diverse teams are smarter. *Harvard Business Review.* https:// hbr.org/2016/11/why-diverse-teams-are-smarter

Shaw, S. (2016, October 8). Student activities to promote diversity, inclusion, and empathy. *Getting Smart.* https://www.gettingsmart.com/2016/10/student-activities-to-promote-diversity-inclusion-and-empathy/

University of Michigan. Inclusive Teaching Initiative. (2017). BARNGA overview and framing material. https://sites.lsa.umich.edu/inclusive-teaching/wp-content/uploads/sites/355/2017/04/BARNGA-framing -and-notes.pdf/

US Chamber of Commerce Foundation. (2020, February). Hiring in the modern talent marketplace. https:// www.uschamberfoundation.org/reports/hiring-modern-talent-marketplace

Vaccaro, A. (2014, March 25). Why diverse teams create better work. *Inc.* https://www.inc.com/adam-vaccaro /diversity-and-performance.html

Wang, J. (2003). Moving towards ethnorelativism: A framework for measuring and meeting students' needs in cross-cultural business and technical communication. *Journal of Technical Writing and Communication, 43*(2), 201–218.

REFLECTION ON
Inclusive Professional Practice

In this section, the authors are motivated to address students' cultural competence because it is essential in the development of their professional skills. Medical and business professionals must be prepared to work in diverse environments, which requires them to learn to interact with others in culturally appropriate ways. The authors' starting point is introducing students to the concept of cultural differences. They raise students' awareness through experiential activities that place students in a simulated marginalized position. For many of the activities in Part V, the simulated experience makes students' values and ways of thinking visible, so they can question them. Critical reflection is essential to move students from a monocultural mindset to an intercultural mindset needed in their professional lives.

PRACTITIONER BEHAVIORS

- Raising students' awareness of cultural differences can bring up strong emotions. How can educators anticipate student resistance?

- How is diversity present in your profession? How do you address inclusivity directly?

- Does your profession have guidelines to recognize and value diversity? How can you use those values to inform your course outcomes, activities, and assignments?

PEDAGOGY

- How does your teaching style reflect culturally appropriate behaviors used by professionals in your field?

- How do you raise students' awareness of social injustice in your field while also protecting the students in your class who may have experienced the injustices you are teaching about?

- How often do you modify your teaching in response to current research on inclusive pedagogy in your discipline?

CURRICULUM

- How can your course materials such as lectures, textbook, and activities reflect the diversity of your profession?

- How do you critically evaluate and revise your curriculum to promote diversity, inclusion, and engagement in your profession? How often do you involve students in evaluating your curriculum?

ASSESSMENT

- How do your assessment processes evaluate students' ability to authentically and meaningfully address equity and diversity in their profession?

PART VI
Inclusive Assessment

As faculty adopt inclusive teaching strategies, Tracie Addy, Derek Dube, and Khadijah Mitchell raise important concerns about challenges faculty face in trying to assess the impact of inclusive teaching. Assessing the efficacy of inclusive teaching practices is imperative to determine whether such practices have the desired impact, the extent of the impact, and identify implementation gaps. The authors emphasize the importance of identify disciplinary challenges and pedagogical goals for equity and inclusion. They assert that any meaningful assessment needs to understand the scope of the project, list expected outcomes, gather data, identify data sources, and develop an assessment plan. They offer examples of assessment projects across disciplines to demonstrate how to design and implement assessment of inclusive teaching practices. They propose an assessment framework to measure the impact of inclusive pedagogy.

Deyu Hu and Michele Deramo developed a teaching rubric to maintain the quality of design, development, delivery, evaluation, and improvement of inclusive teaching in higher education. The authors explain some of the specific standards of their proposed rubric to show how the standards can be adopted for use across disciplines to measure inclusive practices. They suggest educators can use the rubric as a self-check guide to determine if they have met a specific standard or not and what specific actions are needed to reach the standard. The rubric serves as a guide to measure quality of inclusive pedagogy and to identify actions needed to maintain quality.

CHAPTER 14

Measuring the Impact of Pedagogical Efforts for Equity and Inclusion

Tracie Addy, Derek Dube, and Khadijah A. Mitchell

A major goal of this chapter is to provide a practical framework for measuring the impacts of pedagogical efforts for equity and inclusion. While a variety of general resources on assessment exist, few provide specific guidance in this area (Kuh et al., 2015; Montenegro & Jankowski, 2017; National Institute for Learning Outcomes Assessment, 2019). Both instructors recently adopting inclusive pedagogy and experienced implementers can benefit from this chapter content regardless of discipline, class size, type of course, and institutional context. Further, principles are broad enough to apply to graduate and professional school courses and online learning. Additionally, we describe how measuring impacts need not rely solely on quantitative data. Faculty members can also gather qualitative data through focus groups, interviews, student work, and other means.

Our personal interactions and professional development experiences with instructors who described various obstacles to assessing the impacts of their efforts inspired many of the contextual elements of this chapter. Challenges we have heard include, generally, not having the tools or expertise to measure impact, difficulty with defining the scope of the assessment project, uncertainty as to whether to assess impact from the students' or faculty member's perspective, and concern that impacts will be able to be measured only many years later. Empirical data captured from our Institutional Review Board–approved investigation of twelve active implementers of inclusive pedagogy from diverse disciplines who previously underwent professional development on inclusive teaching highlights the challenges that faculty can face with measuring impact. These instructors from a doctoral-granting university reported implementing a variety of inclusive teaching approaches such as: using students' pronouns, reflecting on personal biases, using active learning methods including small groups, assigning groups rather than allowing student choice, including course content from individuals of diverse backgrounds, getting to know students, requiring student office hour visits, and others.

While the faculty implementers were able to identify the types of inclusive teaching methods they used to support their diverse learners, and list several offices on campus that supported their efforts, they were unable to describe any measurable impacts of their inclusion efforts. Instead, their responses either speculated upon what could happen if their efforts were successful, or why it was important to measure impact. Comments included: "Improved vocabulary among faculty and staff for discussing the topic. Impact on student performance in the classroom," "Will benefit all or most students . . . we will be a better school," "This would create a positive and inclusive environment of a group of students/faculty that bring many different strengths," and "The institution is becoming more inclusive and diverse." In other responses, the faculty expressed uncertainty about or a lack of impact: "Not sure" and "Haven't seen it yet."

Further, while the institution provided support for their inclusive teaching efforts, implementers reported that their departments in general did not measure the efficacy of their approaches (mean = 2.08 out of 6 on a Likert scale from strongly disagree to strongly agree; n = 12). Such a lack of contextual information is, arguably, not unique to faculty at this institution.

RATIONALE FOR MEASURING IMPACTS

There is a need for more resources to help faculty and departments measure the impact of their efforts for equity and inclusion. Assessing the efficacy of inclusive pedagogy is also integral given that the demographics of students attending colleges and universities are continually changing, and supporting diverse learners is of critical importance. While in 1990, based on fall enrollments at degree-granting postsecondary institutions, only 21.1 percent of students were non-White, in 2000 the percentage increased to 29.2 percent, and by 2016 the percentage of non-White students was 43.1 percent (Snyder, deBray, & Dillow, 2019). A 2018 survey administered by the American College Health Association found that 18.1 percent of undergraduates identified with a sexual orientation other than "heterosexual," increasing from 6.6 percent in 2008, and 3.1 percent identified their gender as "nonbinary," an increase from 0.2 percent in 2008 (then listed as "transgender") (American College Health Association, 2008; 2018). From 1975 to 2016, the share of international students enrolled in US colleges increased from around 1.5 percent to over 5 percent (IIE, 2018). Further, as of 2011–12, approximately 33 percent of US college students identified as "first-generation students" (Skomsvold, 2014), and in 2017–18, 32 percent of all US college students received Pell Grants, displaying exceptional financial need (Baum et al., 2018). These trends highlight some of the many ways the college classroom is becoming more diverse.

As previous chapters in this book showcase, it is possible to design student-centered classrooms with a focus on equity and inclusion across various disciplines and class structures. Although there is some evidence that doing so can positively impact the achievement of diverse learners (Eddy & Hogan, 2014), assessing the efficacy of a *particular* educational activity, course, or program designed with the goals of equity and inclusion is vital for several reasons. Assessing impact can reassure the instructor, department, or program that their strategies are producing the intended outcomes. Such data inform future plans. When the efficacy of the pedagogical practice is supported by empirical data, the faculty member can share such evidence with students and provide a rationale for using the approach. Further, many institutions evaluate teaching efficacy in their contract renewals and reviews for promotion and tenure and having data that highlights the impact of the faculty's teaching practice can be valuable. At a broader level, such assessments can provide knowledge as to whether progress is being made toward the strategic goals of departments, schools, and institutions in supporting diverse learners (McConnell & Doolittle, 2012).

Of note is that the assessment initiatives described in this chapter have overlap with, but are distinct from scholarship of teaching and learning (SoTL) projects (McKinney, 2006; 2015). SoTL projects are typically considered research and are subject to a variety of procedures governed by institutional internal review boards. A primary aim of SoTL is to disseminate generalizable findings to outside scholarly audiences through scholarly journals, books, and other outlets. Our assessment projects are typically used to inform local efforts, in this case, curriculum and instruction, but are not necessarily designed to be shared on a broad scale to inform the field. Additionally, peer review and having a basis in prior published research are typically not components of assessment but are key components of SoTL. Findings from assessment projects, however, may inform SoTL projects that are later published (Dickson & Treml, 2013).

FRAMEWORK FOR ASSESSING IMPACTS

This section describes a framework for assessing the impacts of pedagogical efforts for equity and inclusion to equip faculty with a tool for measuring impact. Components are described in a stepwise fashion, but the usage of the tool need not be strictly linear to reach the desired outcomes. Centers for teaching and learning may be able to support faculty with using this framework, by helping instructors consider the data they can collect on their students (Sathy & Hogan, 2019). Two resources, "Framework for Measuring Impact" and "Sample Available Tools for Assessing Inclusive Teaching Efforts," are available on the open access companion site for this book.

IDENTIFY DISCIPLINARY CHALLENGES AND PEDAGOGICAL GOALS FOR EQUITY AND INCLUSION

Disciplines may have existing challenges around diversity and inclusion that can inform choices for measuring impact. For example, in STEM fields, women and minorities continue to be underrepresented in their educational attainment and employment (National Science Foundation, 2017). Within humanities disciplines such as classics, groups historically marginalized are sparse (Pettit, 2019). Women are overrepresented in some health professions such as nursing, resulting in the underrepresentation of males

(National Council of State Boards of Nursing, 2017). These are just some of the many inclusion challenges faced by disciplines.

At a basic level, instructors can identify existing disciplinary equity and inclusion challenges in their fields by supplementing their individual observations with the literature. On a more advanced level, instructors may solicit student feedback on issues of inclusion and use this information to frame their teaching efforts. After considering disciplinary concerns, instructors next list their pedagogical goals. For example, an economics instructor who consistently observes a low percentage of female students enrolled in a course might list the pedagogical goal of designing the course to be more relevant to women. The instructor may revise the title and description of the course and integrate examples that highlight the positive contributions of females to the field. Given the high numbers of males in the field of economics compared to females in leadership positions, this pedagogical goal also aligns with disciplinary inclusion challenges (Bayer & Rouse, 2016). As another example, a history instructor may observe that some students are quieter in a seminar course, and thus have as a pedagogical goal to offer alternate modes of participation.

CHOOSE AN APPROPRIATE SCOPE FOR THE PROJECT

All assessment projects should have an appropriate scope. For instance, instructors may desire to measure the impact of a specific class assignment, activity, or small-scale course change; the students' entire experience in the course; or the summation of students' experiences in equity and inclusion at the departmental program level. As an example, a biology department may be concerned about achievement gaps between students from majority groups and those from underrepresented groups. They observe that the problem is most pronounced in the introductory course sequence. The department identifies the scope of its assessment project as the first-to-second year transition period for students who intend on being majors. Members of the department are quick to recognize that the achievement gap may be due to systemic inequality that should be addressed. When they describe this gap, they are also careful to not perpetuate stereotypes and instead use discourse that conveys its structural nature (Quinn, 2020).

LIST EXPECTED OUTCOMES

Once the scope of the project is identified, instructors specify the expected outcomes of instruction, ensuring that they are both clear and measurable. With regards to the economics course mentioned above in which female students were underrepresented, one outcome may be an increase in the number of female students enrolled in the course. The instructor can also assess the experiences of these students with regard to equity and inclusion after the course redesign. If a department is committed to increasing the number of female majors from underrepresented groups after implementing multiple inclusive course interventions, using programmatic assessment in this project with a larger scope, the department can measure whether there is an increase in the numbers of female students in the major, as well as whether the sense of belonging of these learners has improved.

SPECIFY DATA SOURCES AND FORMULATE ASSESSMENT PLAN
Identifying appropriate data sources and having a data collection plan are critical steps. For example, in the hypothetical example of the history instructor interested in hearing from a wider range of students in class, an important metric is the participation rate of students. Such data may be gathered through careful documentation by the instructor during class regarding which students participated vocally during classes and comparing this information to participation after the intervention occurs. For example, the instructor may choose to integrate reflective writing prompts where all students are asked to respond, or clicker questions to promote inclusive participation. Increased numbers of students responding over several courses provides evidence of the efficacy of the intervention. In general, the disaggregation of data by the factor(s) being assessed are key components for measuring impact. Data sources may also be qualitative in nature such as interviews or focus groups with alumni from the course to inquire about their experiences with equity and belonging while enrolled. Another sample data source is an anonymous mid- or end-of-course feedback survey with open-ended questions specific to the scope of the project. Both of these data sources can be analyzed for emerging themes. In general, the outcomes drive the data sources utilized with regard to whether they are quantitative, qualitative, or a combination of both.

GATHER PRELIMINARY DATA/INFORMATION
Comparing pre-/post- or before-and-after change is a recommended approach for measuring impact, depending on whether the assessment goals necessitate the collection of pre-data. Pre-data may include student demographic information, final grades, and other assessments from previous classes. Instructors should determine how best to obtain this information for their assessment project given their institutional context. Possible sources of data may include the department, Registrar's Office, Office of Financial Aid (e.g., Pell-eligibility), or previous class files. Digital tools such as dashboards of student demographics can support inclusive teaching efforts. One example is the Know Your Students tool developed by the University of California, Davis (UC Davis, 2019). The Family Educational Rights and Privacy Act of 1974 (FERPA) law should always be adhered to when considering these data to protect students' privacy (US Department of Education, 2019).

IMPLEMENT PROJECT AND COLLECT DATA
After the necessary preliminary data are gathered, the instructor next implements the pedagogical approach for equity and inclusion. The instructor collects the data to help

measure whether expected outcomes have been met. Several tools might be considered for measuring the impacts of inclusive pedagogy as described in the resource "Framework for Measuring Impact" available on the open access companion site for this book, in addition to qualitative methods such as interviews and focus groups. Disaggregation of the data by student demographics and other factors can help the instructor measure impact (Montenegro & Jankowski, 2017).

ANALYZE DATA, DRAW CONCLUSIONS, AND OUTLINE NEXT STEPS

The final steps involve analyzing findings and drawing conclusions. Outcomes can inform future work to maximize impacts. A hypothetical, simplified example is analyzing whether a departmental-level intervention providing targeted English language support to international students positively impacts students' GPAs within courses in their major. An ultimate goal is to decrease achievement gaps seen between international and domestic students. An analysis of GPA over the four years of implementing the program does not uncover any changes (Figure 14.1). This data inform the department's next steps in surveying international students who are alumni of the institution to provide insight into how their academic experiences within the department may have impacted their learning and reveal any systemic inequalities.

The faculty members in the department discovered that a sense of belonging to the department has been lacking among these students. As a result, the next year, they allocated resources to fund a student-driven learning community for the international students in their major with academic support components and mentorship. The department continued collecting data and found that achievement gaps start to close between international and domestic students (Figure 14.2). One important consideration for this type of analysis is that comparing these two groups (international and domestic

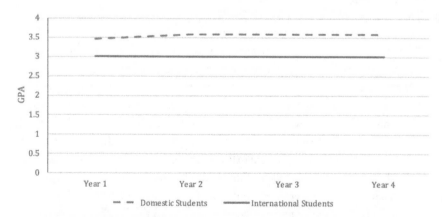

Figure 14.1. GPA comparison (departmental classes only) of domestic and international students following English Language Support Intervention

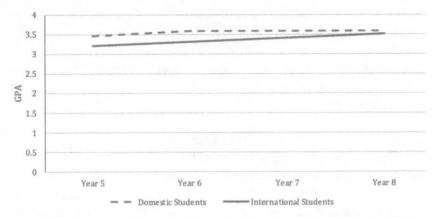

Figure 14.2. GPA comparison (departmental classes only) of domestic and international students following a Learning Community Intervention

students) is localized to a specific departmental context. This type of analysis may therefore be informed by college-level or national comparison data available on domestic and international students. A statistician may also be consulted to conduct more complex statistical analyses considering confounding variables. In general, this example illustrates how the analysis stage of an assessment project measuring the impacts of pedagogical efforts for equity and inclusion will typically involve the disaggregation of data around factors relevant to expected outcomes.

SAMPLE ASSESSMENT PROJECTS ACROSS DISCIPLINES

Below are examples of assessments designed for various teaching contexts.

ACTIVITY, ASSIGNMENT, OR SMALL COURSE CHANGE

An instructor teaching a Great Works of Literature course has for several years included Charlotte Brontë's *Jane Eyre* as a required reading. In previous iterations of the course, students completed a writing assignment after reading the novel and reflected on ways in which it may or may not be considered feminist work. The instructor recognized that there are also other themes within this novel that are important to discuss including race, ethnicity, and culture. With the pedagogical goal of creating a more equitable and inclusive learning activity that engages a racially and culturally diverse class, the instructor redesigned the assignment to foster student reflection on such themes.

In the new assignment, students think critically about how the lens through which they read texts and how their interpretations are shaped by their own racial and ethnic identities and those of the author. First, students write a short, reflective piece on the themes about how race, ethnicity, and culture are implicated in *Jane Eyre*. Then, they read excerpts from Jean Rhys's *Wide Sargasso Sea,* a book written more than one hundred years after the publication of *Jane Eyre* as a response and prequel that focuses on the character of Antoinette Cosway (aka Bertha Mason) and her experiences with racism and assimilation as a woman of Creole heritage. Students are then asked to complete a second assignment that challenges them to reexamine their thoughts on these themes from *Jane Eyre* considering what they have read from *Wide Sargasso Sea,* including if and how they have evolved. Finally, students are asked to respond on a scale from 1 to 10 to what degree they considered the influence of the racial and ethnic identity of the author during their initial reading of the book, their first reflective writing assignment, and the second assignment. They are also asked to reflect upon how their perspectives might be shaped by their own identities.

The instructor analyzed the students' essays for acknowledgment and depth of thought on the topics and the influence of the author's racial background, as well as the students' views on how much they considered the author's racial identity at each step. The instructor also examined how students with different racial and ethnic identities reflect on the activity in their essays. He utilized this information to help revise course activities for future years to best support the learning and engagement of all of his students, by building in time for small group discussions on recurrent concepts that students found important followed by an additional short reflection where students informally wrote on what their peers noted and they had not previously considered.

ENTIRE COURSE OR PROGRAM

As an example of how an instructor might assess larger-scale pedagogical changes across an entire course structure, in a multisection Introduction to Philosophy course the instructors have the freedom to use a variety of pedagogical approaches. An instructor is interested in knowing how her teaching methods impact the achievement of students from varying socioeconomic backgrounds, as she had noticed in past years that there was an achievement gap across various groups but did not have the appropriate data to support her observations.

As described previously, collecting relevant student demographic information is important, and there are a number of validated surveys and questionnaires focused on collecting this information (MacArthur Research Network, 2008; National Cancer Institute, 2019; Svedberg et al., 2016). In this example, collecting data using the same method across class sections allows for downstream analysis. The course would be taught with each section discussing similar topics and content, but utilizing distinct teaching approaches; for example, one might be more lecture-based and another heavily utilizing small group work. At the end of the course, students' course grades can be examined as well as grades on specific assignments of interest, compared with overall GPA, and then analyzed in concert with the preliminary data on students' socioeconomic status. Once this is done for each class section individually, analyses can be performed that compare the sections taught with different methods to determine if there are particular pedagogical approaches that are more efficacious for different groups of students.

SUMMARY

Using equitable and inclusive pedagogical approaches is critical to foster a sense of belonging and achievement for diverse learners. Assessing the impact of such practices is also integral, including whether expected learning outcomes are accomplished after an intervention. Inclusive assessment practices can promote educational equity by placing value on individual student differences in abilities and skills (Hockings, 2010), which improves engagement for all students (Thomas & May, 2010). In this chapter, we present a framework to help instructors take preliminary steps in developing an assessment project that measures impact. We hope that usage of the framework will generate data that encourages reflection on teaching practices, as well as further conversation around diversity, equity, and inclusion.

REFERENCES

American College Health Association. (2008, Fall). *ACHA—National College Health Assessment II: Reference group executive summary*. American College Health Association.

American College Health Association. (2018, Spring). *ACHA—National College Health Assessment II: Undergraduate student reference group executive summary*. American College Health Association.

Baum, S., Ma, J., Pender, M., & Libassi, C. J. (2018). *Trends in student aid 2018*. College Board.

Bayer, A., & Rouse, C. E. (2016). Diversity in the economics profession: A new attack on an old problem. *Journal of Economic Perspectives*, 30(4): 221–242. https://doi.org/10.1257/jep.30.4.221

Dickson, K. L., & Treml, M. M. (2013). Using assessment and SoTL to enhance student learning. *New Directions for Teaching and Learning*, 136, 7–16.

Eddy, S. L., & Hogan, K. A. (2014). Getting under the hood: How and for whom does increasing course structure work? *CBE—Life Sciences Education*, 13(3), 453–468.

Hockings, C. (2010). *Inclusive learning and teaching in higher education: A synthesis of research evidence*. Higher Education Academy.

Institute of International Education (IIE). (2018). *International student enrollment trends, 1948/49-2017/18.* http://www.iie.org/opendoors

Kuh, G. D., Ikenberry, S. O., Jankowski, N. A., Cain, T. R., Ewell, P. T., Hutchings, P., & Kinzie, J. (2015). *Using evidence of student learning to improve higher education*. Jossey-Bass.

MacArthur Research Network on SES & Health. (2008). *Sociodemographic questionnaire*. https://macses.ucsf.edu/research/socialenviron/sociodemographic.php

McConnell, K. D., & Doolittle, P. E. (2012). *Classroom-level assessment: Aligning pedagogical practices to enhance student learning.* In C. Secolsky & D. B. Denison (Eds.), *Handbook on measurement, assessment, and evaluation in higher education* (pp. 15–30). Routledge.

McKinney, K. (2006). Attitudinal and structural factors contributing to challenges in the work of the scholarship of teaching and learning. In J. M. Braxton (Ed.), *Analyzing faculty work and rewards: Using Boyer's four domains of scholarship* (pp. 37–50). Jossey-Bass.

McKinney, K. (2015). SoTL and assessment: Siblings? *SoTL* Advocate. https://illinoisstateuniversitysotl.wordpress.com/2015/07/06/sotl-and-assessment-siblings/amp/

Montenegro, E., & Jankowski, N. A. (2017, January). *Equity and assessment: Moving towards culturally responsive assessment.* (Occasional Paper no. 29). National Institute for Learning Outcomes Assessment (NILOA). http://www.learningoutcomesassessment.org/documents/OccasionalPaper29.pdf

National Cancer Institute. (2019). *Socioeconomic status questionnaire.* https://dceg.cancer.gov/tools/design/questionnaires/reviewed/socio-economic-status-questions-reviewed

National Council of State Boards of Nursing. (2017). *National nursing workforce survey.* https://www.ncsbn.org/workforce.htm

National Institute for Learning Outcomes Assessment. (2019). http://www.learningoutcomesassessment.org

National Science Foundation, National Center for Science and Engineering Statistics. (2017). *Women, minorities, and persons with disabilities in science and engineering: 2017.* Special Report NSF 17–310. www.nsf.gov/statistics/wmpd/

Pettit, E. (2019, January 7). After racist incidents mire a conference, classicists point to bigger problems. *Chronicle of Higher Education.* https://www.chronicle.com/article/After-Racist-Incidents-Mire-a/245430

Quinn, D. M. (2020). Experimental effects of "achievement gap" news reporting on viewers' racial stereotypes, inequality explanations, and inequality prioritization. *Educational Researcher.* https://doi.org/10.3102/0013189X20932469

Sathy, V., & Hogan, K. A. (2019, July 22). How to make your teaching more inclusive: Advice guide. *Chronicle of Higher Education.* https://www.chronicle.com/interactives/20190719_inclusive_teaching

Skomsvold, P. (2014). *Profile of undergraduate students: 2011–12* (NCES 2015-167). National Center for Education Statistics. https://nces.ed.gov/pubsearch/pubsinfo.asp?pubid=2015167

Snyder, T. D., de Brey, C., & Dillow, S. A. (2019). *Digest of education statistics 2017* (NCES 2018–070). National Center for Education Statistics.

Svedberg, P., Nygren, J. M., Staland-Nyman, C., & Nyholm, M. (2016). The validity of socioeconomic status measures among adolescents based on self-reported information about parents' occupations, FAS, and perceived SES; implication for health-related quality of life studies. *BMC Medical Research Methodology, 16*(48). https://dx.doi.org/10.1186/s12874-016-0148-9

Thomas, L., & May, H. (2010). *Inclusive teaching and learning in higher education.* Higher Education Academy.

UC Davis. (2019). *Know your students.* Center for Educational Effectiveness. https://cee.ucdavis.edu/toolsUS Department of Education. (2019). *FERPA.* https://www2.ed.gov/policy/gen/guid/fpco/ferpa/index.html

CHAPTER 15

Is Your Teaching Inclusive?
An Inclusive Teaching Rubric for Higher Education

Deyu Hu and Michele Deramo

As the US population becomes increasingly diverse, so do the higher education campuses. Since universities and colleges train, develop, and replenish the workforce, it is important that higher education institutions effectively educate future workers who have diverse ethnic, racial, cultural, and socioeconomic backgrounds. Doing so can not only provide quality education to all students and thus help the United States remain competitive in the global economy but also address the persistent social inequities, such as achievement, retention, and graduation rates for low-income, first-generation, and underrepresented students of color across both secondary and postsecondary levels (Milem, 2003; Nelson Laird, Engberg, & Hurtado, 2005; Williams, Berger, & McClendon, 2005).

In addition to the external imperatives above, research indicates that there are both learning and social benefits for students educated in diverse learning environments, such as gaining improved cognitive and affective abilities, exhibiting more interest in racial and cultural engagement and public good, and becoming more competent in working within diverse environments (Bowen & Bok, 1998; Bowman, 2010; 2011; Gurin et al., 2002; Johnson & Lollar, 2002). To gain these benefits, universities and colleges must establish inclusive learning environments and provide effective education to all students, including students with diverse ethical, racial, cultural, and socioeconomic backgrounds. This kind of teaching is often referred to as inclusive teaching.

The concept of inclusive teaching is daunting to many faculty in higher education (Nguyen & Nolan, 2013). On one hand, when faculty are asked to infuse inclusive teaching into their classes, they are not clear on why. In fact, students simply do not check their identity at the classroom door. Their prior knowledge, experience, social identity, and many other characteristics play important roles in their learning. Studies show that helping students cope with stereotypes and supporting their social belonging can improve their persistence and academic success (Hurtado et al., 2012; Steele & Aronson, 1995; Walton & Cohen, 2011). On the other hand, even when some faculty are interested in utilizing inclusive teaching in their classes, they do not know how. For example, some faculty state that their classes are about math, science, or engineering. They cannot see how inclusive teaching can be integrated into their classes.

RATIONALE OF THE RUBRIC

To help faculty with their inclusive teaching endeavor, faculty development opportunities should be provided (Jordan, Schwartz, & McGhie-Richmond, 2009; Moriña, Cortés-Vega, & Molina, 2015). As part of such efforts, some higher education institutions have developed inclusive teaching strategies. These strategies, however, often cover only a subset of inclusive teaching strategies and are organized differently across universities. It is difficult for faculty to achieve the best possible inclusive teaching by using this type of scattered and fragmented information.

In our search for a solution, practices in online education shine a light. At the beginning of the twenty-first century, with the rapid increase of online learning there was a growing need to assure the quality of online courses. Many organizations have developed guidelines and standards for this purpose. Among them, Quality Matters (QM) (Maryland Online, 2019) is the most widely adopted standard to ensure the quality of online or hybrid courses. Over a decade after its launch, Shattuck (2015) reviewed literature on its effectiveness and impact on learning and professional enhancement. Results from multiple studies have shown that students' satisfaction, persistence, and performance were better in courses designed or redesigned to meet the QM standards than those that were not. Additionally, QM-related professional development opportunities, such as training or serving as peer reviewers, are correlated with faculty's enhanced self-efficacy in online teaching and significant knowledge gain in online course design best practices.

An inclusive teaching rubric may serve similar functions for inclusive teaching in higher education. Our literature review, however, showed that no such rubric for higher education exists yet. Hence, the purpose of this chapter is to develop an inclusive teaching rubric for the design, development, delivery, evaluation, and improvement of inclusive teaching in higher education. The rubric is based on a literature review of what has been studied in inclusive teaching as well as best practices from the front lines.

THE RUBRIC

The focus of this rubric (see the resource "Inclusive Teaching Higher Education Rubric" on the open access companion site for this book) is to provide particular strategies at the course level, but not at the program or institutional levels. While the two higher levels of integration can greatly enhance the effectiveness of inclusive teaching efforts, we want to empower faculty to start to take actions in their own classrooms since individual faculty can make a difference. In addition, we focus on "the how," but not "the what" to teach in inclusive teaching: these strategies can be used by any faculty in any classroom. Some researchers (Hockings, 2010; Lawrie et al., 2017) limit the contexts of inclusive teaching to education for all students and intentionally exclude studies on any particular group of students. Since our focus is on inclusive teaching strategies, we do not exclude strategies that have a focus on particular groups of students. Moreover, due to space constraints we do not cover each specific standard and discuss some of them only briefly.

STANDARD 1: FACULTY AWARENESS

Bias can be explicit or implicit. Implicit bias, also known as unconscious or subtle bias, goes against our consciously held beliefs and is thus difficult to identify and correct (Banaji, Bazerman, & Chugh, 2003; Greenwald & Hamilton Krieger, 2006). Bias can also be favorable or unfavorable. Studies show that faculty carry unfavorable implicit bias toward underrepresented students in relevant fields and such biases influence students' test scores, how faculty perceive a student's behavior or misbehavior, and their support to students (Anthony, 2004; Milkman, Akinola, & Chugh, 2015; Moss-Racusin et al., 2012; Staats et al., 2017).

In order to address implicit bias, the first step is to acknowledge that we all have biases and be aware of them. There are many ways that faculty can identify their own implicit bias. For instance, faculty can take the Implicit Association Test (IAT) (Project Implicit, 2019). The IAT was designed by researchers at Harvard University, the University of Virginia, and the University of Washington as a self-administered free online assessment for implicit bias. Since its launch in 1998, it has been widely used. A meta-analysis review that summarized sixty-one studies on IAT confirmed its predictive validity toward bias-related behaviors, such as prejudicial attitudes and stereotypes (Greenwald & Hamilton Krieger, 2006; Greenwald et al., 2009). Additionally, faculty can reflect on how their own identity, background, and experience have influenced their interaction with students from different backgrounds (Garibay, 2015). Faculty can also solicit feedback regarding their implicit bias from outside observers, such as a peer or staff in the teaching and learning center, or their students through course evaluations or focus groups. Keeping a journal of interaction with different types of students is yet another way that faculty can use to actively monitor their own implicit bias.

Once faculty are aware of their implicit biases, they can utilize different methods to remediate them, such as learning about issues of social privilege and oppression, starting or continuing personal education on bias, discrimination, and inequity, and seeking support from trusted colleagues. Faculty can also reduce implicit bias through developing an inclusive classroom climate and using inclusive teaching practices (Anthony, 2004; Garibay, 2015; Hurtado et al., 2012).

STANDARD 2: INCLUSIVE LEARNING ENVIRONMENT

In an inclusive learning environment, all students are welcome, valued, and respected because of their differences. Putting students with diverse social identities in a classroom, however, does not automatically create an inclusive learning environment. An inclusive learning environment has to be intentionally designed to achieve meaningful interactions among members as well as a sense of belonging and inclusion (Hockings, 2010; Lawrie et al., 2017).

To promote an inclusive learning environment, it is important to establish community guidelines for interaction early in the class so that there is a tone of inclusivity and students are aware of the expectations of respectful and equitable class interaction. Faculty can engage students in setting up the guidelines so that there is better buy-in from students. The guidelines should also be reviewed periodically or before and after "hot moments" in the classroom to ensure effective implementation. When issues arise, such as offensive, discriminatory, and insensitive comments, faculty should act quickly to maintain a inclusive and equitable learning environment. Moreover, faculty should utilize various opportunities to build a rapport with their students and allow students to build rapport among themselves through collaborative teamwork or cross-cultural communication. Through engaging each student and developing faculty-student and student-student rapport, faculty can achieve effective teaching, including inclusive teaching for all students (Hurtado et al., 2012; Jordan Schwartz, & McGhie-Richmond, 2009).

STANDARD 3: COURSE OVERVIEW AND SYLLABUS

A course overview and syllabus are critical to the success of all students, especially first-generation students, underrepresented students of color, and international students (see Chapter 1, this volume). They can be used to create an engaging and inclusive classroom climate and facilitate both teaching and learning in that faculty can use them to set up inclusivity expectations and disclose terms of participation and other implicit knowledge to help all students succeed (Collins, 1997). As an example, faculty can provide information about office hours, location, what to expect of a visit, and how to prepare for an office hour to help students get the most out of this experience.

Faculty can also include a diversity statement and a statement of fair accommodation for religious or disability-related requests to make all students feel that they are welcome and respected. Including a clear outline of course objectives and corresponding activities and assignments in the syllabus and reviewing them with the class helps all students understand the learning objectives of the course and the purposes of the activities, which are to help them achieve the course objectives rather than doing busy work. In addition, faculty should clarify how students' work will be assessed and how they can meet the expectations of the course. Doing so helps all students, especially historically underrepresented students and international students. Furthermore, faculty should set high expectations for all students because research has shown that faculty's expectations impact students' academic performance (Rosenthal & Jacobson, 1968; Tinto, 1993).

STANDARD 4: INSTRUCTIONAL MATERIALS

Traditional mainstream curriculum is dominated by the Euro-American culture and has marginalized scholarship by and about other cultures. This has led to some students' disengagement in learning as there is a lack of identity affirmation and relevance for them. Studies showed that students' learning, including levels of engagement, attitudes toward learning, and academic performance, can be improved by integrating content relevant to students' backgrounds (Sleeter, 2011; Wlodkowski & Ginsberg, 1995). Therefore, it is a good practice to include course content that represents opinions and experiences from a wide range of groups (Anthony, 2004; Hurtado et al., 2012). To further engage students with the content, faculty can invite students to critique the course content, discuss their experiences, inform them about the limitations of the material, and encourage students to correct any inaccuracies or misrepresentations in the content. Additionally, for science, technology, engineering, and math disciplines, faculty can connect scientific knowledge with social issues, social justice, and social responsibilities as they relate to diversity and inclusion (Garibay, 2015; Part IV, this volume).

STANDARD 5: ASSESSMENT

Assessment can be used to demonstrate the effectiveness of teaching and learning and serve as a guide for educational improvement. Research shows that assessing students early and often can improve their learning (Brown, Roediger, & McDaniel, 2014). This also allows faculty to adjust their instruction to help students from diverse backgrounds if the assessment results reveal such a need. To elicit students' intrinsic motivation and to respect their prior experience, values, and needs, faculty can provide multiple means for students to meet learning objectives and demonstrate their learning (Lawrie et al., 2017; Wlodkowski & Ginsberg, 1995). For example, John Boyer, an instructor at Virginia Tech, teaches the World Regions class with around three thousand students from approximately eighty countries. His students can choose from a variety of assessments, such as weekly quizzes, midterm and final exams, attendance to international events, international film reviews, or World Leader Shadow Twitter assignments to demonstrate their learning. While offering flexibility, the availability of various assessment methods promotes quality of work, individual responsibility, and self-regulation in students (Boyer, n.d.). In addition to assessments, faculty can change the way that they grade student assessments. For example, when subjective grading is used, faculty can adopt blind grading to avoid potential biases (Hanna & Linden, 2012; Malouff & Thorsteinsson, 2016).

STANDARD 6: INSTRUCTIONAL STRATEGIES

A key finding of an inclusive teaching literature review conducted by Lawrie and her colleagues was that pedagogy should meet learners' needs and not create barriers for them (Lawrie et al., 2017). This requires that faculty effectively utilize various instructional strategies for diverse learners and scenarios since relying on a small repertoire of instructional strategies may limit faculty's teaching effectiveness to only a subset of their students. To find out one's preferred instructional strategies, faculty can conduct a self-assessment using the Teaching Practice Inventory (Carl Wieman Science Education Initiative, 2019), which was developed for STEM courses but can be used for other subject areas as well. In addition to utilizing various instructional strategies, faculty should also present information in multiple ways, offer various means of engagement, and make their courses accessible to diverse students (Kumar & Wideman, 2014; Madriaga et al., 2010; Moriña, López Gavira, & Molina, 2015). For instance, students from different racial, ethnic, and cultural backgrounds may have different familiarity with the examples that faculty provide in the classroom. Therefore, faculty should strive to provide varied language and cultural reference point examples to support all students. Additionally, faculty can employ principles of Universal Design for Learning (UDL) to minimize barriers, accommodate differences, and maximize learning for all students. The three main principles of UDL include presenting information in different ways, allowing students to approach learning tasks and demonstrating their learning in different ways, and offering multiple ways to engage students. These principles have been covered in this and previous standards (Lawrie et al., 2017).

DISCUSSION

Hockings (2010) argued that one of the ongoing challenges in inclusive teaching is to capture and communicate the effective practices. Undoubtedly, this challenge should continue to be addressed. Yet an equally important aspect is to synthesize the effective practices into a comprehensive rubric and promote its use as this may greatly advance the integration of inclusive teaching into classrooms and improve learning for all students. This task was made possible by the emerging research in this field. Since Hockings's work, scholars have conducted more research (Lawrie et al., 2017) and proposed many strategies to enhance inclusive teaching. This rubric is the result of relevant research and best practices in the field. While each strategy in the rubric can stand on its own, utilizing them all will make teaching in higher education more inclusive and effective for all students.

We encourage a wide adoption of this rubric and feedback from faculty and faculty developers to advance inclusive teaching in higher education. For example, by using it as a self-check guide a faculty member can determine if she has reached a specific standard. If not, she can then determine the actions to take to reach the standard as well as when the actions should happen, such as before, during, or after the class. For instance, specific standard 1 asks faculty to examine their implicit bias using self-assessment, feedback, or journaling. These activities often happen outside of the classroom. In contrast, specific standard 6 requires the faculty member to both plan and prepare to manage conflict before the class and actually take such actions in the classroom. While faculty can take full responsibility in meeting the rubric, their busy schedule may prevent them from identifying effective strategies and relevant resources. Therefore, similar to the implementation of the Quality Matters exercise, faculty developers can be trained in this instrument and then facilitate its implementation in courses. As research in this field progresses, this rubric, its specific standards, and more detailed guidelines should be further developed and updated. At the same time, research is needed to evaluate the effectiveness of this instrument in advancing inclusive teaching and its impact on student learning, faculty practice, and institutional outcomes.

REFERENCES

Anthony, A. S. (2004). Gender bias and discrimination in nursing education: Can we change it? *Nurse Educator, 29*(3), 121–125.

Banaji, M. R., Bazerman, M. H., & Chugh, D. (2003). How (un)ethical are you? *Harvard Business Review, 81*(12), 56–64.

Bowen, W. G., & Bok, D. (1998). *The shape of the river: Long-term consequences of considering race in college and university admissions.* Princeton University Press.

Bowman, N. A. (2010). College diversity experiences and cognitive development: A meta-analysis. *Review of Educational Research, 80*(1), 4–33.

Bowman, N. A. (2011). Promoting participation in a diverse democracy: A meta-analysis of college diversity experiences and civic engagement. *Review of Educational Research, 81*(1), 29–68.

Boyer, J. (n.d.). *New education approaches.* http://www.thejohnboyer.com/new-education

Brown, P., Roediger, H., & McDaniel, M. (2014). *Make it stick: The science of successful learning.* Belknap Press of Harvard University Press.

Carl Wieman Science Education Initiative. (2019). *CWSEI teaching practices inventory.* http://www.cwsei.ubc.ca/resources/TeachingPracticesInventory.htm

Collins, T. (1997). For openers . . . An inclusive syllabus. In W. E. Campbell and K. A. Smith (Eds.), *New paradigms for college teaching* (pp. 79–102). Interaction.

Garibay, J. C. (2015). *Creating a positive classroom climate for diversity.* https://equity.ucla.edu/wp-content/uploads/2016/06/CreatingaPositiveClassroomClimateWeb-2.pdf

Greenwald, A., & Hamilton Krieger, L. (2006). Implicit bias: Scientific foundations. *California Law Review, 94*(4), 945–967.

Greenwald, A., Poehlman, T. A., Uhlmann, E. L., & Banaji, M. R. (2009). Understanding and using the implicit association test: III. Meta-analysis of predictive validity. *Journal of Personality and Social Psychology, 97*(1), 17–41.

Gurin, P., Dey, E. L., Hurtado, S., & Gurin, G. (2002). Diversity and higher education: Theory and impact on educational outcomes. *Harvard Educational Review, 72*(3), 330–366.

Hanna, R., & Linden, L. (2012). Discrimination in grading. *American Economic Journal: Economic Policy, 4*(4), 146–168.

Hockings, C. (2010). *Inclusive learning and teaching in higher education: A synthesis of research.* Higher Education Academy.

Hurtado, S., Alvarez, C., Guillermo-Wann, C., Cuellar, M., & Arellano, L. (2012). A model for diverse learning environments: The scholarship on creating and assessing conditions for student success. In J. Smart & M. Paulsen (Eds.), *Higher education: Handbook of theory and research*, vol. 27 (pp. 41–122). Springer.

Johnson, S. M., & Lollar, X. (2002). Diversity policy in higher education: The impact of college students' exposure to diversity on cultural awareness and political participation. *Journal of Education Policy, 17*(3), 305–320.

Jordan, A., Schwartz, E., & McGhie-Richmond, D. (2009). Preparing teachers for inclusive classrooms. *Teaching and Teacher Education, 25*(4), 535–542.

Kumar, K., & Wideman, M. (2014). Accessible by design: Applying UDL principles in a first-year undergraduate course. *Canadian Journal of Higher Education, 44*(1), 125–147.

Lawrie, G., Marquis, E., Fuller, E., Newman, T., Qui, M., Nomikoudis, M., Roelofs, F., & van Dam, L. (2017). Moving towards inclusive learning and teaching: A synthesis of recent literature. *Teaching and Learning Inquiry, 5*(1). https://doi.org/10.20343/teachlearninqu.5.1.3

Madriaga, M., Hanson, K., Heaton, C., Newitt, S., & Walker, A. (2010). Confronting similar challenges? Disabled and non-disabled students' learning and assessment experiences. *Studies in Higher Education, 35*(6), 647–658.

Malouff, J. M., & Thorsteinsson, E. B. (2016). Bias in grading a meta-analysis of experimental research findings. *Australian Journal of Education, 60*(3), 245–256.

Maryland Online (2019). *Quality matters.* http://www.qualitymatters.org/

Milem, J. (2003). The educational benefits of diversity: Evidence from multiple sectors. In M. J. Chang, D. Witt, J. Jones, & K. Hakuta (Eds.), *Compelling interest: Examining the evidence on racial dynamics in higher education* (pp. 126–169). Stanford University Press.

Milkman, K. L., Akinola, M., & Chugh, D. (2015). What happens before? A field experiment exploring how pay and representation differentially shape bias on the pathway into organizations. *Journal of Applied Psychology, 100*(6), 1678–1712.

Moriña, A., Cortés-Vega, M., & Molina, V. M. (2015). Faculty training: An unavoidable requirement for approaching more inclusive university classroom. *Teaching in Higher Education, 20*(8), 795–806.

Moriña Díez, A., López Gavira, R., & Molina, V. M. (2015). Students with disabilities in higher education: A biographical-narrative approach to the role of lecturers. *Higher Education Research & Development, 34*(1), 147–159.

Moss-Racusin, C. A., Dovidio, J. F., Brescoll, V. L., Graham, M. J., & Handelsman, J. (2012). Science faculty's subtle gender bias favor male students. *Proceedings of the National Academy of Sciences of the United State of America, 109*(41), 16474–16479.

Nelson Laird, T., Engberg, M., & Hurtado, S. (2005). Modeling accentuation effects: Enrolling in a diversity course and the importance of social action engagement. *Journal of Higher Education, 76*(4), 448–476.

Nguyen, L., & Nolan, S. (2013, May). Your sphere of influence: How to infuse cultural diversity into your psychology classes. *Psychology Teacher Network.*

Project Implicit. (2019). *Project implicit.* https://implicit.harvard.edu/implicit/

Rosenthal, R., & Jacobson, L. (1968). Pygmalion in the classroom. *Urban Review, 3*(1), 16–20.

Shattuck, K. (2015). *Research inputs and outputs of Quality Matters: Update to 2012 and 2014 version of What We're Learning from QM-Focused Research.* Quality Matters.

Sleeter, C. (2011). *The academic and social value of ethnic studies: A research review.* National Education Association.

Staats, C., Capatosto, K., Tenney, L., & Mamo, S. (2017). *State of the science: Implicit bias review 2017 edition.* Kirwan Institute for the Study of Race and Ethnicity, The Ohio State University.

Steele, C. M., & Aronson, J. (1995). Stereotype threat and the intellectual test performance of African Americans. *Journal of Personality and Social Psychology, 69*(5), 797–811.

Tinto, V. (1993). *Leaving college: The causes and cures of student attrition* (2nd ed.). University of Chicago Press.

Walton, G. M., & Cohen, G. L. (2011). A brief social-belonging intervention improves academic and health outcomes of minority students. *Science, 331*(6023), 1447–1451.

Williams, D., Berger, J., & McClendon, S. (2005). *Toward a model of inclusive excellence and change in postsecondary institutions.* Association of American Colleges and Universities.

Wlodkowski, R., & Ginsberg, M. (1995). A framework for culturally responsive teaching. *Educational Leadership, 53*(1), 17–21.

REFLECTION ON
Inclusive Assessment

The chapters in this section provide readers with two ways to evaluate the effectiveness of their course design in promoting inclusivity: scholarship of teaching and learning (SoTL) and an inclusive teaching rubric. A SoTL project that incorporates the student experience will help educators understand how students perceive their course. It can help identify areas for future development. Additionally, SoTL encourages educators to share their work with others. When using either approach educators need to intentionally center inclusion in their analysis. It may be helpful to enlist others to examine the pedagogical, curricular, and assessment choices used in the classroom.

PRACTITIONER BEHAVIORS

- Please use one of the methods mentioned in Chapter 15 to examine your implicit bias. Were the results surprising to you? List strategies you might try to address your implicit biases and mechanisms you could use to monitor your improvement.

- What strategies could you utilize to increase the inclusiveness of your teaching? How would you know if they were effective? How would you like to improve?

- How can you use the rubric to self-check the inclusiveness of your teaching? What actions do you plan to take to make your teaching more inclusive?

PEDAGOGY

- What are your pedagogical goals for equity and inclusion?

- What is an appropriate scope for your assessment project of your inclusive teaching practices? For example, does it make sense to conduct it at the assignment, unit, multi-unit, whole course, or programmatic level?

- What data will you need to know if you have met the goal of your inclusive teaching practice? How will you collect this data?

- How will you analyze the data? How will you use the data to further your goals for equity and inclusion? How will you ensure that the data are not used to further marginalize students?

CURRICULUM

- How can you use a SoTL project to explore the inclusiveness of your curriculum?
- How can you enlist the help of your peers in applying the rubric to your course design?

ASSESSMENT

- How can you develop a SoTL project to co-create your assessment processes with your students?
- How can you use the feedback from the rubric to revise your assessment processes so they are more inclusive?

Epilogue

The authors in this collection have illustrated their deep commitment to creating inclusive learning environments. They demonstrate the variety of ways educators across disciplines and teaching situations can thoughtfully address the needs of traditionally marginalized students and develop equity-mindedness in their classrooms. Higher education must address social inequities to create an inclusive society. Carnevale and Strohl (2013) examined how higher education in the United States reproduces the same social inequalities and biased processes that marginalize students of color: "The postsecondary system mimics the racial inequality it inherits from the K–12 education system, then magnifies and projects that inequality into the labor market and society at large. In theory, the education system is colorblind; but in fact, it is racially polarized and exacerbates the intergenerational reproduction of white racial privilege" (p. 3). Because educational systems have not worked to be equal, they have not achieved equity for underserved students. We return to the words of Carbado and Gulati (2003): "At the most basic level, students perform in society the racial interactions they learn and rehearse in school" (p. 1155). If students learn how to interact with others who are different from themselves in equitable ways, higher education can be a driving force in creating a more inclusive and just society.

This focus on creating an inclusive and just society begins with educators examining their own beliefs and behaviors for implicit biases. By recognizing their implicit biases, educators can more thoughtfully adopt pedagogies and curricula that create a sense of belonging and participation for all students while also demonstrating respect for those who are different. They acknowledge responsibility for eliminating inequalities in their classes.

The contributors to this book have made eloquent arguments for learning more about the students in order to implement student-centered pedagogies that are culturally sustaining. In their work to incorporate inclusive pedagogies, they recommend using surveys and ice-breaker activities to begin building a community of learners. They further include activities to develop a culture of respect for difference. They honor students' different ways of knowing by providing multiple paths to making the course content accessible. Using information from their surveys and their interactions with students, they explicitly discuss how their course content is relevant to students' educational, professional, and civic goals. Through the activities described in the book, students are invited to try different disciplinary ways of thinking. Additionally, students are invited to critically reflect on their developing intercultural knowledge and skills and to examine their role in creating and participating in a just and inclusive society.

The curriculum is more than content to be covered. The educators in this book intentionally work to decolonize their curricula, so it illustrates the diversity of cultures and ideas that led to their discipline's development. They intentionally create a learning environment that is equity-minded, which does not treat all students as the same. Instead, they recognize the unique needs of each student by offering multiple paths and approaches to the curriculum. In the inclusive classrooms described in this book, learning is co-constructed among the students and with the instructors. The educators demonstrate how an inclusive curriculum can help to address the impact of years of "low teacher expectations, biased attitudes and perceptions around language competence, and discriminatory practices in relation to teaching, assessment, and student support" (Gabriel, 2019, p. 1460). Each learning environment is student-centered, and knowledge is individually constructed through social interactions with peers and the instructor. Educators in disciplines that combine academic and professional practice demonstrate how a more diverse curriculum can give students greater access to career opportunities in a global context as employment markets become increasingly internationalized (Gabriel, 2019). Using an intercultural competence framework, these educators help students develop intercultural skills that prepare them to work in diverse organizations.

The equitable and inclusive pedagogies and curricula are supported and reinforced through transparent assessment practices. Each classroom aligns the activities and assessments using course learning outcomes shared with students. They are transparent about the demonstration of learning expected at the end of the course. The two final chapters offer insights into how faculty can evaluate how well their overall course design meets their objectives for addressing equity and inclusion in their courses. Data collected through evaluations of student learning, students' perceptions of their learning, scholarly reflection, and scholarship of teaching and learning can provide insights into how the course advances equity and inclusion.

Catastrophic events like the COVID-19 pandemic bring to wider attention the deep disparities that often run below public attention. Such events exacerbate existing inequalities, so they disproportionately affect communities already marginalized. For instance, as more colleges and universities moved to online teaching in response to the pandemic, more students who have historically been underserved were pushed out of higher education. The National Student Clearinghouse (2020) reported that first-year student enrollment declined by 13.9 percent, led by declines in underresourced and marginalized communities. Two-year colleges, typically the point of entry for underserved students, saw a decline in enrollment of 18.9 percent. Students in these communities already struggle to manage resources to achieve a degree. The exigencies of the pandemic seem to have forced many to defer their enrollment.

Many of the recommendations in this collection to create an inclusive learning environment were created for in-person classes; however, Benander and Rankey (chapter 3, this volume) showed how to make online learning environments more inclusive. Instructors can begin with a statement reflecting their commitment to equity and inclusion in their classes in their syllabus and course learning management system (LMS). Students notice this language, so it is important to continue this inclusive practice in online classes. Next, they can explore the technology available to promote inclusion. For instance, the Canvas LMS allows users to identify their pronouns. While creating an inclusive online learning environment, it is important to keep in mind the digital divide preventing some students from access to the resources needed for online learning, such as a computer and reliable internet connection, as was made evident during the COVID-19 pandemic. Instructors need to provide grace for themselves and to their students during unprecedented times, but this patience and grace is needed at all times for racially minoritized and underresourced students who continue to experience the pandemic of inequality. Offering flexible due dates and a variety of ways to demonstrate learning allow for students to access the course and materials as they are able. Instructors should also intentionally connect students to resources available on campus and in the community to address students' concerns. Students' basic needs for safety and belonging need to be met before they can attend to the learning. Therefore, it is helpful to students to have information about wellness and financial support resources easily accessible in the course in addition to providing academic support information as a best practice in meeting students' needs.

Higher education must address equity and inclusion to close deepening social and economic divides and change civic attitudes and behavior. Bowman (2011) suggested that experiences of diversity are associated with increases in civic attitudes, behavioral intentions, and behaviors, and the effect is greater when there is increased interpersonal interactions with racial diversity than for curricular and cocurricular diversity experiences. When college graduates have greater social and economic mobility, they are more likely to volunteer in society, and contribute to a changing economy (AAC&U, 2015). In the absence of equal access to higher education many low-income, underrepresented minoritized students may be unable to escape the vicious cycle of poverty and disenfranchisement. Caught in this oppressive cycle, many have difficulty developing a sense of privilege and mobility, which overtime widens the economic and social inequities.

Higher education faculty cannot do the work of equity alone. Bensimon (2005) argued that higher education institutions need to play a definitive role to address racial disparities in higher education attainment. These disparities reflect learning inadequacies on the part of institutions, rather than students. Educators need help to fight against a corporate model that is dehumanizing and focused on profits. As faculty work through self-examination, curriculum design, pedagogy, and assessment practices to create inclusive classrooms, they need institutional support in the forms of time, recognition, and compensation. Faculty need *time* to do the difficult work of self-examination, explore best practices in their fields to address equity, and analyze the effectiveness of their modifications. Faculty need course reductions or reductions in class sizes to delve into equity research and consider its implications for their own courses.

At the institutional level, hiring practices and processes need to be changed to diversify faculty and staff, who frequently serve as role models for students. Abdul-Raheem (2016) argued that when an institution invests in diverse tenured faculty, it can help to ensure "adequate and effective cultural diversity education along with minority advocacy of racial and ethnic equity in higher education" (p. 53). He asserted that frequently the lack of diversity, insufficient experience, and biases of hiring committee members can hinder effective recruitment. Such an investment in recruiting has a long-term impact on retention of minority students for whom the increase of minority faculty will serve as examples and representation. Park and Denson (2009) have indicated that increasing faculty diversity can impact students of color positively in the classroom, research, and teaching. O'Rourke (2008) stated that research and experience demonstrate that excellence and legitimacy, two important institutional interests, are better served with faculty diversity. A diverse faculty with a broad range of experiences and perspectives encourage academic excellence. They promote legitimacy by showing that scholarly achievement is attainable by all, even by those who have been historically excluded from pursuing higher education. Faculty diversity should be sustained with explicit institutional policies, infrastructures, and a reward system to support it.

Faculty diversity is only possible when institutions not only diversify the makeup of hiring committees but also provide adequate training and education to committee members to counter misplaced biases. Hiring criteria should include requirements that address candidates' commitment to equity and inclusion. Since faculty play such a primary role in a university, it is important to understand what attitudes they bring toward diversity and their potential to be advocates for equity (Park & Denson, 2009). Additionally, it is equally important for institutions to communicate their values and priorities in the area of promoting equity and inclusion to faculty members, especially in the area of faculty searches.

Institutions must convey strong messages about their commitment to equity and inclusion not only by making intentional efforts to diversify faculty, but also by valuing faculty for their contributions to equity through teaching, research, and service. If universities truly consider equity and inclusion as part of their academic mission, then they are obligated to include it in the criteria used to measure and reward faculty achievement (O'Rourke, 2008). Johnson (2020) argued that though many institutions of higher learning claim their commitment to diversity, equity, and inclusion, the commitment is questionable when it comes to awards, tenure, and promotion. Traditionally underrepresented faculty, especially in STEM, continue to expend energy and time for service that is not valued at the same level as teaching and research for the purpose of promotion and tenure. Faculty doing the important work of equity and inclusion that revolves around supporting students of color, guiding first-generation students, intervening on behalf of them with administrative offices, and sponsoring campus groups need to be recognized for their efforts appropriately. In addition, overrepresented faculty need to step up to shoulder the responsibility of institutional goals to champion diversity, inclusion, and equity as both the student body and the professoriate continue to diversify.

In response to the changing nature of the student body, faculty, teaching, learning environments, and scholarship, institutions need to provide more faculty development opportunities to develop inclusive pedagogies and curricula. Higher education's primary purpose is to uphold democratic values and it meets this responsibility through faculty development (Martínez-Alemán, 2016). Research shows that the issue of multiculturalism as it relates to teaching and learning was identified as one of the most significant issues that faculty development services need to address. However, there was a gap between the perceptions of the need to respond to the issue and the actual number of appropriate faculty development opportunities being made available (Sorcinelli, 2007). Many faculty are reluctant to address issues of diversity and inclusion independently both in and outside of class due to lack of relevant training. They need institutional assistance, support, and time to attend professional development activities like conferences and faculty learning communities to develop their equity skill set. Martínez-Alemán (2016) argued that higher education in service to democracy has the responsibility to provide and broaden opportunities for all individuals to develop their potential, talents, and skills while ensuring that all have the freedom to pursue and produce knowledge. She asserted that in order to fulfill this commitment, institutions are obligated to "prepare faculty to meet these commitments across their primary functions—academic research and scholarship and teaching and learning" (n.p.). She recommended that faculty development programs should consist of "three main components: (1) release time for faculty, (2) monetary rewards for equity-minded teaching, and (3) recognition of equity-minded teaching in promotion and tenure appraisals" (n.p.) so that faculty can develop academic personas that are grounded in equity. Research supports a finding that faculty who participate in diversity training experience personal growth, which is demonstrated in their attitude and curriculum changes. Additionally, their students benefit from an enhanced sense of community, personal growth, and improved conflict resolution skills (Booker, Merriweather, & Campbell-Whatley, 2016).

In order to address inequities of privilege that sustain systemic racism, higher education needs to partner with the Black Lives Matter movement. The Black Lives Matter movement raises awareness of critical barriers to student success. If higher education takes this criticism seriously, it will intentionally implement equity-minded practices and policies to ensure the success of all students. These equity-minded practices may lead to a reduction of the invective language used to incite violence against others. Everyone has a responsibility to reduce the hostility present in today's discourse on diversity, equity, and inclusion. Educators who work in higher education can no longer ignore their responsibility to address the injustice of policies and practices designed to privilege some while marginalizing others. All educators must begin working to create more equitable and inclusive learning environments for students by examining their own beliefs, and by adopting inclusive pedagogies, decolonized curricula, and transparent assessment.

REFERENCES

AAC&U. (2015). *Step up and lead for equity: What higher education can do to reverse our deepening divides.* https://www.aacu.org/sites/default/files/StepUpLeadEquity.pdf

Abdul-Raheem, J. (2016). Faculty diversity and tenure in higher education. *Journal of Cultural Diversity, 23*(2), 53–56.

Bensimon, E. M., (2005). Closing the achievement gap in higher education: An organizational learning perspective. *New Directions for Higher Education, 131,* 99–111.

Booker, K. C., Merriweather, L., & Campbell-Whatley, G. (2016). The effects of diversity training on faculty and students' classroom experiences. *International Journal for the Scholarship of Teaching and Learning, 10*(1). https://doi.org/10.20429/ijsotl.2016.10010

Bowman, N. A. (2011). Promoting participation in a diverse democracy: A meta-analysis of college diversity experiences and civic engagement. *Review of Educational Research*, 81(1), 29–68.

Carbado, D., & Gulati, M. (2003). What exactly is racial diversity? *California Law Review, 91*(4), 1149–1165. https://doi.org/10.2307/3481413

Carnevale, A. P., & Strohl, J. (2013). *Separate and unequal: How higher education reinforces the intergenerational reproduction of white racial privilege.* Georgetown Public Policy Institute. https://1gyhoq479ufd3yna 29x7ubjn-wpengine.netdna-ssl.com/wp-content/uploads/SeparateUnequal.FR_.pdf

Gabriel, D. (2019). Enhancing higher education practice through the 3D pedagogy framework to decolonize, democratize, and diversify the curriculum. *International Journal of Technology and Inclusive Education, 8*(2), 1459–1466. https://doi.org/10.20533/ijtie.2047.0533.2019.0178

Johnson, A. W. (2020, June 30). Institutional mixed messaging. *Inside Higher Ed.* https://www.insidehigher ed.com/advice/2020/06/30/all-faculty-members-should-work-diversity-and-equity-initiatives-and-be-rewarded

Martínez-Alemán, A. M. (2016) Faculty development for educational equity. *Association of America Colleges &Universities, 19*(1). https://www.aacu.org/diversitydemocracy/2016/winter/martinez-aleman

National Student Clearinghouse. (2020, November). *National Student Clearinghouse Research Center's monthly update on higher education enrollment.* https://nscresearchcenter.org/stay-informed/

O'Rourke, S. (2008, September 26). Diversity and merit: How one university rewards faculty work that promotes equity. *Chronicle of Higher Education.* https://www.chronicle.com/article/diversity-and-merit-how-one-university-rewards-faculty-work-that-promotes-equity/

Park, J. J., & Denson, N. (2009). Attitudes and advocacy: Understanding faculty views on racial/ethnic diversity. *Journal of Higher Education, 80*(4), 415–438. https://doi.org/10.1080/00221546.2009.11779023

Sorcinelli, M. D. (2007). Faculty development: The challenge going forward. *Peer Review, 9*(4). https://www .aacu.org/publications-research/periodicals/faculty-development-challenge-going-forward

List of Contributors

EDITORS

RITA KUMAR, Ph.D., is the Executive Director of the Faculty Enrichment Center at the University of Cincinnati and former Professor of English at University of Cincinnati, Blue Ash. Her research interests include problem-based learning, inclusive classroom practice, and faculty development. She serves on the Executive Board of the Women's Network, American Council on Education Women's Network–Ohio. (Ch. 7)

BRENDA REFAEI, Ed.D., is Co-Director of the Learning + Teaching Center and a Professor of English and Communication at the University of Cincinnati Blue Ash College where she teaches developmental, first- and intermediate English composition. Dr. Refaei is an Engaging in Excellence in Equity Fellow. (Ch. 7)

CONTRIBUTORS

TRACIE ADDY, Ph.D., MPhil, Associate Dean of Teaching & Learning, Director, Center for the Integration of Teaching, Learning and Scholarship at Lafayette College. Dr. Addy directs the center for teaching and learning at the college. She enjoys working with faculty across disciplines on teaching excellence and conducting scholarship on teaching and learning. (Ch. 14)

RUTH BENANDER, Ph.D., Professor in the Department of English and Communication, University of Cincinnati Blue Ash College. She has degrees in Teaching English to Speakers of Other Languages and Educational Linguistics from the University of Pennsylvania. Dr. Benander currently serves as the UC Blue Ash College Online Quality and Design Leader. (Ch. 3)

ROSELINE CARTER (she/her), currently the Director of Programs at the Centre for Sexuality, is a registered social worker in Calgary, Alberta. She is passionate about nonprofit leadership and is currently the Director of Programs at the Centre for Sexuality. Since 2004 she has been working in the fields of sexuality, sexual health, harm reduction, and sex work. (Ch. 11)

MUN CHUN (MC) CHAN, Ph.D., is a teaching professor in the Biology Department at Georgetown University. He also works with The Center for New Designs in Learning and Scholarship as a Doyle STEM faculty fellow, focusing on assisting STEM faculty in incorporating Inclusive Pedagogy strategies and goals in their courses. (Ch. 9)

ADAM CHEKOUR, Ed.D., is an Associate Professor of Mathematics at the University of Cincinnati Blue Ash College. His areas of interest include STEM education, measurement and assessment, instructional design & technology and online education. He has presented and published at numerous STEM conferences at the local, regional, national, and international levels. (Ch. 8)

FLOYD CHEUNG, Ph.D., is Vice President for Equity and Inclusion at Smith College. He is also a faculty member in English and American Studies. His scholarship focuses on recovering early Asian American literature and promoting inclusive teaching practices. (Ch. 5)

JORDAN CRABBE, Ph.D., received his B.S (Mathematics) from K.N.U.S.T, Ghana in 2001, M.S (Mathematical Science) from the U.N.L.V in 2007, and Ph.D. (Statistics) from Oklahoma State University in 2013. He is an Associate Professor of Statistics at University of Cincinnati Blue Ash College. His research interests include Nonparametric Statistics and Probability Theory. (Ch. 8)

NATALIA DARLING is Professor of Mathematics at the University of Cincinnati Blue Ash College and teaches developmental and college algebra. Her interests include Culturally Responsive Mathematics and metacognitive learning strategies, and her research and creative activities focus on student-centered technology and encouraging student persistence and motivation in mathematics. (Ch. 8)

MICHELE DERAMO, Ph.D., is the Assistant Provost for Diversity Education in the Office for Inclusion and Diversity at Virginia Tech. She earned her Ph.D. from Virginia Tech in social and cultural theory. She is a member of the Phi Beta Delta Honor Society for International Scholars and the Edward A. Bouchet Graduate Honor Society. (Ch. 15)

DEREK DUBE, Ph.D., is an Associate Professor of Biology at the University of St. Joseph, West Hartford. Dr. Dube teaches at the undergraduate and graduate (M.S.) level, both in-person and online. He conducts research and has published manuscripts both in the field of virology and in science education. (Ch. 14)

CYNTHIA GANOTE, Ph.D., formerly the Assistant Dean for Diversity and Community Engagement in the College of Arts and Sciences, is now a faculty member in the Department of Sociology at the University of Louisville. Her scholarship focuses on ways to address microaggressions with microresistance and on critical and feminist pedagogies. (Ch. 5)

MICHAEL R. GESINSKI, Ph.D., is an Associate Professor at Southwestern University. He earned his doctorate at the University of California, Irvine exploring the synthesis of antiparasitic compounds, followed by a postdoctoral/lecturer position at Berkeley. His research involves the metal-mediated synthesis of complex molecules and the development of innovative classroom activities for organic chemistry. (Ch. 10)

PATRICE GILLESPIE is an Adjunct Professor of Business at the University of Cincinnati Blue Ash College where she teaches Introduction to Business, Fundamentals of Management, Human Resources, Team Building, and Mid-Collegiate Experience Bridging. Patrice brings over 40 years of experience in operations management and human resources into the classroom to provide students with real-world experience. (Ch. 13)

HELENE ARBOUET HARTE, Ed.D., is an Associate Professor at The University of Cincinnati, Blue Ash College. She earned her doctoral degree in Special Education and a master's degree in Early Childhood Education from The University of Cincinnati. Her scholarship includes family engagement, engaging young children in inclusive settings, and college student engagement. (Ch. 4)

KIRSTEN HELMER, Ed.D., is Director of Programming for Diversity, Inclusion, & Equity and lecturer with the Center for Teaching and Learning at the University of Massachusetts, Amherst. Her work focuses on inclusive course and syllabus design, universal design for learning, culture sustaining/anti-oppression pedagogies, microaggressions, difficult dialogues, and trauma-aware teaching. (Ch. 1)

SUSAN A. HILDEBRANDT, Ph.D., is Interim Chair of the Department of Special Education at Illinois State University, where she is Professor of Applied Linguistics and Spanish. Her research focuses on teaching languages to students with disabilities and pre-service teacher knowledge assessment and its intersection with educational policy. (Ch. 6)

DEYU HU, Ph.D., is Associate Director of Research, Training, and Special Initiatives in the Division of Information Technology at Virginia Tech. She has over 15 years of experience in instructional design and development, faculty development, training, scholarship of teaching and learning, and curriculum development. (Ch. 15)

ZEKERIYA (YALCIN) KARATAS, Ph.D., is an Assistant Professor of Mathematics at the University of Cincinnati Blue Ash College. He teaches various mathematics courses at different levels ranging from developmental mathematics to college-level mathematics. His research interests are in the scholarship of teaching and learning, and advanced algebra. (Ch. 8)

GENE KRAMER, Ph.D., is a Professor of Mathematics at the University of Cincinnati Blue Ash College. He is active in SoTL research and is a member of the Academy of the Fellows for Teaching and Learning. He serves as an editor for *The Journal for Research and Practice in College Teaching*. (Ch. 8)

CLAIRE W. LYONS, Ph.D., has been teaching developmental psychology for over 20 years. She specializes in interactive lecturing to very large groups. She has received the James Madison University General Education Distinguished Teacher award. Her research interests include identity development in emerging adulthood and the scholarship of teaching and learning. (Ch. 2)

ANGELA MILLER-HARGIS, Ed.D., is an Associate Professor at The University of Cincinnati, Blue Ash College. She earned her doctoral degree in literacy from The University of Cincinnati. Her scholarship includes curriculum theory, critical literacy in school settings, and ways to improve student engagement and critical thinking in education coursework at the post-secondary level. (Ch. 4)

KHADIJAH A. MITCHELL, Ph.D., is the Peter C.S. d'Aubermont M.D. Scholar of Health and Life Sciences, and Assistant Professor of Biology at Lafayette College. (Ch. 14)

BETH MONNIN, RDH, MS.Ed., is an Assistant Professor at the University of Cincinnati Blue Ash College. She has 25 years of experience in both the educational and clinical areas in dental hygiene. Her educational research interests include culture in the curriculum, diversity and inclusion, radiation safety, dental radiology, and increasing the education of health professionals. (Ch. 12)

LIZZIE NGWENYA-SCOBURGH, Ph.D., an Associate Professor of Organizational Management at the University of Cincinnati, where she teaches Human Resources, International Business, Marketing, and Introduction to Business. A native of South Africa, she has over 15 years in industry & academia with research interests in the field of Cross-Cultural Management, HR Development, and Mindfulness. (Ch. 13)

EMILY D. NIEMEYER, Ph.D., is a Professor of Chemistry at Southwestern University. As Program Director of the grant-funded Inquiry Initiative, she oversaw a transition to an active learning curriculum across the university's science departments. She holds the Herbert and Kate Dishman Chair in Science and teaches courses in analytical, environmental, and introductory chemistry. (Ch. 10)

TAMIKA ODUM, Ph.D., is an Associate Professor of Sociology at the University of Cincinnati Blue Ash College. She earned her Ph.D. in Sociology from the University of Cincinnati. Her research focus includes medical sociology, more specifically reproductive health disparities among poor women and women of color and structures of inequality. (Ch. 4)

MICHELLE OHNONA, Ph.D., is the Assistant Director for Diversity and Inclusion Initiatives at the Center for New Designs in Learning and Scholarship at Georgetown University. She is also a faculty member in the Women's and Gender Studies Program and the MA Program in Learning, Design, and Technology. (Ch. 9)

BRENT OLIVER, Ph.D., is an Associate Professor of Social Work at Mount Royal University. Based in Calgary, Dr. Oliver leads a community-based research program focused on sexuality, gender, and SoTL. Dr. Oliver has worked with community collaborators across Canada on a variety of qualitative and mixed methods research projects. (Ch. 11)

JAMES OLSEN, Ph.D., is the Assistant Director for Programs for Graduate Students and Faculty at the Center for New Designs in Learning and Scholarships at Georgetown University. He is also a faculty member in the Philosophy Department and the Environmental Studies Program where he primarily teaches courses in Environmental Ethics. (Ch. 9)

PAM RANKEY is an Associate Professor in the UC Blue Ash Business and Economics Department. She has degrees in Curriculum and Instruction and Information Technology from the University of Cincinnati. She has served as the college eLearning Director and currently serves as Unit Head for the Business and Economics Department. (Ch. 3)

FABIO F. SANTOS, Ed.D., is an Associate Professor of Statistics at the University of Cincinnati Blue Ash College, where he teaches elementary statistics, applied statistics, and business analytics. His research interest focuses on examining the effects of writing-to-learn and problem-based learning on students' acquisition of structural knowledge. (Ch. 8)

ESTER SIHITE, Ph.D., is an Associate Director in the Office for Inclusion, Belonging, & Intergoup Communication at Stanford University. She was formerly an Assistant Director of Diversity Education in the Center for Multicultural Equity & Access, Diversity & Inclusion Specialist in the Center for New Designs in Learning & Scholarship, and Director of A Different Dialogue. (Ch. 9)

TASHA SOUZA, Ph.D., formerly the Associate Director for Inclusive Excellence, is now the Director of BUILD (Boise State Uniting for Inclusion and Leadership in Diversity) and Professor of Communication at Boise State University. Previously, she was the Faculty Associate for Inclusive Teaching for Humboldt State University and a Fulbright scholar at the University of the West Indies in Barbados. (Ch. 5)

SHAWNA STAUD, RDH, MDH, is an Assistant Professor at the University of Cincinnati Blue Ash College. She has been in dental hygiene education since 2015. She is the clinic coordinator for second-year dental hygiene students. Her educational research interest includes pediatric dentistry. (Ch. 12)

JANNA TAFT YOUNG, Ph.D., has been teaching psychology for over sixteen years. She researches memory, particularly Alzheimer's. She teaches courses like General Psychology and Neuroscience of Memory Senior Seminar. In 2016, she received JMU's Provost Award for Excellence in Part-Time Teaching. She focuses on developing rapport, critical thinking, and peer to peer learning. (Ch. 2)

BECKY VAN TASSEL, M.Ed., is the Training Centre and Community Engagement Manager at the Centre for Sexuality in Calgary, Alberta. Her work has primarily focused on sexuality, inclusion, sexual health, and healthy relationships. (Ch. 11)

TAYLOR W. WADIAN, Ph.D., is an Assistant Professor of Psychology at the University of Cincinnati Blue Ash College. He earned his doctoral degree in Psychology from Kansas State University. His scholarship examines the various factors that produce or otherwise moderate children's, teens', and adults' expressions of prosocial and antisocial behavior. (Ch. 4)

Index

Hurtado, S., 1, 127
hybrid model
    organic chemistry as, 141–44, 142f
    Quality Matters on, 201, 206
    video lecture in, 143
hypertext, 27

IAT. *See* Implicit Association Test
IDC. *See* Intercultural Development
    Continuum
identity, 38
IF-AT. *See* immediate feedback assessment
    technique
Illinois State University, 91
imagery
    of racism, 65–68
    student response to, 67
immediate feedback assessment technique
    (IF-AT), 140
Implicit Association Test (IAT), 5, 202
implicit bias, 107, 168–69, 171, 202, 204, .209.
    See also bias
Inclusive Introduction Questionnaire, 33
inclusive pedagogy, 56, 83. *See also* active
    learning pedagogies; measurements,
    of inclusive pedagogy; microresistant
    pedagogies; *specific topics*
    in behavioral sciences, 58–60
    biochemistry framework in, 130t
    in business classes, 177–85
    CIP in, 5, 10
    as community of learners, 93–94, 96–97
    creating, 9–11
    for culture, 9–10, 42–43, 116–17, 171
    in dental hygiene classroom, 168–71
    dissemination challenges of, 205
    Doyle Faculty Fellowship Program in,
        126–27, 128t, 129, 134–35
    of educators, 4
    for English composition, 103–5, 108–9
    for English literature, 106–9
    for foreign-language, 86–91
    as instructional climate, 94–95, 97
    intercultural, 9
    as language support intervention, 195f

    for mathematics, 115–16
    mindset as, 9
    as perceptible information, 93, 95–96
    pronoun policy as, 23–24, 26, 33, 213
    rationale for, 86–91, 115–16
    scaffolding as, 104, 106–7
    in social sciences, 58–60
    in STEM courses, 129–35
    as STEM strategies, 125–35, 128t, 130t
    success of, 77–80, 144–48, 145f–47f,
        159–63, 171–75, 172f–74f, 185
    as target language, 92
    as tolerance of errors, 93, 96
    transformative learning theory as, 155–64
    world languages and, 89, 95–97
Inclusive Teaching Initiative, 183
Indigenous education, 10
inequity, 71, 91, 156, 158
ingredients, 133–34
Inoue, A., 101, 104
inquiry-based learning, 127
Institutional Review Board (IRB), 171, 190
instructional climate, 94–95, 97
instructional curriculum materials, 204
instructional strategies, 205
instruction outcomes, 193–94
Intercultural Development Continuum (IDC),
    166, 169–71
interdisciplinary model, 126–27
IRB. *See* Institutional Review Board
Irey, S., 76–77
IRIS Center module, 63

Jackson, A., 69
James Madison University (JMU), 31–33
Jane Eyre (Brontë), 196–97
Jankowski, N. A., 13–14
JMU. *See* James Madison University
Johnson, A. W., 214–15
Jones, S, 6

Kandaswamy, P., 11
Kareem, J., 101–2
Kearney, R. C., 167
Kishimoto, K., 11